Law-and-Order News

*An analysis of crime reporting
in the British Press*

Steve Chibnall

Law - and - Order News

*An analysis of crime reporting
in the British Press*

Tavistock Publications

First published in 1977
by Tavistock Publications Limited
11 New Fetter Lane, London EC4
Photoset in Great Britain by
Red Lion Setters, Holborn, London
and printed in Great Britain by
Cambridge University Press

ISBN 0 422 74960 5 (*hardbound*)
ISBN 0 422 74970 2 (*paperback*)

Contents

Preface

This is a book for sociologists, journalists, and that creature much beloved by publishers, the educated and interested layman. Writing for even this apparently restricted readership has posed considerable problems of style and presentation. First, I have had to walk an uneasy tightrope between excessive academicism, the pedantry of the scientific monograph, and the breathless prose of 'journalese'. Inevitably, I have wavered. Some journalists will find the book too academic for their taste, while some academics will find it too journalistic in style. Second, in organizing and ordering the material of the book I have had to cope with contradictory imperatives of presentation. A conventional sociological monograph begins with a review of the relevant literature and a discussion of theory and then progresses to findings and data. The conventional work of journalism, on the other hand, has an inverted pyramid structure. It grabs the reader's attention by opening with the most pertinent, important, or dramatic material in the expectation that the reader may discard the piece before reaching the end. I have attempted to resolve this contradiction by dealing with research findings at the earliest possible stage of the book's development, having briefly situated them in a theoretical context. The implications of the study are then re-examined in a concluding chapter when it is hoped that the empirical material presented will have been strong enough or colourful enough to sustain the interest of the non-academic reader through to the close.

Many people have helped me in researching and writing *Law-and-Order News* and I can only hope to acknowledge a handful of them. The principal acknowledgement is to my informants in Fleet Street and its environs for providing so much valuable data, but my special thanks must also go to Stan Cohen (University of Essex) for his help and advice in supervising my research which was financed, in part, by the Social Science Research Council. I am also grateful to James Curran, Jeremy Tunstall, Paul Rock, Colin Bell, Graham Allen, and Peter Saunders for their criticism and encouragement in the early stages of the research; and to Graham Murdock, Steve Molloy, Lynn Makings, and Martyn Denscombe for their comments on various drafts of the manuscript. Thanks and acknowledgement are also due to the staff of the libraries of Essex University, Cambridge University, Leicester Polytechnic, and the *Daily Mirror* for their technical services; to Marion Duff and Jan Morris for their careful typing of the manuscript; and to *Time Out* and The Leicester University Centre for Mass Communications Research for their general assistance. Finally, my thanks to London Express News and Feature Services for permission to use copyright material from the *Sun* and the *Daily Express*, and to the *Daily Mail* for allowing the reproduction of one of its news layouts.

S.C.
Leicester,
October 1976

Introduction

'The basic interests of the human race are not in music, politics and philosophy, but in things like food and football, money and sex, and crime — especially crime.'

: Larry Lamb: Editorial Director, The *Sun* and The *News of the World* 1975.

Law-and-order news

Newspapers and television do not merely monitor the events of the real world; they construct representations and accounts of reality which are shaped by the constraints imposed upon them: constraints emanating from the conventions, ideologies, and organization of journalism and news bureaucracies. Ideally, we could evaluate the influence of these constraints and the accuracy of media accounts by comparing media depictions with the reality of the events they portray. But, typically, in a highly differentiated society like Britain, the events which capture the interest of the media only become visible through their eyes. There is often no easy method of separating 'sacred' facts from 'free' comment or, more precisely, from profane interpretation. All are contained within complex frameworks of conventional understandings which identify and define news stories. If we cannot always disentangle reality from media interpretation, and if interpretations have a public reality of their own, if they come to represent reality 'for all practical purposes', we should at least be aware of the way in which they are constructed and the influences which direct the process. This, essentially, is the task confronted by this study. It examines the characteristic ways in which knowledge about situations of which the newspaper reader can have little first-hand information is socially constructed by journalists and cast in the form of news. Beyond this, it inquires into the values, ideologies, and interests which inform the construction process. Clearly, this type of study requires a focus to concentrate its efforts, and to this end I have chosen to examine a single field of reporting in one medium, i.e., crime reporting in the press. The analysis is organized around one general theme of media discourse — law and order — which spans a number of specialist fields but is situated essentially in crime journalism and constitutes its most fundamental theme. Crime news and the 'Law-and-order' theme are chosen because they illustrate most effectively, the system of beliefs, values, and understandings which underlies newspaper representations of reality. There is, perhaps, no other domain of news interest in which latent press ideology becomes more explicit than in what we may term 'law-and-order news'. Nowhere else is it made quite so clear what it is that newspapers value as healthy and praiseworthy or deplore as evil and degenerate in society. Nowhere else are the limits of newspaper values such as neutrality, objectivity, and balance revealed with such clarity. Crime and deviance represent, simultaneously, a challenge to newspapers' liberal and consensual view of society and a source of ideological reinforcement. The growth of crime during periods of apparent 'progress', prosperity, and consensual politics presents interpretive problems for the ideology becuase it calls into question assumptions about social order and change[1]. On the other hand, as sociologists from Durkheim onwards have frequently noted, crime and the processing of offenders offers an opportunity for the celebration of conformity and respectability by redefining the moral boundaries of communities and drawing their members together against the threat of chaos. Newspapers, of course, not only seek membership of the same speech communities as their readers, they also aim to reflect and manipulate sentiments within those communities in their provision of information, comment, and understandings[2].

Crime news may serve as a focus for the articulation of shared morality and communal sentiments. A chance not simply to speak *to* the community but to speak *for* the community, against all that the criminal outsider represents, to delineate the shape of the threat, to advocate a response, to eulogize on conformity to established norms and values, and to warn of the consequences of deviance. In short, crime news provides a chance for a newspaper to appropriate the moral conscience of its readership. Steven Box goes so far as to argue that this potential for moral enterprise constitutes the *raison d'etre* of crime news:

'The reason ... why deviant behaviour occupies so much media space is not because it is intrinsically interesting, but because it is intrinsically instructive. It serves to reinforce the world-taken-for-granted by restating social rules and warning subjects that violators will not be tolerated. In this way, the wayward are cautioned and the righteous are comforted.'

(Box 1971 : 40)

The existence of crime news disseminated by the mass media means that people no longer need to gather together to witness punishments. They can remain at home for their moral instruction (Erikson 1964).

More often than not, the columns of law-and-order news are peopled by heroes and villains, personifications of good and evil acting roles in a symbolic drama. The symbolic drama may only occasionally become explicit in journalists' routine accounts of crime, deviance, and police work, but it underlies them, surfacing when once again some apparent crisis of social control develops or when a particularly sensational crime captures the headlines. At times like these crime reporting may function as an important vehicle and repository of newspaper ideology while also indexing the perceived anxieties of its readers. The anxieties it documents tend to be generalized anxieties concerned with the breakdown of order. These vague feelings of unease are repeatedly articulated through the shifting images and scenarios of law-and-order news, finding expression in concern about crime rates, delinquency, wildcat strikes, violent picketing, mugging, terrorism, and so on. But these are not seen as discrete social problems so much as symptoms of an underlying social malaise, a nameless, malignant sickness.

In doing this law-and-order news mythologizes, i.e., it explains away the phenomena it reports by relating them to a single, intangible entity whose existence must remain an article of faith. The malignant sickness is occasionally named. Sometimes it is called 'moral decline', sometimes 'the disease of violence'. At other times it may assume a more human form: 'communist subversives', 'the mafia', 'the criminal mastermind'. But each of these concepts functions in much the same way to provide a simple explanation of diverse and perplexing phenomena; an explanation which cannot be disproved. But again, such an explanation is rarely explicit in newspaper stories. It is more likely to be tacitly evoked by cues in the text or by powerful master labels such as 'violent' and 'criminal' which carry unambiguous connotations and meld together disparate phenomena and their meanings. In law-and-order news, complex and ambiguous reality is constantly reduced to its simplest forms. As we shall see, heterogeneity and diversity of meaning are concealed by a reporting technique which continually projects reality in the same form of binary opposition, particularly 'good threatened by evil' and 'order threatened by chaos'.

All this is the largely unconscious accomplishment of newsmen and their sources. In constructing their public interpretations of events journalists draw upon the widely shared news values of their profession. These values direct attention towards particular features of events — elements of drama, the role of personalities, and so on — and encourage their presentation in simplistic terms. News values, as I will argue later, shape and reinforce the interpretations of law-and-order news, but these interpretations receive further support from many of the 'accredited spokesmen' (Hall 1972) upon whom journalists also draw selectively in their construction of stories. Some Conservative politicians, for instance, collapse together diverse phenomena in much the same way as law-and-order news, identifying them all as symptoms of moral decline. In his major policy speech after the October 1974 general election, Sir Keith Joseph linked together increasing delinquency, truancy, vandalism, hooliganism, illiteracy, drug-taking, drunkenness, sadism, student revolt, vagrancy, and violence in the streets as multiple signs of the decadence of modern British Society. He warned that the country was being

'destroyed from inside' by a moral degene.   ːu̯ by
'mischievous, wrong-headed, debilitating yet seductive' ideas.
Lord Hailsham had reached a similar conclusion ten months
before when he had warned the Junior Carlton Club of the
immanent threat to the rule of law:

> ' "Gentlemen, we live in grave times. The symptoms of our
> malaise may be economic, may show themselves in price rises,
> shortages and industrial disputes. But underlying the
> symptoms is a disease which has destroyed democracies in the
> past, and the causes of that disease are not economic. They
> are moral and political and constitutional, and in order to
> cure it we must recognise them as such." '

(The Times 3.12.73)

As we shall see law-and-order news frequently reflects the type
of definition of the situation suggested by these statements and
others by police sources. They form part of the *ad hoc* montage of
accounts and interpretations by which problematic events are
given a widely available meaning. But, while law-and-order news
tends to be a loose and imprecise piecing together of explanatory
fragments, the pragmatic constructs which result are generally
situated within a particular ideological framework. The men and
(occasionally) the women responsible for these constructs, of
course, rarely see their work as explicitly ideological. Most
professional communicators feel their job is to collect and process
the accounts of their sources, casting them in a conventional news
form for rapid dissemination to their readers. They may recognize
that the process of creating news from source accounts inevitably
involves elements of interpretation and selection but this is seen as
a form of intellectual craftsmanship which creates a predominantly neutral product. But when we subject those products as a
whole to critical scrutiny it is possible to discern a distinctly
ideological system of beliefs, values, and understandings
underlying media accounts. I shall argue that, while this
ideological system may not be common to all newspapers and
their personnel, there does appear to be surprisingly little
variation in commitment from one national newspaper to

another. The ideological system supplies a context within which the moral worth of established and emergent social groups can be evaluated and signified to the public, as well as a framework of tacit interpretations and understandings within which actions and events can be rendered meaningful.

1 Crime reporting and mass communications research

In selecting law-and-order news to illuminate both newspaper ideology and the professional practices of journalists this study is at odds with much of the social science research tradition in the field of mass communications. Crime reporting has habitually been rather ignored by academic researchers or treated as essentially apolitical.

It has been of interest primarily as an example of the worst excesses of journalistic superficiality and sensationalism, a curiosity of no more than marginal importance to the understanding of mass communications. The only aspect of crime reporting which had received academic consideration in Britain until the 1970s was its social and psychological effects, but this was merely a small part of a wider inquiry into the effects, usually upon children, of media portrayals of sex and violence.

This situation might well have continued if it had not been for the developments occuring in the late 1960s which saw a convergence of both style and content between social deviance and political marginality (Horowitz and Liebewitz 1968) and a concomitant 'politicization' of much criminological theory (Taylor, Walton, and Young 1973; 1975). The recognition of crime and deviance as essentially a result of, or a response to, conditions of life in capitalist society rather than as a consequence of personal inadequacy has given a new significance to crime reporting. It is this significance which is explored in this study. The established tradition of academic inquiry provides little help or inspiration in this task because it has tended to operate with a limited problematic which has handicapped attempts to confront the central problems of media content and journalistic practice.

Most recent critics agree that academic, social science research into the mass media lacks theoretical integration and methodological consistency. Denis McQuail (1969 : 17) writes of 'a lack of coherence and a fragmentation of effort' which, in the words of Peter Golding (1975:8) has produced 'a patchwork of structured information not always comparable, reconcilable, or even complementary'. Research has almost invariably been financed by commercial and government interests and has not simple confined itself to the practical concerns of its sponsors, but has frequently been based on woefully inadequate theoretical foundations. Given the nature of its sponsorship, it is not surprising that the great bulk of media research has been aimed at expanding knowledge of the media's audiences — the way in which they use and are influenced by media products[1]. Much less attention has been paid to the social and political content of media products and the conditions of their production.

Analyses of the content of media products have too often been based on naive and simplistic assumptions about the value of quantitative methods, leading to a slavish, mechanical, and largely fruitless counting of words and phrases[2]. The principal problematic of content analysis has been that of bias i.e., to what extent are the media impartial in their coverage of affairs, particularly political affairs? In this, research has reflected the practical concerns of the major political parties and media organizations.

Among the broadcasting media in particular, the quest for impartiality has become a fetish. Television producers and presenters go to enormous lengths to ensure that their programmes appear politically 'balanced', that the healthy dynamics of controversy are not permitted to degenerate into sterile propaganda. Arguments are aired, spokesmen of more-or-less equal 'weight' are selected to represent the various cases, and the television company supplies a professional umpire to see that the contest is carried out fairly and that one side does not monopolize all the play. All is open. The structure of the debate favours neither one side nor the other. Such strict impartiality is not required of newspapers. They are allowed a certain political colouring. They are expected to express opinions, provided they do not allow those opinions to obscure or determine the reality of events. Reporting must continue to appear objective even though we are aware that it cannot be entirely divorced from the opinionizing of the leader columns. Providing one organization does not command a monopoly of the news, partiality is a luxury we can afford. Serious difficulties in the system are only generally seen to arise if the preponderance of papers supporting a particular political party becomes overwhelming, or if papers violate popular expectations of responsibility and objectivity by launching deliberate 'smear campaigns'. Generally speaking, however, the play of market forces ensures that a wide range of opinion is represented in the press as effectively as strict controls ensure that impartiality is maintained by the broadcasting media. As Sir Max Aitken has expressed it: ' "Reduced a little in numbers, the Fleet Street newspapers today offer the public a complete range of opinion and expression totally free from outside direction" ' (O'Higgins 1972:113).

Researchers who accept this conventional wisdom, however, are allowing an important truth to be concealed i.e., the apparently 'wide range of opinion' is really only a *limited* range. All the major media voices sound within a framework of legitimate discourse delineated by the mass parties of our parliamentary system. Opinions and world-views which occupy the margins of that system or fall outside it receive very little representation indeed. Thus the media are, as Stuart Hall puts it 'oriented within a framework of power' and consequently 'structured in dominance', by which he means that they show a systematic tendency to reproduce definitions of reality derived from the political elites. What he says of television programmes is equally applicable to newspaper stories:

'The broadcasting institutions exercise a wide measure of editorial autonomy in their programmes: but ultimately they operate within the mode of reality of the state, their programme content is, in the last instance, governed by the dominant ideological perspective and is oriented within its hegemony.'

has to be
complaints of what want (Hall 1972:1)

It should be stressed that this does *not* mean that journalists and broadcasters never interpret events in ways which are unacceptable to establishment politicians, but that, in the vast majority of cases their interpretations and accounts are grounded in the shared perspectives of the 'liberal consensus'. The range of opinion generally extends from the moderate 'Right' of the Conservative Party to the moderate 'Left' of the Labour Party. While Fleet Street newspapers may exhibit different or shifting allegiances to the two major political parties they are united in their oppositions to policies and parties which seek to alter the social or economic organization of society in any fundamental way. This type of statement might seem banal and obvious *when we think about it*, but its value lies essentially in the fact that we do *not* normally *shifting* think about it. We tend to take for granted the constraining *opinions* parameters within which media discourse takes place, allowing *left to* them effectively to circumscribe a paramount reality which is *right* subject to neither questioning nor thought. This means that we may notice differences of opinion and approach between papers but we are unlikely to draw out the implications of what they share in common — a basic commitment to the established social and economic order, and a characteristic way of interpreting the world. The recognition of this essential similarity of world-view involves us in a new problematic. Issues of bias are no longer central to our appreciation of the signficance of the news media and are replaced by a concern with broader questions of ideological disposition. The significant problem is not whether most newspaper reports betray a partiality towards one political leader rather than another but rather what type of concepts and assumptions do newspapers employ in identifying and making sense of political events. What is the nature of the paramount reality and how is it created and presented to the media's audiences? Certainly, that paramount reality routinely appears to us in a reified form — self evidently true, a matter of

what about personal reasoning carear

'common-sense', what any reasonable man would believe — but, in the final analysis, it is a human creation:

> 'Reality is socially defined. But the definitions are always *embodied*, that is, concrete individuals and groups of individuals serve as definers of reality. To understand the state of the socially constructed universe (of meaning) at any given time, or its change over time, one must understand the social organisation that permits the definers to do their defining. Put a little crudely, it is essential to keep pushing questions about the historically available conceptualisations of reality from the abstract "what?" to the sociologically concrete "says who?".'
>
> (Berger and Luckmann 1967:134)

When we ask this question in relation to the definitions contained in newspapers we direct attention to two areas of inquiry:-

i. The ownership and control of newspaper businesses.
ii. The world of the professional communicator.

The social science tradition of theory and research has certainly not concerned itself greatly with the first of these two areas of inquiry. In Britain, it was not until the early 1970s that the interpenetration of Marxism and academic social science produced a theoretical overview of trends in the economic organization of mass communications pinpointing the relations between the different media sectors. The findings of that study (Murdock and Golding 1974a), however, leave little doubt about the importance of patterns of ownership and control in understanding media products. The authors draw our attention to the accelerating tendency towards monopoly in the media industry, the concentration of ownership in fewer and fewer hands, and the progressive absorbtion of media organizations by large capitalist corporations with interests in a wide range of industries. All this can only restrict the diversity and range of media voices still further while encouraging a reliance on proven formulae and a desire not to 'rock the boat', especially in the choppy economic waters of the seventies. Murdock and Golding (1974b) have indicated the specific implications of concentration for the press:

'As far as the newspapers are concerned, economic pressures mean less space; fewer journalistic resources, especially correspondents; less scope for gathering background material; and increased reliance on a handful of news agency sources. In addition, the overall tone is likely to become politically blander and less sectional in order to avoid offending audience groups necessary to the maintenance of revenue.'

Turning to the second area of inquiry, the world of the communicator, we can say that there has been more research than in the first area, but its contribution to the understanding of British journalism has been less than we might desire. Firstly, the research has been primarily American[3] and secondly, it has usually operated with a central concept of limited utility: the 'gatekeeper' concept[4]. Its deficiencies stem from its foundation in a model of news production which is apparently unable to cope with the creative aspects of communicative work. That model is essentially mechanistic in its conception of the process of news production as a system of cybernetic filters reducing the flow of information reaching the audience. Professional communicators are dichotomized into 'news-gatherers' and 'newsprocessors' whose activities relate to the two stages of production. In the first stage reporters collect the news stories and pass them on to the gatekeepers in their news bureaucracies. Here, in stage two, the stories undergo a process of selection, abbreviation, and organization and those lucky enough to survive in some form emerge at the end of the news funnel and are received by the audience.

While superficially attractive, this model is misleading and can blind us to vitally important elements and processes of news manufacture. The reporter does not go out gathering news, picking up stories as if they were fallen appies, he *creates* news stories by selecting fragments of information from the mass of raw data he receives and organizing them in a conventional journalistic form. As Curtis MacDougall (1968:12) correctly points out 'The news is the account of the event, not something instrinsic in the event itself'. But in the process of news construction the reporter will only rarely utilize his own direct perception of an event. More usually, his raw materials will be the selected and selective accounts of others — his sources. In most reporting situations, the reality of events must be processed by others before the reporter can render his own account. It is within this context of reporter/source interaction, a context largely taken for granted by the conventional news flow model,[5] that the significant 'gatekeeping' takes place. If we wish to understand the selection and construction of news stories, we must examine the procedures which journalists adopt to identify potential stories and select appropriate sources, as well as the ideologies and stocks of knowledge which inform those decisions[6]. We must scrutinize the process of exchange which takes place between the journalist and his source, the bonds which bind the one to the other, and the interests and pre-dispositions of each. This is not to ignore the role of sub-editors and news room executives for their importance lies in the occupational socialization of the reporter rather than in the selection of his copy[7]. By the time that copy reaches the sub-editor the most significant decisions have been made — events have occurred, they have been experienced, accounts of experiences have been constructed for particular audiences, accounts of those accounts have been fashioned and these have either been stored away or transformed into fully-fledged news stories. At every stage selection and processing has taken place.

The gatekeeper concept, then, does nothing to help the integration of the social science tradition of theory and research. The tradition continues to lack a coherent theoretical framework which will enable the different moments in the process of news production to be analyzed as related parts of a whole rather than as discrete events.

These introductory remarks have served as both a theoretical context and a rehearsal for some of the arguments to be developed and documented in the course of this study. It will centre upon the social construction of knowledge by professional communicators, assessing the influence of newspaper ideology, news values, and source relationships on the writing of newspaper stories. I have selected the work of crime reporters for particular attention because theirs is the core specialism of law-and-order news. They form an elite corps of journalists occupying a strategically important position in the process of news creation and dissemination. There are less than twenty-five full-time crime specialists on Fleet Street papers, but the control they exert over our knowledge of the worlds of criminal and policemen is much greater than their numbers might suggest. Their accounts of crime and deviance may often be fragmentary and superficial, but for most of us they are the most complete and detailed available. This makes them powerful accounts, capable of shaping opinion and understanding.

In the course of the study I interviewed fourteen specialist crime correspondents representing eight of the ten Fleet Street daily and Sunday papers which employ such specialists. In addition, a further twenty or so journalists whose experience appeared relevant to the understanding of law-and-order news were interviewed. These included leader writers, journalists who had reported the Northern Ireland troubles, and journalists on the fringes of the crime reporting field. All requests for interviews were made directly to individuals, rather than through organizations and resulted in a surprisingly high response rate of around 75%. Insights gained from these interviews were supplemented by extensive reading of the memoirs and other published works of journalists and policemen, an interview with a Scotland Yard press officer, and brief periods of observation at the Yard's Press Bureau. I have attempted to integrate materials gathered from these sources with others gathered from a careful monitoring of law-and-order news in the national press over the period January 1971 to December 1975 and research into the reporting of earlier selected case studies. The eclectic and pragmatic approach to data collection is one which it is hoped the reader will judge appropriate to the overall aim of the study: to understand newspaper content by relating it to the beliefs, practices, and interests of newsmen and their sources.

The plan of the book

Chapter 2 begins to explore, in general terms, the relationship between the polictical ideology of newspapers and the professional news values of their journalists. The two are seen to intermesh closely enough to constitute mutually dependent elements of a single ideological system.

Chapter 3 moves towards the detailed study of law-and-order news by tracing the development of crime reporting as a specialist field of journalism. It identifies the shifting focal concerns of the specialism, relating them to changes in patterns of crime and deviance in post-war Britain; and it examines the role played by sensationalism and 'cheque-book journalism' in setting the characteristic style of crime reporting.

Chapter 4 is an analysis of law-and-order news during the period 1965-1975, organized around the dominant theme of 'The Violent Society'. It looks particularly at how emergent forms of deviance and criminality were interpreted and classified by the press, at how different phenomena were articulated into one threatening image of law-and-order crisis.

Chapter 5 is concerned principally with the relational background of law-and-order news: the symbiotic relationship between crime reporters and police sources which exerts a considerable influence over their accounts of police work. It uses the reporting of cases of deviance by policemen as both an example of this influence at work and also as a means of shedding light on the character of source relationships.

Chapter 6 draws out further implications of employing social control agencies as primary sources of news by examining the goals and techniques of news management by the police in Britain and the army in Ulster, concluding that much of what we read in law-and-order news may well be 'helpful' to control agencies but does not necessarily correspond with the reality of events.

Chapter 7 explores the wider theoretical implications of the study, looking in some detail at the deficiencies endemic in most Marxist approaches to the understanding of mass communications which simply assert the function of the news media in reproducing a dominant ideology without explaining how it is achieved beyond referring to the media's structure of ownership and control. The chapter once again emphasizes the importance of looking at the world of the communicator and the centrality of crime news to the understanding of how dominant ideology is routinely maintained.

Finally, a chronology of law-and-order events is provided which may help the reader to order and contextualize the happenings mentioned in the study. It may also be of wider interest to students of deviance in post-war Britain.

2 Press ideology: the politics of professionalism

'If the hegemonic viewpoint does not unilaterally have its way at all times, this does not mean that the media serve all viewpoints equally: there is no "perfect competition" in the market place of public opinions, where each individual member of the audience has an equally open chance of structuring the public discourse. Despite the requirements of "objectivity", "balance", "impartiality", etc. the media remain oriented within the framework of power: they are part of a political and social system which is "structured in dominance". Objectivity, impartiality and balance are exercised within a framework and that framework is one which, overall, the powerful, not the powerless — elites not audiences — crucially define ... the media will tend to take over, from the political elites, a way of perceiving an event, as well as a way of explaining or contextualising it.'

(Hall 1973 : 15-16)

An ideology is essentially an integrated framework of categories, concepts, and relevancies grounded in a particular mode of existence (in this case, professional journalism is the mode of existence). This framework is a largely unconscious construction which structures perception and thought, systematically excluding certain realities and promoting and shaping others[1]. At the same time as filtering reality, ideological structures permit events to be 'mapped' i.e., located within wider contexts and related to similar events. In short, ideologies are structures through which the subjective reality of things is fashioned and meaning is imposed on the social world. But structures alone are incapable of this task of reality construction. The functioning of the structures must be organized and regulated by operational rules or codes, or usage. These rules or codes direct the passage of messages through the structures and govern the 'mapping' process. They articulate the ideological system.

This may seem a rather abstract conceptualization and may be difficult to grasp as such, but its meaning and utility should become clearer as we apply it to press ideology.

There are two basic components in the system by which the press identifies and interprets 'the news'. Firstly, there is *the framework of concepts and values* which (a) permits the classification of events into types of stories — political, human interest, crime, show-biz celebrity, etc. and (b) shapes the meaning of the event, rendering it understandable in the terms of the ideological system, and implicitly defining it in a number of ways (for example, as legitimate or illegitimate, as the result of certain processes, as similar to other events, or unique, as worthy of alteration, as likely to have certain consequences as successful or unsuccessful, etc.). This framework of concepts and values is reflected in press language. It underlies and gives meaning to such well-worn phrases as 'the rule of law', 'the national interest', 'the politically motivated strike', 'holding the country to ransom', 'extremist agitators' 'fair-minded moderates', 'wage inflation', 'the silent majority', 'lowering moral and educational standards', and so on. With constant use these phrases become ideological cues, eliciting more-or-less predictable responses. One doubts if they are particularly common in most people's speech, but they are given increased currency every time they appear in the news and editorial columns. They are legitimated as common and immediately understandable modes of expression of *responsible* opinion. As such they fulfil an important insulating function for the ideological structure because criticism of its components becomes linguistically difficult. Those who wish to criticize the ideology must first reject the language of its expression and substitute an alternative — a step which can easily alienate the critic from those he seeks to persuade (Marcuse 1964, Chapter 4). The framework of concepts and values and its language is an essentially *political* component of press ideology because it derives from and reproduces the dominant meaning system of the political elite. The press, in fact acts as an agency for the wider dissemination of that meaning system and contributes towards its cultural hegemony by utilizing a similar model of society, system of categories, and way of understanding events. The second component of press ideology, however, is more distinctively *professional*. The operational rules or code of usage of the ideology are primarily supplied by *the professional imperatives of journalism*. These roughly correspond to what are conventionally termed 'news values' — the criteria of relevance which guide reporters' choice and construction of newsworthy stories. News values are tacitly accepted and implicitly understood by journalists who generally experience severe difficulty in articulating them (Galtung and Ruge 1965, Halloran 1970, Tunstall 1971a). But although news values may be difficult to explicate few journalists indeed would deny their existence or the influence they exert on press representations and accounts of reality. They are learnt through a process of informal professional socialization — reading newspapers, talking to more experienced colleagues, and observing the selection procedures of sub-editors. As one crime reporter put it:

'There is this intangible thing called a news story — I don't know how you recognise it, it's experience, I suppose. It's an odd quality. You can put six reporters in a court and they can sit through six hours of court verbiage and they'll all come out with the same story.'

This 'odd quality' or news values remains predominantly taken for granted and lies behind the more conscious typifications of news stories with which reporters also operate. For instance, the typification 'Man bites Dog' encapsulates a whole plethora of news values which stress the relevancy of the unusual, the unexpected, the dramatic, etc. (Tuchman 1973). The same news values are common to most news organizations although they may not be ordered in quite the same way from one organization to the next. Each will have its own, largely implicit, news policy and will disseminate the policy to its journalists by according appropriate weightings to the news values. This will enable a paper to develop a distinctive style. 'After years of having your copy changed by the subs I suppose you simply learn by experience the sort of stuff they want and how to get it in the paper as written' (*Daily Mirror* reporter). The values and their weightings quickly become associated with reader expectations and are justified in terms of pleasing readers and 'giving them what they want'. News values are thus translated into conventions of the craft of journalism which constrain not only what types of reality the reporter can accommodate in his accounts but also what kind of sense he can make of acceptable events. Thus, while it can be seen that news values are part of the *professional* stock of knowledge of an occupation it can also be seen that they operate in a distinctly *political* fashion by systematically excluding large segments of the social world from representation and discussion in the news media. The effect of this is that public knowledge of those segments is impoverished. Just how large and significant the segments are should become clear when we examine the contents of the operational rules of relevancy in more detail. Suffice it to say now that, considering their apparently different origins the operational rules articulate with the framework of concepts and values surprisingly effectively. But this is perhaps less surprising when we realize that, as components of an ideology, they are both grounded in the shared interest of media controllers, that they both rest on the same economic infrastructure.

The two components of the ideological system will now be analyzed in greater detail. First, I will attempt to sketch out the ideology's framework of concepts and values. This will inevitably be something like a caricature, a line drawing with minimal texture or shading; but it should suffice to identify its main features.

The framework of concepts and values [2]

Underlying the press's representations of reality is a belief in the essential justice and desirability of the present organization of society. While there may be anomalies within the distribution of rewards and an unacceptable side to the face of capitalism, the economic and political institutions of Western Liberal Democracy ensure a quality of life unsurpassed in the history of civilization. But the scale and complexity of social organization as well as the frailties of human nature and performance make reform a constant necessity. Just like a delicate piece of machinery, society requires continuous supervision and regular overhauls. Modifications to the machine become necessary, occasionally, in the interest of efficiency, but its overall design is accepted as entirely satisfactory. Any changes that are needed to improve society can be accomplished by the established agencies whose members newspapers trust to act as responsible mechanics, although they realize that the process may be an infuriatingly slow one.

For most papers the society founded on a modified free enterprise economy and democratic political institutions is characterized by a very high degree of consensus — a fundamental agreement about the nature of society, what is valuable within it, and how social life should be regulated and controlled. There is an implicit assumption that people generally have shared conceptions of what is desirable, they have common goals. Debate centres on the most appropriate means to attain these goals. The business of politics is apparently conducted within a generally accepted framework of rules and conventions which ensures that debate remains 'civilized' and deep-seated animosities are not generated. Differences of opinion are not allowed to 'get out of hand' and endanger the smooth running of the system and the stability of the consensus. As one *Daily Express* leader put it (21.2.74):

> 'When all the shouting has died down and the last vote has been cast and counted this truth will remain: there is greater unity between a Tory and a Labour man who both support Leeds than there is between two Socialists (or Tories) one of whom supports Leeds while the other follows Liverpool. In Britain, thank God, sport, not politics, is the great divider.'

In newspaper ideology fundamental social, economic, and political divisions tend to be things of the past, no longer relevant to serious discussions about the problems of modern Britain. Another *Daily Express* editorial (20.12.73) expresses this idea well:

'It is clear that the "them" and "us" attitude in Britain today is wholly, permanently and dangerously out of date. We just cannot afford the old attitudes. Employers still living in the Edwardian Age ... are an anachronism; so are trade union leaders whose thinking stopped at the 1926 General Strike.

Once we could have laughed indulgently at this Olde Englande approach. Not any more. It is Mr. Heath's job ... to spell out the national objectives. These objectives would be the same whichever party holds power: to pretend otherwise is to play[a] silly political game ...'

Politicians or union leaders who employ the rhetoric of class struggle are seen to be living in the past — 'They think they are the whiz-kids of the seventies. So they are of — of the 1870s' (*Daily Express* 1.6.73). But they are not only out of date, they are also irresponsible because talk of class conflict only mystifies the public, promotes bitterness and division, and diverts attention away from what the Press see as the 'real' problems of the economy — inflation and low productivity. The 'national objectives' on which we can all agree are the overcoming of these problems through increased efficiency and co-operation. This can only come about through the subordination of selfish, sectional interests to an overriding 'national interest'. As the *Daily Mail* (2.3.74) put it after the first General Election in 1974 had produced a rather inconclusive result:

'The people are calling for co-operation, not confrontation. This uncertain verdict is itself a mandate for moderation ... We want a nationally minded government which puts the national interest first every time.'

According to a number of papers, to identify class interests is to commit a dangerous heresy and to encourage 'the politics of envy'. Anthony Shrimsley, who has been political editor of both the *Sun* and the *Mail*, has spelt out the disruptive implications of this kind of activity:

'Men and women who once believed in fairness and justice have allowed themselves to become the standard-bearers of a kind of politics which lives on envy and malice and divides the nation at a time when such division could be fatal.'

(Daily Mail 4.7.74)

Any challenge to the hegemony of the national interest may be seen as subversion of the consensus, the very foundation of the stable, free, and peaceful life which newspapers claim we generally enjoy. To deny the national interest and to move outside the conventional structures of political participation is to leave the realm of politics and enter a twilight world of anarchy and disruption. In newspaper discourse, legitimacy is only available to those who respect the rule of law and the democratic processes which it symbolizes. Nowhere is this conception of politics more clearly demonstrated than in the coverage of the Northern Ireland troubles. The press have generally been more than willing to accept Parliament's definition of the Irish problem as one of law and order rather than politics because, as the *Daily Mail* (17.4.74) put it, 'without law and order there can be no politics'. The major political parties have maintained a fairly united front on Ulster policy and the press has not generally challenged its wisdom. The *Guardian* expressed the general sentiment well when an editorial of October 1974 declared: 'The Irish troubles, mercifully, have not become an election issue' (9.10.74). From the beginning of their campaign in 1970 the IRA were regarded as a gang of ruthless subversives attempting to impose their own brand of anarchy and tyranny on an unwilling population. They were men in love with violence for its own sake. In no way could they be seen as political actors:

'There is a myth that the IRA are a band of patriots crusading for a united Catholic Ireland. They are not ... They are lepers, not leprechauns ... their myth never was much more than a front for most of them. Behind the front lies something more sinister ... The destroyers. What we loosely call Marxists. The idea of international revolution. Of international rebellion against all that most of us hold dear.'

(Sun 15.6.74)

or in the words of the *Express* (5.12.73): 'Neither ideology nor religion has any part in this struggle. It is simply a matter of the People versus Anarchy'. The identification of direct action and extra-parliamentary opposition with anarchy and destruction is a recurring theme in press representations. The consensus and its institutions are continually threatened by the subversive activities of a small but significant minority composed of agitators, militants, criminals, degenerates, and extremists of all kinds. The rule of law and the democratic processes which it symbolizes are constantly haunted by the spectres of chaos and tyranny. As the *Sun* put it: 'The price of liberty is ETERNAL vigilance' (1.8.72). We must 'beware of the aggrophiles', 'the strife-makers', 'the people whose interests are in destruction', 'who get their kicks from stirring up trouble' (*Sun* 16.1.73). Those in public positions of responsibility who fail to condemn 'the wreckers' must be 'judged to be condoning the subversion which is threatening British democracy' (*Daily Express* 20.12.73). At the heart of that democracy lies the sovereignty of the rule of law. Newspaper ideology holds that, 'when the Law is no longer supreme, this country will be finished' (*Sun* 4.1.74). This means that: 'It is one thing to change the law through Parliament. But the law of the land, however unfair, however oppressive, must be obeyed until it is repealed' (*Daily Mirror* 20.12.74). The sanctity of the legal code, enshrined in the popular tautology 'the law is the law', must be respected even by those who believe that particular laws are immoral. As one paper said of the Industrial Relations Act:

'The Sun does not love the Indistrial Relations Act. We have said all along that it is likely to do more harm than good ... *But it is the law of the land*
The unions have a right to try to get it changed. They have the right to work for the return of a Labour Government which is pledged to repeal it.
But they do NOT — repeat NOT — have the right to set themselves up as being above the law.'   (*Sun* 20.4.72)

Newspapers insist that the law, like the other institutions of democracy, must be protected from the destructive activities of the wreckers. The wreckers, however, can apparently be beaten given a concerted effort on the part of the sensible, moderate, majority of citizens — a re-assertion of consensual values, norms, beliefs, and interests and a genuine 'tightening of belts' and spirit of co-operation in pursuit of a national interest. Only within such a climate of public support and encouragement can the forces of law and order ensure that a state of normality is maintained, that reasonableness, peace, and moderation prevail. When 'chaos' threatens the railways, or the power stations, or the schools, or whatever, the press generally council 'the public' to stand firm, united by a bond of common suffering and inconvenience, silently defiant. But they must refrain from expressing their justifiable anger by 'taking the law into their own hands'. They must wait patiently for their elected representatives (encouraged by their self-appointed representatives — the media) to get things back to normal.

But, despite its emphasis on law and order, press ideology is profoundly *liberal*. It recognizes that we live in a plural society of competing points of view in which no side can justifiably claim a monopoly of truth. There is something to be said for most arguments. There is good and bad in most people. There is, however, a small minority of people whose activities put them 'beyond the pale'. Again, the expression of dissent in Ulster provides a good example. As long as extra-parliamentary opposition was restricted to civil rights campaigning it could be treated as a legitimate area of controversy about which sensible and responsible people could hold different opinions. But as soon as the relatively peaceful protester gave way to the petrol bomber and then the gunman, and opposition became insurrection, responsible debate had to be restricted to the discussion of the most effective means of eradicating the behaviour. But repression remains either a last resort or, as was the case with internment, a temporary 'holding' measure until a more permanent solution could be found and things could return to normal. Imprisonment is a necessary evil but it should be used constructively whenever possible — our prisons should not become mere dustbins for criminals. While prisoners should not be 'molly-coddled', prison regimes should be humane enough to allow treatment and rehabilitation for all but the most serious and hopeless cases. The ideology upholds a welfare model of crime and deviance. Most ordinary lawbreakers are more sick than evil. Their lawbreaking is an expression of their differentness, their apartness, their sad inability to live by the sensible rules of normal society. They are not inherently evil but rather weak-willed and inadequate. Their weakness and inadequacy, however, makes them vulnerable to the tiny minority of people who are genuinely evil (Young 1974). These people form the hard core of wreckers whose motives are entirely selfish and destructive. Their corrupting influence can be discovered at work behind all kinds of deviant activity — behind the drug taker is the pusher, behind the prostitute is the pimp, behind the striker is the agitator, and so on. The deviant does not typically exercise free will and choose to engage in his activities, he is duped and manipulated by more sinister individuals. We are all open to suggestion:

> 'The Trots and the Reds know all there is to be known about making the tail wag the dog. The only people who can stop them are the big body of honest, ordinary trade union members … The fanatics have great staying power, and will wait for any sign that the moderates are flagging. They will try to infiltrate new organisations as they have infiltrated existing ones …'
>
> (*Sun* 1.8.72)

The press encourage us to stand firm in the face of the threat but warn that the introduction of repressive measures would only be 'playing into the hands' of the wreckers by alienating liberals. The state must not repress but it should control and regulate where necessary. This applies to the economic and welfare spheres as much as to the sphere of social deviance. For the most part newspapers accept that a certain amount of 'state interference' in the workings of the economy is unavoidable and, despite the lament of some papers for the old virtues of self reliance and family responsibility undermined by the welfare state, it is also accepted that the post-war expansion of the social services has done much to improve the quality of life. This expansion must

[handwritten margin note: this is a shared ideology imposed by norms politically correct]

now be consolidated and we must guard against, on the one hand, excessive monopolistic tendencies which would eliminate our freedom of choice, and on the other hand, the kind of 'softness' and decadence which destroys industriousness and encourages welfare 'scroungers'. As the *Daily Mail* (29.3.73) commented:

> 'The real problem is that there is a large and growing number of people who are defrauding the public ... who, worse still, see nothing wrong in doing so ... and who are, in fact, encouraged by such cynical bodies as the Claimant's Union to regard living off the state as a way of life. Worst of all, by giving the social services a bad name the scroungers injure the cause of those who really deserve help — the sick, the handicapped, the elderly and the fatherless children.'

This, then, is the essence of press ideology, or, at least, of the ideological framework of concepts and values. We can now identify the master concepts of the framework — the British way of life, the national interest, the democratic process, the rule of law, anarchy, law and order, subversion, militants and moderates, minority and majority, the public, private property, free enterprise, state interference and monopoly, and perhaps a handful of others such as family life. The dominant values of the ideology are set out in the table below.[3] They provide criteria for evaluating existing and emergent forms of behaviour.

Positive legitimating values	Negative, illegitimate values
Legality	Illegality
Moderation	Extremism
Compromise	Dogmatism
Co-operation	Confrontation
Order	Chaos
Peacefulness	Violence
Tolerance	Intolerance
Constructiveness	Destructiveness
Openness	Secrecy
Honesty	Corruption
Realism	Ideology

Positive legitimating values	*Negative, illegitimate values*
Rationality	Irrationality
Impartiality	Bias
Responsibility	Irresponsibility
Fairness	Unfairness
Firmness	Weakness
Industriousness	Idleness
Freedom of choice	Monopoly/uniformity
Equality	Inequality

Those actors who want their actions and beliefs signified as legitimate by the news media must contrive to associate themselves with the positive legitimating values. The politician seeking a 'good press' must appear 'firm but fair', his approach must seem honest and open, his policies moderate and flexible, never allowing dogmatism to distort his perception of economic and political realities, and finally in his public and private behaviour he must be seen to uphold the values of family life — love, respect, loyalty, faithfulness, consideration, etc. Similarly, the legitimacy of emergent forms of behaviour is assessed according to criteria derived from positive values. Their aims can be identified as constructive or destructive, open or secret, rational or irrational, responsible or irresponsible and so on; while the means employed in pursuit of those aims can be identified as legal or illegal, moderate or extreme, violent or peaceful, fair or unfair, etc. This process of evaluation can only be accomplished, of course, by means of shared background assumptions concerning the meaning of 'fairness' 'violence', 'moderation', and so on in typical contexts. These background assumptions constitute the most unconscious part of any ideological system. They are part of a stock of common sense knowledge (Schutz and Luckmann 1974) and as such they really only become accessible when realized in concrete evaluations.[4]

The professional news imperatives of journalism

By and large, journalists share the same stock of common sense knowledge as their readers. They are not responsible for its creation, although they do contribute towards its stability and survival. It is not part of the *professional* component of press ideology. The operation of the framework of concepts and values is ordered and controlled by at least eight professional imperatives which act as implicit guides to the construction of news stories:

1. Immediacy
2. Dramatization
3. Personalization
4. Simplification
5. Titillation
6. Conventionalism
7. Structured access
8. Novelty

*professional
imperatives
guide to construction
of TV production
(will depend on
Broadcast?)*

1. *Immediacy:*

News is about what is new, what has just happened. This means that it is centrally concerned with the present rather than the past, change rather than inertia, and events rather than long-term processes. This means large and important segments of reality are not communicated because they cannot be successfully cast in the conventional news form. The process of selection is constrained both by the medium of news and the timetable of newspaper production. Newspapers predominantly report 'developments' occurring between the two most recent printing deadlines, supplying only enough 'background' information to make the foreground event intelligible at a mundane level. The consequences of this 'event orientation' of news (Galtung and Ruge 1965; Murdock 1973) are spelt out by Paul Rock:

> 'Developments which unfold very gradually tend to be unreportable by the daily press unless some distinctive stage is reached. Phenomena which do not change appreciably have a lesser chance of being recorded unless they were expected to develop. There is thus a constant strain within the reporting enterprise to adapt the world of events to the timetable of the newspaper ... Newspapers must demonstrate that significant change has occurred during the time interval that elapsed between editions. This requirement may lead to nothing more

*not really relevant
in TV but a moveable
topic / story is*

than a special selection of what is newsworthy, but it may lead
to the imposition of development upon recalcitrant phenomena. Western newspapers are unable to contend with slow-
moving historical cycles; they are far better equipped to
accommodate rapid, expected change. They are, moreover,
generally incapable of reporting what seems to be an indeter-
minate or fluid situation. Process may be forced on occurrences
whose direction is indecisive.'   (Rock 1973:76)

News, then, is a form of communication which encourages
what Barthes (1972:151) has described as the 'miraculous evapora-
tion of history' from events. When cast as news stories events
tend to be denuded of the historical context and history of development which gives them meaning for their participants. As
Marx (1846) pointed out, without history reality becomes
vulnerable to the interpretations of a dominant ideology: '... we
must pay attention to this history, since ideology boils down to
either an erroneous conception of this history, *or to a complete
abstraction from it.*' The professional imperative of immediacy
protects the political interpretations of newspaper ideology by
robbing the reality of events of its historical dimension, a
dimension which might throw doubt on the interpretations.
Reality becomes as immediate and convenient as instant coffee.
The processes of its production and the social conditions within
which they take place are rendered irrelevant to the purposes of
consumption. Things happen, get described by newsmen and are
ingested by passive consumers with their coffee and cornflakes.
They are understandable, not as historical developments, but as
manifestations of the peculiar present, the strange times in which
we live. If we feel that this level of 'explanation' supplies an
insufficient depth of understanding we are invited to buy the
packaged interpretations of newspaper ideology displayed in the
leader columns and littering the shelves of the news stories.

2. *Dramatization:*
The event-orientation of news is reinforced by an emphasis on the
dramatic. News is commercial knowledge designed in a situation

of competition with profit in mind. Its purveyors are concerned with grabbing the attention of prospective audiences by making an 'impact'. This stress on impact contributes towards the predisposition to communicate concrete happenings and to neglect underlying patterns of motivation and belief. Actions lend themselves far more easily to sensational treatment than do thoughts. This is a consideration essential to the understanding of the manner in which, for instance, political dissent is reported. It leads to a concentration on the form rather than the content of opposition. As John Whale (1971:48) put it: 'Journalists are better at reporting the fact than the matter of protest. The antics of the unilateral nuclear disarmers were always better copy than their arguments.'

But the 'antics' of protesters are not only good copy, they form the basis for the evaluation of the general worth of the protest. The presence or absence of violence during a demonstration becomes perhaps the most significant factor in judging and signifying the legitimacy of the cause it represents, as dramatization directs attention away from the meaning of the event for its participants. The search for impact sensitizes the reporter to any violent form of expression which is then taken up and isolated from underlying political convictions. Meaningful action is transformed into spectacle for passive consumers of news; a tendency noted by Graham Murdock in his discussion of the press coverage of the London demonstration against the Vietnam war in October 1968:

'Readers are...placed in the role of spectators, encouraged to participate vicariously in the performance through projecting themselves into the situation and/or identifying with the central characters. In many ways therefore newspapers are part of the entertainment business...The presentation of events in terms of the theatrical and spectacular follows logically from journalists' conceptions of what attracts readers, but it nevertheless has important consequences...By presenting the demonstration participants as performers within a spectacle the press coverage emptied their actions of their radical political content. For once the demonstration was conceived as play-acting and therefore both transitory and 'not for real' it become simultaneously both entertaining and capable of being contained and assimilated ... by choosing to work through the medium of public spectacle, demonstrations invariably open themselves to the possibility that they will be appropriated as entertainment.' ₘₒᵣₑ ᵥᵢₑʷₚₒᵢₙₜₛ   (Murdock 1973:165-66)

Thus the imperative of dramatization has the effect of trivializing dissent and focusing public attention on the symptoms rather than the causes of 'social problems'. As Hartmann and Husband have noted in their analysis of race relations, in the news media:

'The subjective skills of the newsman when applied to the reporting of race produce an emphasis on conflict, negativeness and the unusual that ... sets "newsworthiness" at odds with reporting underlying trends and background information. It is the discrete event which is more able to encapsulate the elements of conflict and excitement, and which can be condensed into a forceful news story. The underlying processes of urban living and the "reasons" for prejudice and discontent are, on these criteria, less amenable than are the manifestations of violence, crime and individual tragedy which are the more visible symptoms.'   (Hartmann and Husband 1974:159)

3. *Personalization:*

News is not simply about instantly packaging drama, it is about personalities. The cult of the star is perhaps the most pervasive product of the cultural fetishism of modern society. Modernization brings with it a proliferation of celebrities (Alberoni 1972; Taylor 1975). The development of industrialization and the growth of cities and geographical mobility, coupled with the development of a mass entertainment media has resulted in a widening of community horizons:

'The media of mass communication begin to present to the public persons who belong to the extended community and who become an object of interest, identification and collective evaluation. With the progress of visual information persons in the entertainment world begin, to an increasing degree to make their mark. Their lives, their social relationships, become an object of identification or a projection of the needs of the mass of the population, a bench-mark for positive or negative evaluation, the chance to have experience in the domain of the morally possible, and a living testimony to the possibility of achieving a rise in personal status.'   (Alberoni 1972:96)

The celebrity is increasingly a focus of attention not because of what he does but because of what he *is* or what he represents. He is an image, an embodiment of popular fantasy, a projection of the ideal and an object of commercial interest and exploitation. More often than not this commercial interest and exploitation transforms the public person into a commodity susceptible to the fluctuations and caprice of consumer demand. The fickleness of the entertainment consumer means that new products must be continually on offer. A steady stream of talent must be discovered and processed. In Daniel Boorstin's words (1963), 'we have discovered the process by which fame is manufactured'.

We have taken this short detour by way of the stars because the pervasive emphasis on celebrities in our culture has important implications for the news media. The more that news enters the market place of entertainment the more it is obliged to recognize and promote the cult of the star. The consequence of this is not merely that front pages are occupied by the famous arriving at Heathrow, but that issues increasingly become defined and presented in terms of personalities, catering for the public desire for identification fostered by the entertainment media. Politics becomes a gladiatorial spectacle in which the conflict of policies is reduced to the clash of personalities as THATCHER ATTACKS CALLAGHAN or vice versa. Events are to be understood not by reference to certain structural arrangements and social processes but either (a) as the work of individuals or (b) through their effects on individuals.[5]

The first mode of understanding is obviously consonant with

those components in the press's ideological framework which interpret collective deviant activity as a consequence of the work of corrupters, the tiny minority of wreckers who play on the weaknesses of the normally moderate and reasonable majority. The professional imperative of personalization encourages their identification and isolation as objects for the projection of negative popular fantasies. A whole social demonology is established and the genre of exposé journalism is enriched by stories of the form 'We name the men behind the ... industrial chaos/drugs and pornography racket/student unrest/land speculation', etc. Men like Hugh Scanlon, Mick McGahey, and Tariq Ali achieve a notoriety out of all proportion to their influence. Again, the effect is to direct attention away from structural causes and deviant motivations, and this is also true of the second mode of understanding events and processes — through their impact on individuals. This appears to be based first on the tacit assumption that 'ordinary people' can only grasp the meaning of abstractions when they are presented in vivid personalized terms which allow for identification. Thus inflation becomes intelligible by examining its effect on the housekeeping of a Greater London housewife, while violence can be understood through an interview with a mugger's victim. Now, I am not suggesting that this type of approach is irrelevant to an understanding of the phenomena of inflation and violence, but rather that it conveys only one dimension of the phenomena. Moreover, it tends to merely reinforce the 'everyday, common sense' impressions which the reader already has of the phenomena. This is because the professional socialization of popular journalism encourages the reporter to adopt the perspective of his readers, recording those aspects of news events which are directly relevant to their practical activities. Dave Morley (1974) has noted this orientation in his analysis of media coverage of industrial conflict:

'The basis of this approach lies in the media presenter usually taking the point of view of the consumer — who fails to get his goods and services because of the dispute ... But this

elevation of the consumption sphere is very misleading — precisely because it neglects the sphere of production and our different relations to the means of production, which generate the structural conflicts, which cause the disputes by which we *are* all inconvenienced ... From this standpoint interviews with hospital workers representatives repeatedly enquired what their action meant "in terms of the patients", while a representative of the striking London teachers was asked: "I'm sure a lot of people will be wondering, where do the children fit into all this ... aren't they suffering as a result of your battle with the government?".'
                                                                    (Morley 1974:13)

The 'elevation of the consumption sphere' in the context of the imperative of personalization results in the dominant meaning of a rail dispute being signified by a stranded commuter at Southend, or the dominant meaning of the Glasgow dustmen's strike being conveyed by a squaddie loading a dustcart. The victims of structural conflicts and collective motivations are of 'human interest' in a way in which the conflicts and motivations are not.

4. *Simplification:*

A fourth tendency inherent in journalists' conceptions of news is the oversimplification of reality, the elimination of the shades of grey that lie between black and white, the glossing over of the subtle complexities of motivation and situation which make human action intelligible at a level beyond the mundane one of 'common-sense', 'cliche', 'folk wisdom', and taken-for-granted assumption. This simplifying tendency is intimately bound up with practical standards of professional competence. The popular news story must be quickly assimilable and easily comprehended by readers of widely differing intellectual abilities. Arthur Christiansen, one of the most successful editors of the *Daily Express*, defined a bad news story as: '... a story that cannot be absorbed on the first time of reading. It is a story that leaves questions unanswered. It is a story that has to be read two or three times to be comprehended.'

dumbing down

For the popular journalist, then, good reporting involves 'pruning down' the reality of a situation, trimming its rough edges and moulding its shape to fit the pre-existing forms of news. Reality must accommodate news, just as news must trade off reality. Whenever possible, social situations must be reduced to the binary oppositions which provide the materials and dynamics of spectacle and drama — good vs bad / pros vs antis / unions vs Government / moderates vs extremists / Callaghan vs Thatcher. Loose ends must be tied up and the story must remain uncluttered by 'unnecessary' impediments to immediate comprehension.

Among mass-circulation papers the imperative of simplification applies equally to news and leader columns. The chief leader writer of a tabloid daily told me that, in writing editorials for his paper 'simplicity is the keynote' and this entails 'pruning the message down to the minimum' because 'I don't think our particular readership is going to stay with a long leader however interesting and well-reasoned it may be'. However, he recognizes that pruning the message may well reduce the depth of readers' understanding: *audience*

making story easy to read

'At times one has a thesis one believes in and thinks is important, but one has to reject it completely on the grounds that it is not one that can be put into a form that is acceptable for our readers. More often one has to reject parts of it, simplifying, even sometimes over-simplifying the argument, in the hope that you can get the key points home ... A leader is a firm opinion put forward by the paper. I think it should be a balanced opinion ... [that] comes down firmly on one side — I never have gone in for fence-squatting leaders. But, of course, the need for brevity and clear concision makes it less possible to do justice, actually to spell out the two cases.'

I asked him if he ever felt he was underestimating his readership:

'Yes, sometimes, but not very often. I know we have a lot of intelligent readers ... but I do think that a very big majority, are not stupid (I never think our readers are stupid), but lack a high academic training and the ability to follow a complicated argument. And the little bit of good that one is doing is in taking complicated arguments that these people need to understand and finding ways of putting them across simply. I don't regard this as writing down to people, really ... I think that any newspaper should be tending to stretch its audience a little further rather than slipping back and becoming more trivial and over-simplified. But I still think that it's very, very easy to lose touch with the mass of the readers by going out too hard to talk to the cream. If a paper like ours has any purpose at all it is to keep in touch with the ordinary, not-so-well-educated, not-so-well-informed reader. Give the readers what they want, but try to make them want a little more. But the emphasis is on the little, if you try to make them want a lot more too fast you lose touch all together. Even from a purely commercial point of view it's fatal, obviously, but I'm not thinking primarily of the commercial side.'

Simplification, then, is an accommodation to perceived audience needs which tends to dichotomize complex reality, facilitating the presentation of events in a dramatic and personalized form.

5. *Titillation:*

Jock Young writes of newspaper journalists:

'They have discovered that people read avidly news which titillates their sensibilities and confirms their prejudices ... They hold their readers' attention by presenting material and sexual desiderata in an alluring, although forbidden, form ... They fascinate, titivate, and then reassure by finally condemning.'
(Young 1974:239)

This may not apply so much to the *Financial Times* as it does to the *Sun*, but it is a generalization of considerable importance in understanding the genre of popular journalism[6].

The advertizing executives of monopoly capitalism have long realized that, carefully handled, sexual titillation can sell anything from cars to carpets. It also sells newspapers, either in the form of nudes or news: tasteful nudes and scandalous news. It is the scandalous news which will concern us here. If the press lives by disclosure, it thrives on scandal. The popular press has turned salacious gossip into an art, providing its readers with vicarious enjoyment without the need for involvement, the age-old recipe of the voyeur. But while the press develops and caters for the voyeuristic predilections of its readers it studiously distances itself from the activities portrayed. It maintains a self-righteous moral rectitude which denies the desirability of illicit pleasure. The *News of the World*, of course, supplies the classic example of this combination of titillation and condemnation. Its present owner, Rupert Murdock has said of the paper: 'The "News of the World" used to be like a morality play. It used to write about people who were in trouble for doing wrong, or for being adulterous with their neighbour's wife, or whatever, and they always came to a sticky end' (*Guardian* 28.8.74). Ignoring the implication that the paper is no longer like that, this is a very clear statement of the *News of the World*'s commercial formula — the simultaneous portrayal and condemnation of the more exotic and lurid forms of deviance. This applies primarily to expressions of sexuality but it also operates with regard to other forms of illicit hedonism such as drug taking or occultism. Such deviations become a spectacle which may be glimpsed without involvement or contamination. The reader can sit over his cornflakes in mild moral indignation while today's SHOCK HORROR PROBE into yesterday's SEX/DRUGS/WITCHCRAFT ORGY unfolds its unseemly content.

Titillation becomes a suitably commercial context in which to set the activities of personalities — pop stars, footballers, actors, criminals, and even, occasionally, politicians.

When Lord Longford's pornography investigators discussed this emphasis on titillation with Hugh Cudlipp and other members of the IPC editorial board, it was suggested that the 'undue pre-occupation with sex' might be a result of popular disillusion with politics and the need for diversion from what many young people felt to be an over-controlled and uniform society (Longford 1972:323). It might equally be argued that the commercial imperative of titillation trivializes reality and diverts attention from politics and social problems, substituting superficial salacity for genuine understanding and thus clearing the ground for the interpretations of newspaper ideology.

6. *Conventionalism:* codes and conventions

The interpretations of newspaper ideology provide the basic materials for the operation of conventionalism — the situating of emergent phenomena in existent structures of meaning. To understand this imperative we must briefly examine paradigm shifts in journalism over the last century. Of particular importance are changes in the status and meaning of 'objective reporting'. Towards the end of the nineteenth century the journalist's traditional role of independent commentator on events gave way to that of professional translator and negotiator between audiences and institutions. As James Carey notes:

> 'In this role he does not principally utilise an intellectual skill as critic, interpreter and contemporary historian, but a technical skill at writing, a capacity to translate the specialised language of government, science, art, medicine, finance into an idiom that can be understood by broader, more amorphous, less educated audiences.'   (Carey 1969:32)

This process of professionalism accompanied the growth of mass circulation papers and was characterized by a commitment to 'objective reporting'. Carey argues that objectivity was originally grounded in a purely commercial motive — 'the need of mass newspapers to serve politically heterogeneous audiences without alienating any significant segment of the audience' — but was subsequently rationalized into 'a canon of professional competence and an ideology of professional responsibility'. But it might also be noted that objectivity reflected nineteenth century positivist precepts of knowledge[7], the desirability of amassing a large collection of ill-digested 'facts' commonly accepted by historians of the period. Moreover, objectivity may have represented a means of legitimating 'the fourth estate' and allaying the fears of the bourgeoisie about the subversive potential of popular journalism. In any case, the paradigm of objectivity severely restricted the journalist's role as critic. Its overthrow has proved a lengthy affair, although its biases and limitations have long been apparent to sceptical journalists. It still retains its hold on newsmen's accounts in the residual form of the media's structure of access, which will be examined shortly. However, the need for interpretative reporting is now widely recognized and justified by a belief in the need to reduce the ambiguity of news by organizing the immediate chaos of isolated news events into a more coherent framework of knowledge, i.e., in a world of complex and fast-moving events, the public require expert interpretative aid if they are to successfully understand the meaning and significance of the news. To some extent, background information must be provided and the historical nature of news remedied by supplying the reader with an interpretative context. But if this context is to be immediately intelligible it must be familiar. Thus, there is a tendency for new events to be cast as well-known scenarios. We are offered a normalization of the potentially problematic, a collection of familiar images. For example, each new expression of protest against government policy, or American imperialism, or in favour of higher grants is reduced to 'just another student demonstration'. Each new expression of industrial conflict becomes just another strike to endure. As Graham Murdock puts it:

'The news process therefore establishes its own links between situations, links not at the level of underlying structures and processes but at the level of immediate forms and images. Situations are identified as the same if they look the same. In this way news rewrites history for immediate popular consumption.'   (Murdock 1973:165)

Within the paradigm of interpretative reporting the journalist is once more a purveyor of meanings and a potential critic, but the range and variety of his criticism have been greatly reduced in the process of paradigm change. The independent and innovatory qualities of interpretation have been largely replaced by organizational commitment and conventionality of meaning and style. Instead of aiding his audience to come to terms with old realities in new ways, the journalist now tends to help his audience to come to terms with new realities in old ways. It is this tendency which led Galtung and Ruge to remark that all 'news' is to some extent 'olds'. As 'olds', fresh thought about new phenomena becomes unnecessary, they merely require locating within the existing frameworks of press ideology and to this end the newspapers help their readers by supplying 'cues' and 'signs' for correct identification and location. This was succinctly expressed by a crime reporter who suggested that news stories were really 'simple clichés set to music — you select the right cliché and you write it up to suit the particular circumstances'.

Thus we receive our news extensively predigested, coded, and packaged in conventional parcels. As Burgelin (1972:323) has observed: 'Mass communications are plainly not just so much raw material of which the consumer ... can make absolutely anything he likes; they are products which have already been extensively pre-structured ... by the conditions under which they were manufactured.' In part, this pre-structuring takes the form of standardized formats and conventionalized selection procedures but it is also reflected in recurrent explanations legitimations and evaluations of social phenomena.

These structures of meaning have become incorporated into journalism's stock of knowledge and as conventional wisdoms they constitute both a source on which the journalist may draw in arriving at understandings of phenomena, and a conservative constraint on the construction of stories in that they provide 'ready-made' interpretations of new phenomena. The interpretations, of course, draw on and sustain newspaper ideology, but it would be misleading to isolate them from wider cultural beliefs and understandings. As Stuart Hall says of the news media's frameworks of meaning:

'They are widely shared, though not by everyone, and are not understood in the same way by groups who have different life-situations and projects ... These maps of meaning give plausibility, order and coherence to discrete events, by placing them within a common world of meanings. Culture is knitted together by these overlapping, partially closed, incomplete mappings of problematic social reality. Such "structures" tend to define and limit the range of possible new meanings which can be constructed to explain new and unfamiliar events. In part, such normative structures are historical constructs, already objectivated and available as the informal social knowledge — "what everybody knows" about a social situation. They have been routinised and sedimented over time ... They contain or make use of their own "logic-in-use", which serves as a set of loose generative rules which governs the way the "explanation" can be used. Such normative definitions contain strong predispositions to "see" events in certain ways: they tend to "rule in" and "rule out" certain kinds of additional inferences ... At the level of everyday comprehension, the common sense world is "classified out" in stereotypical ways which simplify and crystallize complex social processes in distinctive ways. At this level, then, they surface in the form of informal "models", ad hoc explanations, proverbs, maxims, routines, recipes, truncated social myths, images and scenarios. At the level of social life as a whole they "surface" as full-blown ideologies ...

(Hall 1974:299)

The journalist's conventional interpretations, then, both inform and reflect a somewhat fragmented, but more-or-less hegemonic, ideology. They are the bits and pieces of a world view pressed into the service of occupational pressures. There are, in fact, two ways in which they can 'work' for the journalist. First, they can enhance his personal understanding of social phenomena, enable him to make sense of the world. Or, second, knowledge of conventional interpretations can enable him to produce *public* accounts acceptable to his various audiences (editors, readers, sources) while allowing him to employ alternative interpretations in his *private* construction of reality. By employing these interpretations the journalist can be sure that he is on tested ground, that he will not give offence and that his reporting is likely to be seen as 'responsible' by editors as well as reputable and influential individuals outside the news organization.[8] Moreover, conventional interpretations are convenient. They allow the journalist working under deadline pressures to produce copy rapidly with a minimum of thought and preparation. But, whether the reporter internalizes or distances himself from these interpretations, the imperative of conventionalism (like the other professional imperatives) is so closely bound up with the phenomenon of 'news' that it will exert a significant influence on his perceptual apparatus and subsequent construction of stories. They will tend to act as 'inferential structures' (Lang and Lang 1965) filtering acceptable reality and moulding events to fit pre-conceptions. Interpretative conventions, in short, contribute towards overall frames of reference within which phenomena are defined and signified. The study by Halloran and his colleagues of the 1968 London anti-Vietnam war demonstration provides a striking example of the operation of inferential structures:

> 'During the month or so prior to 27 October ... the newspapers defined the event as likely to be a violent confrontation of the forces of law and order (as represented by the Police) and the forces of anarchy (as represented by the radical groups participating), with the result that when these predictions were contradicted by the peaceful behaviour of the vast majority of the marchers, the discrepancy was resolved by concentrating attention upon those aspects of the event which were violent.'
> (Halloran 1970:90)

The reality of the event was subordinated to considerations of the 'event as news'.

7. *Structured access:*

The imperative of structured access is a residue of the objectivity paradigm in journalism which requires that news stories be firmly grounded in the authoritative pronouncements of experts in the fields covered by the stories. It survives largely because it helps to situate the media within the State's framework of power, defining their relationship to the plurality of institutional elites in the wider society. In the press the structure of access ensures that newspaper accounts and representations are 'structured in dominance'; that there is a systematic tendency to take up definitions of situations and events articulated by those in legitimate institutional positions, and to exclude definitions developed by those who lack formal qualifications to comment (Hall 1972; 1973). From his privileged position of access, Tony Benn has drawn attention to the possible consequences of this denial of direct public communication to the voice of non-institutionalized dissent. He argues that the coverage of demonstrations regularly contains 'discussions among the usual panel of pundits' who talk 'absolutely predictably' about the significance of the event and the problem of law and order. He goes on:

> 'But the only thing we shan't get, either before, during or after is any opportunity to hear, first-hand, at length, and in peace, the views of those who are organizing these demonstrations ... In part they are protesting against the very denial to them and others of any real access for their views on the mass media. All they can be certain of is that their demonstrations will be fully covered on the mass media and undoubtedly that knowledge itself stimulates the demonstrations. If law and order were ever to break down, in part or in whole, in Britain, the policy of restricted access and unrestricted coverage would have to bear a very considerable part of the responsibility.'
>
> (Speech at Bristol 18.10.68)

Benn is pointing to the way in which the structure of access mediates between the reality and the public signification of events, and causes the media to systematically 'over-assess' (a) accredited spokesmen of the State and powerful organizations and (b) certificated experts who are looked to to provide 'impartial' comment and evaluation. This structure of access has its ultimate and implicit base in what Howard Becker has termed society's 'hierarchy of credibility'.

> 'In any system of ranked groups, participants take it as given that members of the highest group have the right to define the

way things really are ... those at the top have access to a more complete picture of what is going on than anybody else. Members of lower groups will have incomplete information and their view of reality will be partial and distorted in consequence.'
(Becker 1967)

Thus, it is argued, members of soceity tend to place greater reliance on the statements of those in powerful positions of authority, those who are in possession of all the 'facts'. Journalists do tend to be less credulous than most when it comes to believing the accounts supplied by the 'official sources' they cultivate, but it does not prevent them reproducing those accounts in preference to those of less powerful sources. They will often take informal accounts to official sources for confirmation or denial. One Fleet Street crime correspondent told me that whenever possible he uses his police contacts to test the veracity of information derived from other sources: 'you don't know what to believe because they [the non-police sources] are all on the fringes of criminal activity'. But despite the rhetoric of truth-seeking with which he may surround his activity, the journalist is primarily interested in the *acquisition* of official accounts (irrespective of their veracity) because his editors expect him to obtain them, and to obtain them quickly. Thus the production demands of the news organization largely dictate the reporter's priorities and relevance structures and encourage the fairly uncritical reliance on official sources reported by this *Guardian* journalist: 'I think we accept Scotland Yard statements too easily, for the sake of convenience. They must feed us information that they want to put out which we accept because it's convenient.'

Perhaps nowhere is this problem of interpretation of source accounts and the possible manipulation by sources more acute than in Northern Ireland, where conflict has sharpened many people's awareness of how the news media may be used to advantage. As a result, journalists covering the troubles sometimes experience severe difficulties in maintaining the conventional hierarchy of credibility operative in other situations. Robert Fisk, then Belfast correspondent for *The Times*, summarized the difficulties in a BBC documentary:

'The overall problem in Northern Ireland, particularly, is that whereas in Britain one tends to trust the authorities automatically and assume that criminals are always saying things which are untrue, in Northern Ireland, as far as extremists are concerned you generally distrust them in the same way — when I read a statement from the IRA I start from the principle that it's untrue and then see if it's true. When a statement comes from the army or the police or the government, I read it very carefully but I don't accept it at face value because there have been numerous occasions when I have found it hasn't contained all the truth, or it's only contained part of the truth, or, on one or two occasions, it hasn't been true at all.'

('Inside the Press', BBC I, 26.1.75)

The journalist, however, finds himself under enormous pressure to accept the 'official version' of events. When he records an interview with an IRA source he may be accused of providing 'a forum for the enemy', and when he attempts to report dispassionately on terrorist activity he lays himself open to 'accusations of condoning, even encouraging offensive conduct' (*Daily Mail* 14.5.73). The type of 'responsibility' expected of him was spelt out in 1973 by the then Northern Ireland Secretary, William Whitelaw in an address to the Parliamentary Press Gallery (15.6.73). He pointed to the dangers of lowering the morale of the Security Forces, referring to one soldier who had asked him 'Whose side are the newspapers on? Ours or theirs?', Whitelaw then went on to comment:

'... newspapers, television and radio, I believe, perform a valuable public service and perform it in Northern Ireland with real responsibility. But it is not at all easy to persuade a serving soldier liable to have a bullet in his back or whose comrade was blown to pieces by a blast bomb that journalists were perfectly entitled to maintain friendly contact with those sources out to kill and maim them ... Publish and be damned in some circumstances is an admirable precept. But there may be times when to follow that maxim of the communication business — and that is the danger of Northern Ireland — can have a diametrically opposed effect to what we all want ... In the fight for freedom can one be neutral? Surely one is either for it or against?'

Whitelaw's invective, however, was only echoing sentiments already expressed in editorials and features. In November 1971, the Chief Leader writer of the *Daily Express* (11.11.71) had warned:

'While British troops are involved in fighting a terrorist-anarchist organisation ... there is no room for impartiality ... There is no question here of political censorship ... people who bomb, kill and maim in order to smash the fabric of society put themselves outside the normal conventions, which include freedom of speech ... the soldier or the policeman who never knows where the next shot will come from deserves support in a hazardous and desperately difficult task. The snide remark which undermines his morale is almost as bad as the sniper's bullet.'

On the same day the *Daily Mail* had deplored the appearance of the 'apologists of violence ... lounge suited and sitting in a [television] studio', commenting, 'even Hitler could have put up a good case on Panorama'. His message to readers and journalists was clear: 'all newspapers and all TV producers must take a far more critical attitude towards what is, directly or indirectly, IRA propaganda'.

Editorials like this serve to explicitly define the limits of access, impartiality, and objectivity in a situation where implicit working definitions have become problematic. They reorientate the position of newspapers *vis-à-vis* the state and they reassert the framework within which responsible reporting and debate may legitimately take place.

8. *Novelty:*
Each of the professional news imperatives discussed so far intermesh to support and articulate newspaper ideology. But there is at least one imperative which introduces an element of randomness into newspaper accounts, even though it too may

facilitate the use of the ideological interpretations and stereotypes. That imperative is the one which demands that stories be
'kept alive' by the search for fresh 'news angles':   *fresh or hype*

> 'When you're working for a pop paper where there is always
> this desperate search for a thing called an angle, it isn't enough
> that something has happened, there must be an angle, there
> must be something different, we must have something that
> somebody else hasn't got, and because we've got something
> that somebody else hasn't got it must be right up the top. The
> plain facts are distorted round to suit this particular angle.'
>
> (Crime Correspondent)

The imperative of novelty encourages speculation, often
speculation supported by only slender evidence. In some cases
when deadlines become oppressively close, almost any story may
suffice, almost any fresh twist of interpretation may become
acceptable. At times like this reporters occasionally file copy which
is distinguished by little more than the doubtful reliability of its
sources. The stories which result are often idiosyncratic but they
may also be collectively shared and managed. Stories of IRA
reprisals after the trial at Winchester of those responsible for the
bombing of The Old Bailey in 1973 provide a revealing example.
The story that finally appeared in a number of papers involved an
IRA plot to kidnap ten English villagers as hostages against the
release of the convicted bombers. The idea originated from an
Irish journalist covering the trial who had floated it in conversation
with a fairly junior member of The Provisionals. A journalist who
covered the trial for an English 'quality' newspaper now takes up
the narrative:

> 'You'd got the position where there was a little ring of people
> who agreed this was a good story but it was also a dodgy story
> so it needed more than one person to run it to give it credi-
> bility. It was decided to run it and so it was put to the police: was
> this a possibility? Well, what can the police say? If they say,
> "no this is absurd and ridiculous" but it actually happens,
> they are completely in the can. So the police never discount
> anything as a possibility.

I didn't write it at all. I rang my news desk and told them what it was and how it had arisen, and I said, "look, the other papers are going to be using it and when they come out there's going to be a big flap on the night desk because we haven't got it" (there's always a flap when you haven't got a story). I said, "this is ridiculous and I don't intend to be a party to it", and the attitude of the office was "fair enough, don't, we won't care if the other papers run it all over the front page and the back page as well, we won't carry a word of it because if that's your judgement then fair enough. If you prove to be wrong then you'll have to answer for it". The next day some of the other reporters were discussing it, saying "good yarn" and everything, and one of them came over to me and said, "you know, I respect you for not running that story. The trouble with us, you know, is that we've got to keep the meal ticket going". The bloke was genuinely ashamed about it.'

This type of collective speculation may result in stories which are not in keeping with newspaper ideology but it is, perhaps, more likely that speculation will be guided by the news imperatives and will draw upon conventionalized interpretations.

It should now be clear that the professional news imperatives of journalism provide the necessary support for newspaper ideology. They add to the plausibility of ideological accounts and representations through the provision of working definitions of news and practical rules for the accomplishment of reportorial work. But this social organization of reporting can only supply *foundations* for the plausibility of newspaper accounts to those whose practical purposes are bound up with the assembling of those accounts i.e., newspapermen themselves. The consumer of news will have different practical purposes and will utilize different criteria in judging the plausibility of the interpretations he meets in his newspaper. These consumer criteria of plausibility are not really the subject of this study but it is perhaps worth speculating that they are also likely to make reference to the utility of interpretations for various practical accomplishments. Paramount among these accomplishments is probably commonsense

understanding. That is, as recent commentators have suggested
(Mepham 1973; Morley 1974), the power of newspaper interpretations lies in their ability to make events intelligible at a mundane,
'commonsense' level, to provide a guide for practical activity and
to alleviate the need for further investigation and consideration.
The self-confident and assertive style in which the interpretations
are communicated complements their general claim to represent
the opinions of all right-minded people and encourages their
ready acceptance as self-evident and 'obvious'. They may be
absorbed as part of a routine and habitualized way of making
sense of the world which typically operates below the threshold of
consciousness. This commonsense mode of understanding trades
off myths and stereotypes which provide simple, comfortable,
ready-made pictures and explanations of things. It does this
because it is grounded in everyday practical concerns which allow
no time to probe beneath the surface of things. The interpretations of popular newspapers tend to fit admirably into the
commonsense world of everyday life because they make few
intellectual demands on the reader. They promote a peculiarly
restricted mode of understanding by signifying the definitional
characteristics of a phenomenon and its causation by reference to
highly selective aspects of the phenomenon. This process 'works',
it is suggested, because the aspects selected are ones to which most
readers can easily relate. Thus, the elevation of the consumption
sphere and the role of agitators in the signification of industrial
disputes (Morley 1974) is effective because readers can readily
identify themselves as consumers and have usually met someone
apparently intent on 'stirring up trouble'. Moreover, the
acceptance of these elevations releases the reader from any further
obligation to the onerous task of making sense of the peculiar
present. The significations of political dissent in conspiritorial
terms or delinquency in terms of meaningless violence similarly
derive their effectiveness from their apparent ability to 'explain
away' the phenomena i.e., to provide simplistic understandings
which pass as sufficient for all practical purposes. I do not wish to
imply that readers are necessarily credulous in their approach to
news[9]. On the contrary, suspicion of newspaper accounts is

deeply ingrained in our culture — it is part of 'what everybody knows' that one has to take what the papers say 'with a pinch of salt'. But I would suggest that it is easier for most readers to reject the open, substantive (factual) content of newspaper accounts than the more latent and implicit interpretive schema in which that content is embedded. These schema are easily absorbed into the common stock of knowledge in a largely subliminal fashion.

The process of 'backdoor' absorbtion provides the context of the examination of law-and-order news which now follows. But in the final analysis, the degree to which newspaper accounts of reality are accepted as credible must remain an open question.

3 Blood-soaked cheque-books: the golden age of crime reporting

' "We believe in the sensational presentation of news and views, especially important news or views, as a necessary and valuable public service in these days of mass readership and democratic responsibility. We shall go on being sensational to the best of our ability." '

Silvester Bolam of The *Daily Mirror* (Cudlipp) 1962 : 116)

This chapter traces the development of crime reporting as a specialist field of journalism, relating it to concurrent changes in the pattern of crime and social deviance in post-war Britain. Both in this and the following chapter we shall be looking at how crime reporting, as the journalistic core of law-and-order news, has interpreted and signified these changes, particularly, at how it has grouped them into identifiable crises of law and order. In framing the image of these crises and delineating the contours of the surrounding debate, law-and-order news takes on a vital political significance and becomes the object and prize of urgent political conflict. Those in powerful institutional positions, of course, are constantly aware of the importance of media representations, and regularly compete to have their particular definitions, conceptualizations and understandings adopted by media discourse, but the ideological struggle for dominance develops a singular importance during crises of stability. As Claus Mueller (1973) has pointed out, this is because they constitute a potentially acute challenge to the hegemony of powerful groups and their ideology of liberalism:

'The insistance on law and order in advanced industrial societies of the West clearly demonstrates the dilemma of political systems in search of legitimation. The very moment law and order becomes the dominant theme and constitutional rights are mutated or simply negated in order to grant more coercive power, to the state, the political system's inability to solve these structural problems from which conflicts arise becomes apparent.'   (Mueller 1973:180)

It would perhaps be more accurate to say *may* become apparent because, as we shall see, the typical reaction of the news media serves to further obscure those structural problems by reasserting the legitimacy of prevailing social arrangements. The press, particularly, becomes a repository and disseminator of the collective fantasies of the established order as it struggles to keep chaos at bay. The role of these collective fantasies at times of widespread social change has been analyzed by Christopher Booker in his intermittently perceptive study of post-war Britain (1970). He writes:

'As a society loses its organic homogeneity, lines of stress appear between its component groups — between class and class, between generation and generation, between rulers and ruled. Two things then happen. First, as each group becomes more conscious of its own identity so it tends to project a group-fantasy embodying its dreams of self-assertion, and its aggression against other groups. Obviously the group-fantasies of the "under-privileged" of the lower classes, the young, the rising ethnic group, tend to be "vitality" fantasies (making up what we may call the basic "left-wing" fantasy) associated with change, revolution, vigour, freedom and the future. While the group-fantasies of the established order, which feels itself to be threatened by this new aggressive force and reacts with aggression of its own, the upper classes, the older generation, the dominant racial group, take the form of "orderly" fantasies associated with stability, law and order, discipline, resistance to change and the better days of the past.'   (Booker 1970:64)

While much of Booker's theorizing rests on questionable foundations (notably the highly deterministic model of a 'fantasy cycle' he uses in his analysis), his conceptualizations of right and left-wing fantasy can be heuristically useful to the student of law-and-order news.

Right-wing order fantasy may be legitimately identified as a constant theme in crime reporting. It appears to generate the everyday predispositions and interpretative conventions of the genre, the tone of shocked indignation and the undertones of vicarious salacity or celebration apparent in so much crime journalism. This is presumably because fantasy, lies at the root of sensationalism. It is a latent presence in routine stories of robbery and rape just as it manifests itself in headline news of crime waves, menace, bombs, and butchery. It links crime reporting firmly to the related genres of thriller and detective fiction. This, of course, carries significant implications for our overall understanding of criminality and the multi-faceted phenomenon of law-breaking. As Robert Roshier (1971a) has observed of newspaper selectivity: 'The dangers of our experiencing crime through the "fantasy world" of crime fiction are almost certainly no more important than the dangers of our experiencing it through the selective reporting of actual events.' Roshier's study, however, focused more on mundane, day-to-day crime reporting of the trivial, senti-mental, human interest type than on the more sensational, front-page crime news. But it is the reader interest generated by sensational crime news that provides the *raison d'être* for crime as a specialist field of journalism. Sensational stories are the bread and butter of crime journalism, not simply the jam. Mundane court reports and human interest stories can usually be left to generalists, stringers, and freelancers. If we wish to understand the development of specialist crime reporting and its contribution to law-and-order news we must make sensational stories our primary concern.

The remainder of this chapter consists of an essentially impressionistic account of the development of crime reporting, and its changing social context, in post-war Britain. I have attempted, wherever possible, to buttress my impressions by referring to more detailed studies of the phenomena described or by drawing on original interview material.

The development of crime reporting

Ths history of crime reporting as a specialist field of journalism is characterized by:-

  i. An increasing reliance on one major institutional source — the Police.
  ii. A long-standing tradition of source suspicion and secrecy.
  iii. The increasing autonomy and complexity of the crime reporter's role.

Before the First World War there were no crime correspondents as we understand the term today. This, of course, does not mean that newspapers were devoid of crime news. The nineteenth century saw the development of the tradition of sensational crime reporting in the Sunday newspapers and in the specialist publications such as the *Police Gazette* and the *Illustrated Police News*. The imperatives of dramatization, personalization, and titillation were stressed just as much in the reporting of the Jack the Ripper murders and the scandalous divorce cases of the 1880s and 1890s as they were to be in the 1940s and 1950s. Journalists scurried to acquire last letters from the death cell with almost as great an urgency. There was even a strain of investigative crime journalism epitomized by W.T. Stead's exposure of child prostitution in the *Pall Mall Gazette*. But the emphasis in nineteenth-century crime reporting was on the coverage of court cases and post-trial developments (Tunstalll 1971a:92). As popular journalism continued its expansion in the 1920s and the competition for circulation became more acute, information about the earlier stages of the criminal justice process took on a greater importance. The police, of course, exercised virtually monopolistic control over such information and were by no means predisposed to release it. The forerunner of the modern crime reporter was not so much a court correspondent as a 'leg man' who used to tour London police stations searching for scraps of information for the use of more senior colleagues. His responsibilities were initially limited, but his increasing contact with the police (especially contact of an informal nature) and the relationships he began to form on his beat steadily contributed to the security of his role and the extension of his autonomy. The use of the police as a news source has always posed severe problems for the pressman. Fifty years ago, it was an even more cautious and secretive organization than it is today. Its members generally regarded journalists with a deep-seated and unconcealed suspicion. One of the Metropolitan Commissioners of the time was lucky enough to survive an attempt on his life when a box of poisoned chocolates was sent to him anonymously. The degree of animosity towards the press may by judged from the fact that the first suspect brought in for questioning in connection with this outrage was a crime reporter. However, the steady growth of crime as a field of specialist reporting and, perhaps more pertinently, embarrassing complaints in Parliament about the existing system of informal information dissemination (consisting typically of policemen selling information to reporters in pubs), persuaded the Commissioner to make the first half-hearted attempt to institutionalize dealings with the Press and the Scotland Yard Press Bureau was founded in the mid-twenties. The new arrangements consisted of just one civil servant issuing twice daily bulletins to the eager but frustrated newshounds. Fleet Street's solution to this problem was to intensify specialization. Journalists were selected to work with the police on a regular basis in the hope that the barriers of suspicion and hostility could be broken down by frequent interaction with individual journalists who could prove themselves trustworthy and sympathetic. Thus the primary task of the crime reporter was the winning of trust and respect from sources who were not generally predisposed to accept him. If he failed in this task his professional existence was in jeopardy. As we shall see later, this obligation to cultivate and protect his relationships with his sources continues to impose a powerful constraint on his construction of stories.

By the end of the Second World War the policy of careful cultivation was bearing fruit. In 1945, the specialist journalists formed themselves into the Crime Reporters Association which was to have the dual function of pressure group for better facilities for gathering information, and business-like organization whose members the police could distinguish from less responsible practitioners of Fleet Street journalism. At Scotland Yard the conservative control of retired military personnel over the

Commissioner's office was broken by the appointment of Sir Harold Scott to the post of what the press rejoices in calling 'London's Top Cop'. Scott was immediately aware of the importance of the press, both in formulating the public image of the Force and as an ally in the fight against crime. He was disturbed by the atmosphere of secrecy surrounding Scotland Yard. As he wrote in his memoirs a few years later (1954:83-4): 'I well remember the horror of one of my senior officers when I announced that I had agreed to allow a press photographer to take a picture of one of my morning conferences. I had to dissuade him from hiding his face behind a sheet of paper when the photograph was taken.' One of the crime reporters of the time similarly noted that 'the higher-ups at the Yard regarded the crime reporters as almost as big a nuisance as the criminals themselves' (Firmin 1948:9). The new Commissioner set about reorganizing the existing facilities for the Press, appointing a Public Information Officer and extending the size of the Press Bureau, and instituting a fresh press and public relations policy.

This new, more open, policy, while far from satisfying most journalists, ushered in a new era of crime reporting which was to reach its heyday during the fifties when money and resources for crime stories were relatively freely available.

The post-war 'crime wave'

The developments in police/press relations of the late 1940s took place against the backdrop of Britain's post-war 'crime wave'. In conditions of commodity shortage, social disruption, and general austerity the incidence of (reported) indictable crime rose dramatically. The figures for 1947 were 50% up on those of 1939 and the rate of (reported) robberies with violence was three times the pre-war rate. But the figures really gave no indication of the extent of property crime and the wide-scale evasion of government regulations surrounding commodity consumption. David Yallop writes of the time:

'The years 1945 to 1952 were vintage years for anyone of criminal inclinations living in this country. With virtually everything rationed, with the necessities of life officially declared luxuries, the situation was Savile Row tailor-made for the black market ... Many a middle-aged businessman owes his present successful position to the judicious buying and selling that he did in those early post-war years.'   (Yallop 1971:22)

Racketeering, then, quickly became a familiar part of commerce. The rackets themselves appear to have been run predominantly by amateurs and part-time professionals recruited from the ranks of returning servicemen or, more often, from the pool of young working-class adults who had been too young for war service, and the 20,000 deserters who had brought their war service to a premature end (Hughes 1963). The war created a vacuum in the London underworld which was quickly filled by Jack 'Spot' Comer and Billy Hill who negotiated an alliance through which they were able to monopolize control of protection rackets and the lucrative gambling and vice business of the West End. Their only real challengers were the gangs of Italian and Maltese extraction who had established themselves at the centre of the prostitution syndicates; but compromise kept conflict, and thus police inter-vention, to a minimum (Lucas 1969; Wilkinson 1957; McConnell 1970; Sparrow 1969; Pearson 1972; Payne 1973). However, protection, gambling, and prostitution rackets were not the most public of crimes in the sense that they did not attract quite the same media interest as certain other types of criminal activity. They were, after all, nothing new[1].

It was essentially murder and delinquency which exercised the talents of crime reporters and moral entrepreneurs in the decade after the war. In 1945, 218 murders became known to the police, a figure which was not to be significantly exceeded until the 1970s. Most were, of course, the product of domestic violence, facilitated by the ready availability of weapons smuggled home by returning servicemen. But British society was already beginning to exhibit the changed pattern of murder noted by Colin Wilson in his assertion that 'the "cerebral" murder, the resentment-murder, has become the typical crime of the twentieth century' (Wilson 1972:2). He was referring to the increasing incidence of apparently 'motiveless' murders of a particularly gruesome and lurid nature, at first in the USA and then in Western Europe. According to Wilson (1969; 1972), these crimes differ from the typical murders of earlier periods in that they were committed neither for economic gain nor in the heat of anger, but rather reflect a Nietzschean 'will to power' on the part of social 'outsiders'. It is unnecessary, here, to subject Wilson's perspectives on murder to critical analysis. At the very least, they serve the useful function of directing our attention to a phenomenon of considerable importance in the development of both crime reporting and concern about law and order. Spectacular atrocities such as those of Neville Heath in 1946 and Haigh a few years later[2] contributed towards a developing focal concern of crime reporting which was to expand and deepen over the next two decades. They were also cases that produced set-backs to the general reduction in friction between the police and the press. In both instances controversy centred on the publication of prejudicial information. During the search for Heath after his first killing the press were prevented from publishing his photograph, a move which might have cast doubt on evidence of identification at his trial but which would probably have saved the life of his second victim. Before Haigh's trial, the police were obliged to issue three separate confidential memoranda to newspaper editors to prevent the continued release of prejudicial information about his crimes (notably information about his vampiric activities). But, as we have seen, Commissioner Scott was too aware of the importance of cordial press relations to let these conflicts of interest completely sour relationships. Soon after his appointment he had invited the news editors of the London dailies to meet him to discuss the crime situation and he had quickly enlisted the aid of *Daily Express* crime correspondent, Percy Hoskins and the BBC in making the radio crime prevention programme, 'It's Your Money They're After'. But, although the programme was adjudged a success, it made little impression on the overall crime figures which, in turn, did little to boost the sinking morale of a police force which was 10,000 men below its establishment in 1947. The Police's grievances — low pay and overwork, were aggravated by the apparent insensitivity of 'do-gooders' in Parliament and the 'irresponsibility' of certain sections of the media (Yallop 1971). In parliament, 1948 saw the passage of the controversial *Criminal Justice Bill,* a liberal reform measure aimed at abolishing corporal punishment and opening up the debate on capital punishment. Police opposition to the Bill was crystallized by the murder, in February, of P.C. Nat Edgar by a 22-year old army deserter, Donald Thomas. As we shall see, the killing of policemen has played a particularly prominent role in the development of law and order crises since the war, becoming a potent symbol of lawlessness. The case of Donald Thomas attracted a considerable amount of media attention and a good deal of moral indignation when his sentence was commuted to life imprisonment. The reprieve was in line with a Commons' amendment to the *Criminal Justice Bill* which had suspended hanging for five years. The *Daily Express* (22.4.48) communicated the outcome of the Thomas trial to its readers under the headline: '4.50 p.m. AT OLD BAILEY. THE NEW DEAL FOR KILLERS HAD BEGUN' (Yallop 1971:31). The indignation implicit in the *Express* headline appears symptomatic of a growing frustration within the right-wing order fantasy of the early post-war years. To say this is, of course, to move into the realm of speculative generalization for which anything approaching conclusive evidence is impossible to assemble, but if we set aside for a moment our justifiable reservations regarding the validity of concepts like 'collective mood' a coherent pattern of change seems observable. There can be little doubt that the end of the War in 1945 produced a widespread euphoria, a release of collectively-experienced tensions, and a raising of expectations, which eventually, found expression in a variety of forms. These ranged from optimistic enthusiasm for a new age of equality and prosperity — (left-wing fantasy?), through the more mundane pragmatic approaches of the 'back-to-work and business-as-usual' school, to nostalgia for a golden pre-war age which was to be recreated anew (right-wing fantasy?). The more extreme forms of optimism, however, must surely have suffered considerable frustration, as growing economic difficulties and continued conditions of austerity were experienced in the late forties. For those caught up in 'right-wing' fantasy, and this seems to have included a significant proportion of the press (Smith 1975), that frustration could only have been compounded by the apparent increase in violent crime among the young.

By 1947 the number of adolescents imprisoned was 250% up on the figures of 1939 and it seemed to many that an increasing number of working-class youths were reacting to conditions of commodity shortage by acting out a type of gangster fantasy. Their 'unhealthy' preoccupation with crime was reflected in the output of the entertainment media. Yallop reports that the popular radio serial, 'Dick Barton, Special Agent' was condemned by the Chief Constable of Gloucestershire as 'crime propaganda' and he demanded that it be banned, a move supported by *The Police Chronicle*. In the same year (1948) the British gangster film, 'No Orchids for Miss Blandish', opened to a chorus of hostile reviews in the Press: 'A nasty film and a wicked disgrace to the British Film Industry' (*Daily Express*); 'About as fragrant as a cesspool' (*Daily Mirror*); 'Without doubt it is one of the most undesirable pictures ever turned out by a British studio' (*Star*); 'A "D" certificate for disgusting' (*The Times*); 'Repellent. All the morals of an alley cat and the sweetness of a sewer' (*Observer*); 'I advise the Plaza management to take it off at once' (*Daily Herald*). It was, in fact, eventually banned by organizations representing over a thousand cinemas (Yallop 1971:27)[3]. The unanimity of the disapproval indicates that it was not simply right-wing papers that were beginning to experience frustration within order fantasies. In all newspapers 'Youth' was an emergent theme (Smith 1975). The 'teenager' began to make his first appearance on the streets and in fashion shops as austerity gradually receded at the close of the forties and commercial interests begin to appreciate his consumption potential and manufacture a collective identity for him. The working-class adolescent was implicitly invited to develop new patterns of consumption and accept new objects of identification as compensation for an impoverishment of his culture which was beginning to take place in the early fifties under the impact of housing redevelopment[4].

Again, there is insufficient evidence to established definite causal linkages but it would be surprising if the effects of social dislocation did not contribute significantly to the general increase in juvenile crime which by 1952 had become a pre-eminent concern of the law-and-order lobby both inside and outside Fleet Street. If contemporary newspapers are any guide, 'Cosh boys' stalked every street and alley-way in the imagination of the order fantasists. In 1951 four policemen were shot dead. One of these, P.C. Baxter, like his colleague P.C. Edgar, was killed by a young army deserter, Derek Poole, who died in a spectacular sten-gun battle with police after the killing. In July 1952, a 19-year old Glasgow bank clerk, Edward Finlay shot two policemen investigating a theft from his bank and then killed himself. One of the policemen, P.C. MacLeod died of his injuries.[5] The murders brought vociferous condemnation of the *Criminal Justice Act* and demands for the restoration of corporal punishment.

The climax of the post-war law-and-order crisis was precipitated in November 1952 by the killing of P.C. Miles on the roof of a Croydon warehouse during an exchange of fire between police and a 16-year old burglar, Christopher Craig. Craig was accompanied by Derek Bentley, an educationally sub-normal 19 year-old who was eventually hanged for his part in the affair.[6] The press quickly identified appropriate interpretative structures for the event, depicting it in terms of familiar scenarios — most notably Chicago gangsters and gun battles but also the siege of Sidney Street. The reality of the event became submerged in the immediate image of dramatic violence and youthful lawlessness projected by the newspapers which, as David Yallop (1971:90) points out, prejudiced any hope of an impartial trial for the two youths: 'Responsibility for the hanging of Derek Bentley rests on many shoulders; some of those shoulders are probably still hunched over typewriters in Fleet Street today.'

Sensational crime and cheque-book journalism

Craig and Bentley supplied the newspapers with convenient personifications of delinquency while the case itself became the centre of Fleet Street competition, a proving ground for ambitious reporters. To appreciate the tension and conflict[7] generated within crime reporting circles by potentially sensational cases like this in the forties and fifties we can do no better than turn to the autobiography of one of the most successful popular journalists of the time Harry Procter of the *Daily Mail* and *Sunday Pictorial*. *The Street of Disillusion* contains an extraordinary chronicle of Procter's dealings with the infamous during the growth period of post-war crime reporting and 'cheque-book journalism'. He comes across as the archetypal newshound, ruthlessly wheeling and dealing to gain exclusives and outwit the opposition. Moreover, his writing conveys vividly the unique blend of commercial competition, detached professionalism, and social concern which continues to characterize crime reporting. Procter's chapter on the Craig/Bentley case is worth examining in a little detail because it is particularly revealing of the reaction of the popular press of the period to spectacular crime. He first locates the significance of the events:

> 'When news of this terrible shooting burst upon a shocked world, newspapers, Churches and the Government were gravely concerned about a wave of violence sweeping the land; about the young teenage thugs, carrying coshes who were daily finding victims and bludgeoning them for a few pounds, a few shillings, sometimes even for a few coppers. The terror-problem of the times made the Craig-murder focus a grave social problem of that day.'   (Procter 1958:180)

He then goes on to detail how he 'tactfully and gently' approached Craig's family and won their cooperation in 'throwing light upon the problem of why so many of our teenagers were practising violence and thuggery', enlisting the aid of a female colleague to befriend Craig's mother and sister. Their visits to the Craigs' home became almost daily and they managed to establish a relationship of exchange well-suited to Procter's professional and commercial interests:

> Eventually the Craig family regarded Madeline and me as their truest friends. They gave us all their confidences, they sought

our help over every problem. And for weeks Madeline and I, as paid and skilled journalists, had the tough task of keeping away the opposition reporters and photographers. The opposition never allowed us a day or night free from anxiety ... When the trial opened at the Old Bailey I had to organize my forces like a military operation. My long experience of the Old Bailey made me realise that the task of taking Mr. & Mrs. Craig and daughter Lucy to that great Court of Justice every day for perhaps a week without allowing even a "yes" or "no" for quotes to the opposition, was a formidable one ... The ordeal was almost as mentally shattering for us as it was for the tragic Craig family. We had to guard our professional interests. But, in addition, we had a moral obligation to see that the Craigs were not bullied or tormented by the opposition, it was our duty to try and make their ordeal a little less unbearable. We succeeded. Not one opposition reporter got one word with either Captain Craig, Mrs. Craig or Lucy Craig ... One pirate reporter "flammed" an interview for his Sunday paper with Lucy, but Lucy denied, through a solicitor, that she had ever seen or spoken to the reporter.'   (Procter 1958:180-82)

The extraordinary lengths to which newspapers were prepared to go to protect their exclusives are vividly documented in Procter's account — the chauffeur-driven Rolls-Royce to convey the Craigs to the Old Bailey, the spiriting away of the Craigs into a country hide-away after the trial, and so on. But so, too, are the popular journalist's hierarchy of loyalites and priorities. Procter's deepening association with the Craig family served his profes-sional purposes admirably but it also created a conflict of obligations when the time came to write his reflections on the Craig/Bentley case. However, there was never any doubt about how that conflict should be resolved. The practical concerns of circulation with their attendant ideology of popularism ('giving the readers what they want') and conservative conception of professional responsibility (condemnation of law-breaking) inevitably took preference over all other loyalties. Procter showed his story (based on an interview with Craig in Brixton Prison which

Procter had managed by posing as a relative) to the boy's family:

' "I am going to condemn your son", I said. "Not because I bear him any grudge — I don't ... But it is my solemn duty to condemn him so that he is not glorified in the eyes of millions of other young boys ... My duty is to assure these boys that Christopher Craig was a coward. I am going to destroy any Craig legend which might exist ... I think it is wickedly wrong for any newspaper — particularly a popular newspaper which is read by teenagers — ever to glamorise crime or compliment criminals. It is our duty to write about criminals with contempt; they must be cheapened, ridiculed, never martyred".'

(Procter 1958:185)

But even Procter's 'candid pen picture' of Craig was insufficient to satisfy his news desk. They demanded another front page story of condemnation. This time they wanted Craig's father to condemn his son:

'I went alone to my room and wrote the story of the confidences Niven Craig had made to me ... I told how Niven Craig now realised that, through neglecting to ensure proper religious instruction for his son, and by sparing the rod, he had been to a large part responsible for Christopher Craig growing up to be a thug. It warned other parents how like indulgence towards their children, under the easy slogan of freedom for youth, could lead to like tragedies. And much more on these lines.'

(Procter 1958:186)

Procter eventually managed to convince Craig's father that he should allow publication provided the article was not treated sensationally. By the time MY FAILURE : BY CRAIG'S FATHER appeared on the front page of the *Sunday Pictorial* it was too late to do anything about it, but the story ended Procter's friendship with the Craig family. The executives of the *Sunday Pictorial* immediately directed Procter to turn his attentions to the Bentley family from whom he succeeded in buying the right to publish Derek Bentley's last letter from the 'death cell'.

Procter's coverage of the Craig/Bentley case illuminates,

particularly effectively, the *modus operandi* of the cheque-book journalist, the ruthlessness of Fleet Street competition in the early fifties, the centrality of crime news to that competition, and the typical orientation of the popular press towards crime and criminals. Crime made good copy but it had to be treated in a 'responsible' fashion which wedded the news media to the repressive apparatus of the State. No national newspapers called for the reprieve of Bentley who had offered no physical violence towards the police before his arrest, was in police custody when P.C. Miles had been shot, and for whom the jury at his trial had recommended mercy. At the height of the post-war law-and-order crisis they supported the State's executive in an act which David Yallop has called 'judicial murder' designed to encourage the others:

> 'The execution expediently demonstrated the Executive's determination to solve the problem of juvenile crime, particularly crimes of violence, once and for all. The Executive felt that Bentley's death would encourage the youth of this country to think twice before they went out armed with revolvers, knuckle-dusters, coshes, knives, razors and chains... His death, in fact, was a categorical statement of intent to all delinquents, "if his death does not encourage you to mend your ways, then take care; you may be next to hang". Derek Bentley had become the scapegoat for a whole generation.'
>
> (Yallop 1971:270)

The 'Angry Youth' theme

Bentley's execution in 1953 seems to have marked an easing in the post-war law-and-order crisis. The height of the youth-fever seemed to have passed, rationing had ended and political opinion appeared to be developing a deepening consensual hue. Even the ever-upward trend of the crime rate had been halted to such an extent that the new head of London's CID, Sir Robert Jackson, was able to feel that he was taking command of 'a victorious army'. All this hope, aspiration, and confidence crystallized in the symbolic form of the Coronation. If those caught up in order fantasy could be said to have a collective mood it was effectively captured in a letter to the *Daily Mail:* 'Let the youth in this country take the lead during this Coronation Year in creating a new spirit of honesty, purity, unselfishness and love ... under the Divine Guidance of God and the Leadership of Her Majesty.' The ideological apologists for the prevailing order were able to interpret the remorseless march of history as a procession of achievements. Sociologists among the apologists were able to adopt an increasingly optimistic view of social change, reading it as progressing towards a more affluent, orderly, and egalitarian future. As Shils and Young (1953) put it:

'Over the past century, British society ... has achieved a degree of moral unity equalled by no other large national state. The assimilation of the working class into the moral consensus of British society, though certainly far from complete, has gone further in Great Britain than anywhere else, and its transformation from one of the most unruly and violent into one of the most orderly and law-abiding is one of the great collective achievements of modern times ...'[8]

But by the end of 1953 the problems of youth were again threatening the dreams of order, tranquility, and conformity. In July a youth was stabbed during a fight near Clapham Common, an event which was soon to acquire a sinister significance as the 'Teddy Boy' became identified in the press as a new and menacing type of delinquent early in 1954 (Parker 1965). The emergence of the 'the teds' as a social problem has been carefully documented by Stan Cohen and Paul Rock (1970) and it is unnecessary to review it here in any detail.[9] The important points to be drawn out for our present purposes are first, the press were largely responsible for the definition and dissemination of the Teddy-Boy style and the investing of 'Edwardian' dress with its subsequent connotations of mindless violence; and second, the activities of the Teds became a focus for the projection of threatening images of gang violence and disorder for four years in the

mid-fifties. The Teddy-Boy became a sombre variation on the
theme of youth, a theme which increasingly gripped the
imagination of the popular press. As the virile, vibrant image of
youth emerged as 'a powerful but concealed metaphor for social
change' (Smith 1975:242) epitomizing the era of shifting styles
and spectacular consumption, so the cult of the rebel and the
manace of the Teds developed through the films of Brando and
Dean, rock and roll riots, racial violence in Notting Hill, and
finally, the knifing of a policeman during a Teddy-Boy
disturbance in London. Violence and vitality became the two sides
of the youth coin minted by the media. In fact, the moral panic
surrounding the Teddy Boy carried such momentum that it
continued long after the style began to decline in 1957. As Cohen
and Rock note, the killing of P.C. Summers by Ronald Marwood
was held up as evidence that the Teds were not dead despite their
increasing submergence in the commercially-inspired cult of the
'clean-cut kid'. By the end of the fifties the powerful image of
youthful revolt symbolized by the Teds had been largely
overtaken by more wholesome counter images promoted by pop
singers like Bobby Vee, Pat Boone, Frankie Avalon, and Cliff
Richard (Farren 1972). The Teddy Boys pre-eminent position in
the demonology of 'The Affluent Society' was about to be
usurped by the dishevelled figure of The Ban-the-Bomber as
political deviance emerged as a focal concern of law-and-order
fantasy between 1958 and 1962.

The spectre of political deviance had lain more-or-less dormant
since the War. There had, of course, always been the occasional
discovery of a Soviet spy to fuel press paranoia during The Cold
War — 'Atom bomb spy', Klaus Fuchs, had been imprisoned in
1950 and Burgess and MacLean had defected the following year.
The occasional revelation about the enemy within had been
sufficient to maintain anxiety and vigilance, and to 'keep in' the
hands of crime reporters in the field of spy journalism and to
keep up their Special Branch contacts (Lucas 1973); but it was
never enough to sustain panic. Similarly, the IRA arms raids on
British depots in the mid-fifties had inspired concern, provided
welcome copy and revived memories of the IRA's pre-war bombing

campaign in England, but they had not pushed political deviance to the front of the Fleet Street stage. But by 1960, the fifth column had apparently come out into the open and was regularly to be seen marching between Aldermaston and Trafalgar Square (Parkin 1968; Taylor 1970; Steck 1965; Driver 1964). The decade of consensus politics preceding the arrival of the CND offered Fleet Street few inferential structures* within which extra-parliamentary opposition could be easily accommodated apart from the conspiracy models of spy journalism and the angry youth theme. While there was little to support the conspiracy model in the early history of the movement, it acquired an increasing appeal in the early sixties with the formation of the Committee of 100 and the activities of the 'Spies for Peace'. The fear of secret conspiracies became all the greater with the discovery in 1961 of the Portland spy ring and the arrest of Lonsdale, Houghton, Gee, and the Krogers. However, perhaps the greatest significance of the reporting of the Campaign for Nuclear Disarmament was as an unwitting rehearsal for the coverage of the growth of extra-parliamentary opposition in the late 'sixties'. It introduced the theme of protest and demonstration which was to receive increasingly complex orchestration in the pages of our newspapers with demands for civil right in Ulster and the growing visability of New Left politics at home and abroad.

The golden age of crime journalism

Although CND must have exercised the imagination of order fantasists, in discussing its coverage we have moved away from the territory of the crime reporter into that of the political journalist and the general news reporter. The focal concerns of the crime correspondent in the fifties were still the activities of professional villains and amateur killers. The reporters, themselves, generally regard the period as the Golden Age of their craft when resources for investigation were plentiful and crime was 'straightforward'.

*Inferential structures are frameworks of preconception within which news selection may take place and new events can be given meaning and significance (Lang and Lang 1965).

Their definition of the situation is supported to some extent by the findings of Roshier's study (1971b) which indicate that, despite a lower rate of recorded crime than in subsequent years, the proportion of newspaper space devoted to crime in 1955 was greater:

Table 1 Percentage of news space (minus advertisements) devoted to crime news, features and articles.

	Sept 1938	Sept 1955	Sept 1967
Daily Mirror	5.6	7.0	5.6
Daily Express	4.4	5.6	4.4
Daily Telegraph	3.5	3.4	2.4
News of the World	17.8	29.1	11.0*

(Adapted from Roshier 1971b)

*September - November

In the sphere of professional crime, black-market fiddles were dying out with the end of rationing and the underworld was settling down to consolidating its control over illegal gambling and vice. The modern pattern of underworld organization and method of operation was being established. The characteristic unit of organization was no longer the 'craft team' of pickpockets, burglars, and small-scale robbers, but the semi-permanent competitive 'mob' of friends and associates whose everyday existence is grounded in on-going protection rackets or gambling, prostitution, and fraudulent concerns. The mobs formed the recruiting ground for 'project thefts' — lorry high-jacking, pay-roll snatches, bank robberies etc. — which became an increasingly prominent part of the crime scene in the fifties (Phelan 1953; Fordham 1972; McIntosh 1971, 1976; Mack 1975), culminating in the Great Train Robbery of 1963 (Fordham 1965; Williams 1973). In London, it was a time of considerable upheaval. In 1955 the coalition between Jack 'Spot' Corner and Billy Hill began to break up and they began to compete for the title of King of the Underworld (Hill 1955). But while Hill enjoyed a brief victory, the struggle left his organization weakened and open to challenge by the rising figures of the sixties — the Krays, the Richardsons, Frank Mifsud and Bernie Silver. The more public exploits of the mobs kept the crime correspondents busy, but there was little attempt to probe beneath the surface happenings to uncover the shifting organization of professional crime, its economic infrastructure, and the necessary contribution of police corruption towards its continuance. Britain's Gangland remained a mysterious world which periodically erupted into open violence for no coherent reason. Apart from these periodic eruptions, the crime reporter's attention was usually diverted elsewhere, especially in the direction of 'bloody murder'.

The fifties was the decade of sensational murder. 1953 was a year memorable for two notorious sex-murder cases — the brutal rape and killing of two girls by Alfred Whiteway (The Thames Towpath Murders) and the relevations which emanated from 10 Rillington Place, Notting Hill, the home of John Reginald Halliday Christie who had killed eight times since 1940. The Christie case, in particular, attracted enormous newspaper interest (in contrast to the case of Timothy Evans, convicted of two of Christie's murders, which was defined in Fleet Street crime reporting circles as a 'fish-and-chippy' murder — dull, sordid, unglamorous, mundane). Harry Procter (1958) tells us that Fleet Street reporters were 'running round in circles' to acquire Christie's life story, willing to pay up to £5,000. Similar sensationalizing and journalistic competition accompanied the trial of Ruth Ellis, the last woman to be executed in Britain. The case provided the press with all the classic ingredients of tragedy and romance that go to make a first-class human interest story and they transformed it into the archetypal crime passionnel.

Crime reporters look back to the murders of the fifties with profound nostalgia, an attitude captured in one reporter's words: 'Murder is not what it used to be'. Death today seems to them much more nasty, brutish, and short:

> 'The pattern of murder has changed a great deal. All our murders used to be frightfully cunning and a cleverly worked

out plan laid down. It is much more violent and quicker now —
stabbing, shooting. Poisoning has almost disappeared apart
from that one recent case [the case of Graham Young].'

(Crime Correspondent: popular daily)[10]

The decline of murder reporting is attributed to a number of
factors. Two, in particular, are often mentioned. First, crime
correspondents point to an apparent falling off in public interest:
'In the early days you could spin out a murder for three weeks.
Now it will only last a few days. There are no queues at the Old
Bailey anymore now the death penalty has been abolished and
you no longer have the ritual of the black cap' (Crime correspondent: popular daily). Some journalists argue that the public have
become desensitized and bored through over-exposure:

'As the years have gone by shooting has become quite common,
stabbing, break-ins, bank robberies ... they're not scarce
currency ... The big investigations still get lots of space in the
paper, but of a different kind. The old murder stories: I don't
think the public would stand for them anymore, they were
definitely over-written. The whole technique has been cut
back. One tends to write much shorter.'

(Crime correspondent: popular daily)

Second, the decline of public interest has been accompanied by a
decrease in newspaper resources devoted to murder reporting.
This, in turn, has led to a change in the organization of reporting.
During the heyday of murder reporting, trusted journalists were
almost automatically attached to murder squad detectives for the
duration of provincial investigations. Before the war these
journalists were primarily 'hangers-on'[11] but, as personal
contacts between senior detectives and specialist reporters
improved, the crime journalists became an integral part of the
police inquiry — supplying investigative expertise and acting as
confidant and companion to the detective. Ward Rutherford
(1973) in his book on Edward Paisnel, the Jersey sex-criminal,
describes the arrival of Scotland Yard detective, Superintendent
Jack Mannings, on the island in 1961. He was accompanied by a
retinue of Fleet Street crime correspondents:

'Mannings, despite a reputation for parting only reluctantly with information, is on ribald good terms with the national newspaper crime men. Ashcroft and Le Brocq (senior Jersey Police officers) had had only limited dealings with them and these were not always happy from their point of view, so that the reporters who often appeared when Mannings was about and who seemed, with his apparent blessing to make themselves at home at police headquarters, were regarded with suspicion, and on several occasions thrown out of the building by zealous officers.' (Rutherford 1973:42)

During the fifties and early sixties specialist crime correspondents would form a natural retinue for the Scotland Yard detective on provincial cases. This even applied to correspondents from the London evening papers. In 1961, the *Evening Standard* assigned two reporters to cover investigations into the murder of a girl at Earls Colne in Essex. They were there for seven weeks. This could only happen now in very exceptional cases. Pressure on police resources and increased efficiency has meant that murder investigations tend to be of shorter duration, and the pressure of Fleet Street resources means that journalists can afford less time to cover them. To some extent, these structural changes have influenced the quality of relationships formed on 'out-of-town' assignments. A crime reporter from the popular Press recalls 'the old days':

'... nearly everybody went on a job, you know, from all the papers. They would know each other and if you didn't know the coppers you would get a more experienced colleague saying to the police Superintendent, "This is so-and-so, he's been on his paper a couple of years. He's only just started crime. I can vouch for him". So then you'd be in, you'd be part of it. And the copper would say "Right, this is the form. I suggest this is tomorrow's story, and there's another little thing here, you could perhaps use that tomorrow". And there'd be this trust going and you'd have the story made for a week, even before you started. They wouldn't make up the story for you, they'd give you certain information. The coppers used to say, "Look, we've found this bloody diary, it's got some good names in it, but would you keep that for a couple of days and not mention it''. But I don't think you could do that now because (a) the story's not running as long or as frequently as it used to be, and (b) you don't get the same bunch of reporters who are known to particular coppers going on these jobs anymore.'

The atmosphere of exclusive camaraderie which attended these gatherings comes over strongly from the above account. It is an atmosphere which is only very occasionally recaptured today. It grew out of a *modus operandi* which also encouraged a particular form of news account — an account embodying the professional imperative of personalization. The personality in question was generally the investigating officer:

'I think a lot of policemen did get lots of publicity, years ago, when we used to write about ''The Big Five'' and policemen's names were household words — I can think of Capstick and Spooner — you don't find that anymore ... There used to be days when we had placards, you know, ''Capstick of the Yard''. I think that ought to come back, personally. The public identify with that very well, like the film stars. I think it would be good for the Yard to have that ... There are so many of them now. When we used to talk about ''The Big Five'' it was exciting and dramatic, but there were then only four or five big investigators. Now the whole C.I.D. set-up has grown so enormously — it must be four times bigger than it was only six years ago, and I suppose there are something like 16 Detective Chief Superintendents at the Yard — plus the fact that you don't get the same length of reporting — cases that last six weeks or longer, these don't happen in the same way.'

(Crime Correspondent: Popular daily)

The image of the police

The 'Golden Age' of murder reporting was also the period, more than any other, which featured the policeman as folk hero. It was the age of 'Fabian of the Yard' and 'The Blue Lamp' when policemen were 'like film stars' and a hungry press feasted from their casebooks. Things began to change in the sixties as the increasing media accent on newness, vitality, and irreverence symbolized by youth began to undermine the acceptability of the established police image. The friendly bobby and the painstaking sleuth began to appear rather slow and old-fashioned. They represented the old order and the old values of safety and dependability which were altogether unsuited to the irresponsible, exciting, aggressive, glamorous mood of the times which the newspapers found themselves articulating. For a time, criminals seemed to represent the theme of vitality and imagination more effectively than the forces of law-and-order, hence the guilty admiration and sympathy accorded the Great Train Robbers[12] and the aura of glamour surrounding the Krays during part of their reign in the East End. From being the unchallenged subjects of media adulation the police suddenly became controversial, a suitable subject for critical scrutiny. In 1959 a Royal Commission on the police was set up following a spate of minor scandals. Soon after the Commission reported (1962), more dramatic indiscretions were uncovered in Sheffield and at West End Central Station in London (see chapter 5). The wave of interest in the police was sufficient to produce two 'Penguin Specials' in two years. The opening words of the first of these books summed up the shift in attitude among certain sections of the public and the media: 'There is a new readiness in Britain today to take a fresh look at institutions which we have long taken for granted. Among them are the police who are a microcosm of some of the more intractable and interesting problems of human society' (Whitaker 1964:11). The new mood, of course, did not extend to all members of society. The reputation of the police was the subject of continuous negotiation between 'The Progressives' and 'The Establishment'[13]. The police themselves remained essentially spectators to the debate, apart from the occasional act of ventriloquism with senior crime reporters, but they were not left unaffected. They tended to interpret the new climate of scepticism and questioning as an 'anti-police mood'. Former Metropolitan Assistant Commissioner, Sir Richard Jackson, has traced its development during the sixties in his autobiography:

'The attack developed on many different fronts; it was sometimes crude, sometimes subtle ... The whole campaign was part
of a general revolt against authority. It went with protesters
who sat down in the road and agitators who threw ball-bearings
under the hooves of police horses.

In the old days children were taught to trust the police and go
to the nearest Bobby if they were in difficulty. Now an entire
generation has been taught — not perhaps by their parents but
by pressures of publicity all around them — to dislike and
distrust the police and to despise what the police stand for ...
As the new mood spread both criminals and the police soon
realized that any complaint against a policeman was certain to
find a ready and credulous audience, and would be so publi-
cized and magnified by the media of modern mass communication that, even if the complaint could be ultimately disproved,
the truth would never really catch up the lie. For several years
now there has been a growing feeling in the police, and
particularly among C.I.D. officers, that the odds are stacked
against them; that the barriers protecting criminals are being
reinforced and that the public is indifferent or hostile.'

(Jackson 1967:134-37)

The press inevitably attracted a large proportion of the blame for
blackening the name of the force. Police witnesses giving evidence
to the Royal Commission presented files of unfavourable press
cuttings and complained that 'inaccurate or distorted reporting of
police news' was partly responsible for any deterioration in
relations with the public which might have occurred. This was
strongly denied by witnesses from the National Union of
Journalists who assured the Commission that 'they regarded it as
their duty to do all they could to put the police in the best
possible light'. The Commission concluded that there was 'no
general lack of sympathy for the police' in the press, and that the
Police's impression that they receive 'a bad press' was due to their
isolation from the rest of the community which 'inclines them to
be over-sensitive to criticism'.

The NUJ's stated 'duty' of depicting the police 'in the best possible light', however, was in conflict, not with the desire to glamorize the activities of criminals, but with the emergent themes of popular journalism in the sixties — speed, vigour, change, technology, and science etc. But the long-term resolution of this contradiction was not to create new heroes to replace the police because such a resolution would have been incompatible with a newspaper ideology which stressed the pre-eminent importance of law and order and social continuity. What seems to have happened instead is that the image of the police was slowly remoulded and polished to suit the emergent themes. The dominant image of the honest, brave, dependable, (but plodding) 'British Bobby' was recast as the tough, dashing, formidable, (but still brave and honest) 'Crime-Buster'. The solid, solitary figure of 'The Bobby-on-the-Beat' became steadily transformed into the hard-bitten 'Squad-Man'[14]. The new image was that of Barlow rather than Dixon — less lovable but better equipped to deal with 'The Modern Villain'. The New Copper was ruthless in the pursuit of right. He had to be, because the criminals with whom he was forced to deal were 'not playing games'. The old conventions of 'fair play' were just no longer operable because the police were not involved in a contest any more, they were fighting a 'war against crime', an increasingly violent war in which the use of firearms in robberies increased five-fold between 1961 and 1967.

Robberies, themselves, increased by over 150% while *armed* robberies increased by over 400% during the sixties.[15] The acceptability of the 'Tough Cop' image was increased by supplying it with a technological gloss consonant with the spirit of the times. Just as Sean Connery, the cinematic James Bond, was equipped with every ingenious gadget the fertile imaginations of filmakers could conjure up, so the new policeman was also a man of the technological age, from the two-way personal radio on his breast to the massive computer records system with which it could link him. This new accent on police technology, coupled with the increasing complexity of organization and differentiation within the Metropolitan Police (Laurie 1972; Bunyan 1976) added a comparatively new area to the crime reporter's sphere of competence. He began to exhibit a growing interest in the changing police bureaucracy, in the creation of new squads and divisions, in manpower and equipment, and in the internal workings and politics of the Force. This reportage took place against what was, if anything, a background of worsening police-press relations until 1967 and the appointment of a new head of public relations at Scotland Yard.

The appointee, Mr. G.D. Gregory, was recruited from industry and brought considerable experience in the publicity field. He immediately set about a task of image-reconstruction, gathering a number of men with newspaper experience into his staff and making sure that the Public Relations Department was never considered a quiet field into which ineffectual policemen could be put out to graze, as it is in some provincial forces. It is significant that one of Gregory's first moves was to sponsor the investigations of a young freelance journalist, Peter Laurie. It was a move which Laurie maintains was met with hostility by many senior officers at the Yard and amazement from many more junior. Having been instilled with a fundamental suspicion of journalists, the policemen he met found it difficult to know how to react:

'I was armed with the Commissioner's approval, expressed in a letter of introduction which I carried on me, so that I could hardly be ignored; yet, on the other hand, I was and still am a journalist by trade. As one detective put it: "Ever since we first began, we've had it drummed into us: 'Journalists are bad. Never speak to journalists'. And here you are with carte blanche to come and go. Quite frankly, you're a bit of a facer".'

(Laurie 1972:12)

But, although it may have created some confusion in the ranks, the new press and public relations policy was to pay dividends the following year when a series of anti-Vietnam war demonstrations in London directed media attention towards police behaviour and the control of crowds (see chapter 4).

The decline of the golden age

The sixties, then, saw the policeman become a different type of folk hero, and Scotland Yard renew its concern with the business of image creation. The same decade was a time of change for crime reporting and, indeed for the whole newspaper industry. Certainly, the demise of cheque-book journalism[16] and the gradual passing of the golden age of murder reporting[17] cannot be divorced from upheavals in the economic infrastructure of the newspaper enterprise, upheavals experienced most acutely by the popular press, the stronghold of crime journalism. During the boom years of the 1950s, Fleet Street suffered only one casualty, the *Sunday Chronicle*, but in the first two years of the sixties four newspapers closed (*Sunday Graphic, Empire News, Sunday Dispatch, News Chronicle*). In 1964 the struggling *Daily Herald* was forced to undergo metamorphosis and re-emerge as the *Sun*, a new brash, bright newspaper of youth. In 1966 *Reynolds News* folded and by 1969 the new *Sun* found itself in even greater trouble than the old *Herald*. The trend continued into the seventies with the merger of the *Daily Sketch* into the *Daily Mail*. The crisis of newspaper publishing was largely attributable to the arrival of commercial television, but its impact was not crucially upon circulation but upon advertising revenue. In newspaper publishing the most important circulation variable is not size but quality. To attract the maximum advertising revenue newspapers must now aim at specialization and a concentration of readers in the upper income levels. The enormous market offered to advertisers by commercial television has completely disrupted the economics of the mass-circulation paper.

'Before the advent of commercial television, newspapers such as the Daily Express and Sunday Express which had readerships covering a wide range of social groups were sought after by advertisers selling in the mass market. Now advertisers who seek blanket coverage of the mass market can get this more effectively from television. Newspapers tend to be used largely to supplement television and fill in what it misses — the specialist markets and the light television viewers.'

(Hirsch and Gordon 1975:40-1)

Pressure on advertising revenue had the effect of tempting newspapers to strive for a more affluent readership; not, perhaps, to attract the Grade A readers of the quality press (successful business and professional men), but at least to increase the proportion of B and C1 readers in their circulation figures. The most celebrated instance of this 'upmarket' trend was, of course, the *Daily Mirror's* 'Mirrorscope', a page of serious feature writing designed, in part, to counteract the paper's 'cloth-cap' image. The impact of the 'upmarket' trend on the sphere of crime reporting was more subtle but still significant. Primarily, it took the form of stagnation and shortage of resources, a general lack of expansion, an increasing concentration of Scotland Yard and London crime. It was not until 1969 and the arrival of Rupert Murdoch's revitalized *Sun* that crime reporting began to sail out of the doldrums. Not only was crime reporting an integral component of Murdoch's sensationalist formula, but the *Sun* was so immediately successful that other proprietors and editors were obliged to take stock of the declining position of crime journalism in their own papers. The launching of the *Mirror's* Crime Bureau[18] in 1970 was indicative of this renewed interest in crime. The real resurgence of crime reporting, however, had to wait on the emergence of a new focal concern, a new law-and-order crisis. The wait was short, and ended abruptly with the arrival of political terrorism as an urgent social problem in Britain. In the next chapter the social construction of meaning which accompanied the emergence of political terrorism will be examined with the context of the more generalized law-and-order crisis of which it formed a significant part.

4 Bombers, muggers and thugs: the press and the violent society

' "The war in Bangladesh, Cyprus, the Middle East, Black September, Black Power, the Angry Brigade, the Kennedy murders, Northern Ireland, bombs in Whitehall and the Old Bailey, the Welsh Language Society, the massacre in the Sudan, the mugging in the tube, gas strikes, hospital strikes, go-slows, sit-ins, the Icelandic Cod-war etc ...
    They are obviously themselves and nothing more. But they are all part of the modern scene. And it may be that they are all standing, or seeking to stand, on different parts of the same slippery slope.'' '

Lord Hailsham (Griffiths, *New Statesman* 1.2.74)

This chapter traces the emergence of 'The Violent Society' as a pre-eminent theme in law-and-order news. The notion of 'The Violent Society' is seen to result from the convergence of a criminal violence theme, originating in the mid-sixties, and a political violence theme which developed a few years later. The implications of the analysis are that interpretations generated in one domain of newspaper discourse (e.g. crime news) can easily be, and have been, transposed through linking concepts (e.g. the violent society) to other domains (e.g. political and industrial news). This transposition is accomplished in spite of the structural organization of reporting around domains of specialization which one might expect to create a bias in favour of the isolation of events as discrete phenomena. The ubiquity of the interpretations can best be understood as a function of an over-arching newspaper ideology and the professional news imperatives controlling its usage. It is largely the practice of popular journalism that has articulated the vague anxiety of members of a society undergoing rapid social change by making available such powerful 'blanket' conceptualizations as 'The Violent Society' and 'Law-and-Order crisis' to cover a whole range of diverse phenomena.

The analysis offered parallels that developed quite autonomously by the Mugging research team at the University of Birmingham (Jefferson et al 1975), who similarly identify the late sixties and early seventies as a period of law-and-order crisis and accord the mugging scare a position of prominence in its development. The Birmingham team also draw attention to the 'convergence' of separate activities under common labels, the 'mapping together' of moral panics which is achieved via the notion of thresholds of societal tolerance. The transgression of these thresholds allows behaviour to be redefined and related to activites which pose a more serious threat to social legitimacy and order. Violence constitutes the most extreme threshold.

Figure 1 *The violent society: convergence of themes*

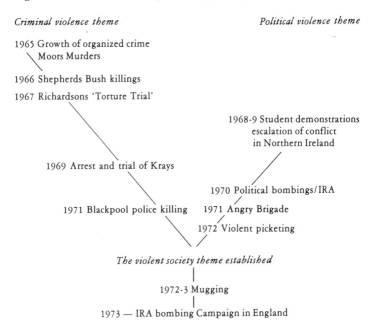

Criminal violence theme   *Political violence theme*

1965 Growth of organized crime
     Moors Murders

1966 Shepherds Bush killings

1967 Richardsons 'Torture Trial'

                                              1968-9 Student demonstrations
                                                     escalation of conflict
                                                     in Northern Ireland

1969 Arrest and trial of Krays

                                              1970 Political bombings/IRA

1971 Blackpool police killing   1971 Angry Brigade

                                 1972 Violent picketing

              The violent society theme established

                         1972-3 Mugging

              1973 — IRA bombing Campaign in England

It may be helpful in reading the rest of the chapter to keep in mind the general theoretical framework around which it is organized. This can be represented in diagramatic form.

Before we begin the detailed analysis of the development of the Violent Society theme, however, it is worth pausing to make a few observations on the general reporting of violence in popular journalism.

A note on the reporting of violence

The political ideology and professional imperatives of popular journalism are a source from which at least five sets of informal rules of relevancy in the reporting of violence appear to be derived. They guide journalists' treatment of violence by asserting the relevance of:

1. Visible and spectacular acts.
2. Sexual and political connotations.
3. Graphic presentation
4. Individual pathology
5. Deterrence and repression

The first set of rules derives predominantly from the professional news imperatives and stresses the relevance of 'visible and spectacular' violence. Its effect is that the violence most likely to receive coverage in the press is that organized in acts involving sudden physical injury to apparently innocent strangers, especially in public places — these are the type of attacks commonly typified by the phrase 'violence in the streets'. Concern about this type of violence is evident in newspaper accounts throughout the post-war years, from the cosh boys and teds of the fifties to the skinheads and football hooligans of the sixties, and culminating in the moral panic surrounding mugging in 1972 and 1973. The operation of this set of rules has reinforced a limited concept of violence which has tended to ignore at least four phenomena which might otherwise have been included:

a. 'Privatized' violence within the family — wife and baby battering, child neglect, and so on — which have only

recently surfaced as social problems.
b. Unsafe or unhealthy working conditions resulting in death or injury.
c. The large-scale poisoning of the environment by industrial concerns.
d. The 'mental' violence involved in boring and repetitive jobs, inadequate housing, and so on.

It is arguable that each of these phenomena has been responsible for as much human suffering as that attributable to 'violence in the streets', but each has received comparatively little consideration. This imbalance of coverage reflects wider ideological definitions of violence articulated by those in powerful institutional positions; but this is not surprising when we consider the biases in access to the media and routine procedures of news-acquisition. To a large extent, newspapers rely on their news sources to identify areas of public concern. Those news sources are typically elite personalities such as M.P.s or members of powerful organizations such as the Police. The social problems nominated by such sources are likely to reflect their particular values and interests and may not correspond to problems experienced by members of less powerful, privileged, or organized social groups. Therefore the emergence of fresh social problems in the press must wait on the formation of pressure groups and the attention of established moral entrepreneurs[1].

A second set of informal rules stresses the relevancy of certain connotations surrounding the violent act. One of these is a sexual connotation which derives its prominence from the imperative of titillation. This does not just mean that sadism is newsworthy but that readers appear to be particularly interested in women who commit violent acts. The reasons for this interest are arguable but they are probably informed by sexual stereotypes which portray women as naturally passive and submissive, the aggressive woman appearing excitingly wicked and unnatural by contrast. Thus figures such as Ruth Ellis, Myra Hindley and, more recently, the Price Sisters, and Rose Dugdale exercise an enormous fascination for newsmen and readers alike. A second relevant connotation of violence is the political connotation. This reflects newspaper ideology which views political violence as a dangerous and threatening phenomenon, totally foreign to a system of decision-making based upon consensual agreement about the rules of the political contest. Because of this subversive quality, political violence is to be the subject of exposure and constant vigilance. As we shall see, it was to provide a developing theme in the reporting of violence throughout the late sixties and early seventies.

A third set of rules refers to the relevance of various moments in the process of violence, identifying the most significant moments as the act and its effects rather than its causal context or motivation. Undoubtedly, this relevancy hierarchy is closely related to the pragmatics of news presentation. A violent act is more amenable to dramatization than are the conditions and processes which shape its development. Its effects can be vividly portrayed by photographing victims; its meaning captured in a single, simple, graphic, and immediate image. The causes of violence are more complex and intractable, less open to instant empathic understanding. They cannot be checked and verified by the established procedures of news reporting because they are theoretical constructs which can only *inform* the collection of empirical material. They cannot themselves be directly observed and recorded by busy journalists in pursuit of 'facts'.

When excursions are made into the realm of theory and attempts are made to untangle the twisted origins of the violent impulse, a fourth set of rules of relevance appears to become operative. These rules are heavily influenced by newspaper ideology and guide journalistic choice between competing theories of violent behaviour. They apparently stress the significance of those theories which attribute violence (and crime in general) to individual pathology, parental failure, or the corrupting influence of undesirable media output, rather than to social conditions. The virulent streak of individualism inherent in bourgeois ideology resists any suggestion that people's actions may be attributable to processes of deprivation and modes of social organization beyong their responsibility. A recent *Daily Mail* (5.6.75) editorial conveys this point forcefully:

'Some crimes are committed because the wrongdoers are sick. They need treatment.

Some crimes are committed because wrongdoers are placed under intolerable personal provocation. They may, in certain circumstances, be excused.

Most crimes are committed because of human wickedness.

Those who perpetrate them should expect to be punished.

This is a simple statement of what the majority of men and women believe to be true.

In recent years, however, sociologists, psychiatrists and penal reformers have sought to shame the public into thinking otherwise: Don't blame the criminal, we are told, blame his social background ...

We are people, responsible people. Not the puppets of social conditioning.'

Most sociologists would probably go along with the *Mail* in rejecting any purely deterministic model of human action, but they would also argue that man is never entirely free or entirely responsible for his actions. Men may not be 'conditioned' by their background and environment in a crude Pavlovian sense, but neither are they left totally unaffected by their life experiences. These life experiences influence the formulation of beliefs about the way the world operates, the type of person one is, 'realistic' expectations for the future, the type of action appropriate in a given situation. These experiences are not random. They are organized in sub-cultures with distinctive patterns of behaviour and relationships based on social class, geographical location, work, age group, and so on. Each culture will have differing attitudes towards law-breaking and violence and a differing 'stake' in the dominant moral and political order. It is through sub-cultures and sub-cultural options, rather than through an individual, independent moral assessment, that most people develop normative precepts of acceptable behaviour. If cultural location does not determine action, it does influence the predisposition to act in a certain way. Moreover, sub-cultures themselves develop as responses to particular problematic situations — the situation of working on a shop floor and doing a menial task, the situation of being black or Jewish, the situation of being a policeman or a teacher, the situation of being young or poor, or living in a deprived area, etc. They are pragmatic adaptations to real problems, ways of coping with life in a given situation. Therefore, it would seem imperative that any adequate explanation of violence must pay some attention to the life situations of the people involved in its commission, and must attempt to understand what it is like to be in that situation and to have the cultural options associated with it. To simply attribute crime and violence to wickedness is to ignore all this and to reduce the complexities of human motivation to the simplest of tautologies: People are bad because they are bad. Few newspapers, however, are prepared to go this far. Instead of drawing a direct causal link between wickedness and violence they look for intervening variables which may remove the constraints of 'civilization' and 'unlock the violent impulses' which lie beneath them. Their search generally reveals two contributing factors. The first is lack of parental control which allows violent impulses to develop unchecked; and the second is the pre-occupation of some sections of the entertainment media with vicarious violence which renders us immune to its horrors and encourages imitation. The first contributing factor was identified by Home Secretary, Reginald Maudling in a widely-reported speech on the day of a large 'pupil power' demonstration in London in 1972: 'If only parents and families as a whole used a little more authority to ensure that their children had a little more respect for law and order, the problems of the police would be eased.' The *Daily Mail* splashed his speech on the front page under the headline 'PARENTS MUST BE TOUGHER'. (18.5.72). A few weeks earlier the Home Secretary had obliged the *Sunday Mirror* by identifying a second contributing factor, expressing his fears about violence in the media for the paper's three-part investigation of 'screen violence':

'I am not suggesting there is necessarily a direct cause or con-nection [between media output and human behaviour] — but what we see on the screen must affect our attitudes. The whole of advertising is built on this assumption. I have heard sensible men say they see so much screen violence that it has no effect at all on us — without realising that they mean they may be coming to accept violence as a part of normal life. A real danger comes if we stop noticing or being shocked by violence.'

(30.4.72)

Press anxiety over screen violence, however, reached a peak the following year with reports of attacks and, eventually, a murder which were apparently inspired by the film 'Clockwork Orange'. But while the whole debate on film censorship was opened up in the press and opinions diligently collected from accredited spokesmen such as Lord Longford and John Trevelyan, very few column inches were devoted to discussing the situation of the adolescents who sought to identify with characters in 'Clockwork Orange'. Instead of locating the crimes in their social context by examining the everyday experiences of the adolescents involved, the newspapers for the most part, isolated the film as an over-whelmingly corrupting influence, characterizing it as the film which turned an ordinary grammar-school boy 'into a mindless, savage killer' (*Sun* 4.7.73). Once depicted as an evil and inhuman influence it passed as an explanation of the crime absolving journalists and readers from further investigation.

The fifth set of rules of relevancy refers to the salience of competing approaches to the prevention and treatment of violence and parallels the attribution of violence to individual wickedness. It stresses the significance and deterrent value of repressive control rather than the appropriateness of large-scale programmes of social reform and reorganization. Even when a link between social conditions and violence is recognized, its consideration generally takes second place to calls for tougher action against the offender. Take, for example, this editorial from the *Daily Mirror*, a paper which has perhaps done more than any of its competitors to draw public attention towards the role of social conditions in the generation of youthful violence:

'... We need to know more about the springs of violence.
HOW FAR is poverty in a rich society and the misery of
deprived families a cause?
HOW FAR is educational inequality a cause?
HOW FAR is dull and repetitive work a cause?
These are problems for social and political action by govern-
ments.
But the rest of us do not have to sit back and wait for that.
Trade unionists should blacklist rough necks.
Sports fans should boycott grounds where hoodlums run amok.
Parents should boycott films which exploit violence ...'

(*Daily Mirror,* 'Shock Issue on Violence' 19.9.72)

Having set out these journalistic rules of relevancy we should
now be in a position to understand more clearly the precise
directions which newspaper concern about violence has taken in
the last decade.

I. *The criminal violence theme*

'At three-thirty one in the afternoon of August 12th 1966, the total picture of
British crime changed suddenly, dramatically and completely.'

(Judge Gerald Sparrow 1969 : 9)

The early sixties was a time of rapid and large scale social change
which produced strain and dislocation in numerous sections of
British culture. Economic growth and a high level of employment,
coupled with technological innovations, prompted changes in
patterns of work, leisure, and consumption; while the growth of
state welfare provision, the reorganization of housing, the influx
of commonwealth immigrants etc. all contributed to a growing
sense of uncertainty and ambiguity in the spheres of social and
family relationships. There was a widespread feeling that social
life was moving and changing faster than people could
comprehend, a feeling which engendered both excitement and
anxiety. It was a time of mild anomie when the 'attack on
traditional values and life styles' became a media cliché. The
prevailing atmosphere of uncertainty was reflected and sustained

by the mass media. As we have seen, the image of youth provided the press with its most potent symbol of changing values and styles of life, representing both the glamour, spontaneity, and creativity of the 'New Age', and its irresponsibility, violence, and iconoclasm. Concern about the activities of youth became a dominant theme in the mounting anxiety evident in newspaper accounts in the years after 1963. Stan Cohen has argued convincingly that the reaction to the emergence of the Mods and Rockers in 1964 articulated fears and resentments generated by more fundamental social changes:

'The Mods and Rockers symbolised something far more important than what they actually did. They touched the delicate and ambivalent nerves through which post-war social change in Britain was experienced. No one wanted depressions or austerity, but messages about ''never having it so good'' were ambivalent in that some people were having it too good and too quickly ... Resentment and jealousy were easily directed at the young, if only because of their increased spending power and sexual freedom. When this was combined with a too-open flouting of the work and leisure ethic, with violence and vandalism, and the (as yet) uncertain threats associated with drug-taking, something more than the image of a peaceful Bank Holiday at the sea was being shattered.'

(Cohen 1972:192)

To the supporters of traditional values and the established order the vandalism, hooliganism, and amphetamine 'abuse' which increasingly commanded the attention of news reporters and leader writers were merely the more visable symptoms of a deeper social malaise. The official crime statistics for 1965 did little to dispel their fears. The figures showed that indictable offences of violence against the person (known to the police) had increased by 324 per cent in ten years.

By the end of 1965 organized crime was again causing grave concern. In London, particularly, robberies were running at an unprecedented level and the sensational disappearance of 'Ginger' Marks and the growing notoriety of the Krays and Richardsons

Table 2 Violence against the person: indictable offences known to the police

		1945	*1955*	*1965*	*1974*
Murder Manslaughter } Homicide Infanticide		492	279	325	600
Attempted murder, threat and conspiracy to commit murder		219	213	302	502
Felonious wounding		545	1,042	2,174	4,240
Malicious woundings		2,747	6,034	21,702	56,500
Other offences against the person		797	338	1,065	1,939
	Total	4,743	7,884	25,548	63,781

Adapted from Criminal Statistics, England and Wales.

began to focus the crime reporters' spotlights on the closed world of London's gangland. In December the *Sun* warned that 'Britain's big cities are being taken over by ... an engulfing wave of crime' (15.12.65), a statement given additional significance by accounts of sadism and child murder emanating from a courtroom in Cheshire where Brady and Hindly were on trial. To the popular press, the 'Moors Murders' quickly became symbolic of the dark side of the permissive society, the nightmare edge of a libertarian dream which had gained ascendancy during 1965 with the suspension of capital punishment. The case 'raised the temperature' of media anxiety about lawlessness. The anxiety eventually boiled over in August 1966 with the shooting of three policemen in Shepherds Bush[2]. Examination of the crime's interpretation by the press clearly reveals that the meanings attributed to it derive predominantly from a species of order fantasy. For most of the newspapers the crime represented both an attack on a symbol of societal order, and evidence that the threshold of a new era had been overstepped, that 'The Violent Society' was with us. The *Sun* followed the Police Federation in once again warning that 'London and other major cities are in danger of being taken over by large-scale criminal organisations' (13.8.66). The *Daily Sketch* regretted that 'comparisons with Capone's Chicago are inevitable' (13.8.66), an assertion echoed in the *Daily Express* headline: 'Armed police hunt killers of three detectives: THIS IS LONDON 1966' (13.8.66). More than any other event the shootings dramatized the value of the police as the thin blue line between order and chaos, between stability and 'anomic terror'. The *Daily Mail*'s editorial (13.8.66) perhaps expressed this most clearly:

'In Britain the policeman is still the walking sign which says that a society has reached and takes for granted a certain stable normality of public order and decency ... That is why the death of a policeman by violence is felt so deeply by us all. The deaths of the three men at Shepherd's Bush, senselessly and deliberately gunned down on the job of maintaining that order and decency, come as a frighful shock that seems to rock the very earth. A dazed incredulity is followed by the realisation that order is not to be taken for granted. The jungle is still there. There are still wild beasts in it to be controlled.'

The editorial effectively captures the revelatory quality which the shooting held for the press: 'The realization that order is not to be taken for granted'. The theme was taken up the following day by the *Sunday Telegraph:*

'The events of Friday have cast a lightning flash over the whole murky landscape of crime in this country. The police need not only the physical but the overwhelming moral support of the population. Throughout the whole range of petty crimes into the more serious offences too often today public sympathy and sentiment is on the side of the offender. He tends to be regarded as the hero; he should be regarded as an outlaw ... The hope must be that the most recent tragedy will lead to a growing awareness of where we are being led by the steady erosion of respect for law and order and by sentiments of softness towards offenders ...'

The newspapers' brief period of disillusion with the police and grudging admiration for the criminal which followed the Great

Train Robbery and the police scandals of the early sixties was brought to a close by the shootings. Liberal and reactionary newspapers joined in identifying the real heroes, united by a common sense of outrage and calling for improved police pay and conditions. The *News of the World* signified the crime as 'The final, sickening answer to the theorists, to the namby-pambies, to the misguided do-gooders' and called for 'TOUGH ACTION NOW' (14.8.66). The *Mirror* opened a fund for the dependents of the murdered men, reminding its readers that 'they were typical members of a police force which is acknowledged to be the finest in the world' and that 'the fight against crime is not a private matter ... the police need and have the right to the support of us all' (15.8.66).

The debate surrounding the shootings was defined exclusively in terms of the most effective techniques of repressing violence. The issues to emerge were the return of capital punishment and the arming of the police. On the first issue the papers were divided. The *News of the World* offered a platform to the recently retired Metropolitan Assistant Commissioner, Sir Richard Jackson, who declared that the abolition of capital punishment for police murder had given criminals 'a licence to kill'. The *Sunday Telegraph* joined him in calling for the restoration of hanging for police murder; while the *Daily Mail* remained ambivalent and the *Observer* counselled dispassionate reasoning and analysis of the evidence. The newspapers, however, were unanimous in their opposition to the arming of the police which, they argued, would only serve to 'push Britain further up the escalator of social anarchy and violence'. Arming the police might also tilt the balance of public sympathy and support which had swung firmly behind the force. When the *Sun's* crime reporter, Robert Traini, wrote his retrospective piece on the shootings it was this theme of public support he took up. If anything good could be said to have come from the killings, he suggested, it was the demonstration of public sympathy for the police:

'For years, this ideal of co-operation between police and public, of goodwill for the guards from the guarded, has been under attack. From the irritated motorist ... to the theorists and reformers, right up to the allegations of sheer thuggery and corruption the carping has gone on incessantly. So much so that the police and the public were irresistably drawing apart. Now in a burst of gunfire on a sunny afternoon, all that is changed. The carping, it becomes obvious, has done no more than chip away the edges from a monument of goodwill.' (*Sun* 16.8.66)

The social construction of meaning surrounding the Shepherds Bush killings, then, introduced 'The Violent Society' theme and saw the re-alignment of the British Press firmly behind the war against crime and behind the front-line troops in that war, the police. The liberalizing drift which had begun, imperceptibly in the early sixties had been decisively corrected. Fresh battle lines had been drawn, deep-seated values and beliefs reaffirmed. 'Law and order' and 'backing for the police' had been staked as standards for newspaper ideologists to rally round[3]. Violence itself had been established as an essential index of social change and the inferential structures for its interpretation had been set. From 1967 the theme of violence was to be elaborated in a number of variations. The anxiety about criminal violence was to be kept alive in the late sixties by the rising crime statistics and the spectacle of the Kray Twins, reaching a fresh peak, as we shall see, in the summer of 1971 with the killing of policemen in Reading and Blackpool. During the period it became increasingly linked with the theme of youthful violence which can be traced from its origins in the 1940s through the teds and the mods and rockers to the football hooligans and skinheads of the late sixties. The same theme of youthful violence is also present in newspaper coverage of political dissent at the close of the 1960s and it is to this that we now turn.

II *Political violence theme*

'Never play with insurrection' — Karl Marx, *The New York Tribune*

Student dissent and the birth of the law and order campaign
The growth of what has come to be termed 'The Violent Society'

coincides with an acceleration in the break-up of the liberal consensus associated with the 'affluent fifties'. The mid-sixties witnessed the first rupturing in the fabric of cultural hegemony so effectively woven since the war, as groups appeared at the margins of the political spectrum to challenge dominant definitions of social and political issues. The emergence of radical student groups, squatters, claimants unions, and the black power and radical feminist movements are examples of this process. The opposition evidenced in these groups was extra-parliamentary in character. It openly rejected the conventional avenues of political influence and structures of power. It sought to make its voice heard on the street through autonomous and unofficial 'rank and file' actions and organizations, eschewing leaders and bureaucracy and all forms of 'institutionalized' conflict. Its politics, then, were those of direct action by, or in support of, the 'oppressed and disadvantaged' sections of society. The social base of the new opposition lay generally outside the central productive sphere of capital and organized labour. Its support was drawn predominantly from the *lumpen* sections of the middle and working class; on the one hand, students, young professional workers, bohemian drop outs, etc., and on the other, the homeless and unemployed, deviant minorities, and so on. Large numbers of people from this marginal sphere gradually ceased to behave in expected ways. An influential section of the student body began to stage lightning take-overs of university property and generally disrupt 'normal' academic life. Homeless families and young people began to take over empty accommodation. Welfare claimants began to form themselves into organizations to 'demand their rights'. Roman Catholics in Northern Ireland began to shout their grievances on protest marches. Each group was attempting to seize the initiative from bureaucrats and policy administrators, refusing to 'sit back quietly and wait to be processed' and seeking, instead, to exercise some control over their situation.

To most conventional politicians and journalists in 1968 these developments were bewildering. But, as far as the journalists were concerned, at least they were colourful and out of the ordinary. As such they were open to appropriation by the news and entertainment industry in their portrayal of the peculiar present. A pattern for such appropriation had been established only shortly before by newspaper coverage of 'hippies and flower power' in 1967. The depiction of hippie life style went through each of the three stages already described by Jock Young: fascination, titillation, and , finally, condemnation (see chapter 2). Initially the hippies were seen as fascinating and essentially harmless eccentrics, a bizarre and picturesque addition to the 'Swinging-London scene'. But once they began to lose their novelty value the press found a fresh new angle in the role of sex and drugs in their life style. But although its depiction may have served the function of titillation, it was simultaneously threatening to conventional notions of morality and was hence a candidate for condemnation. The darker side of flower power began to be emphasized. In the summer of 1967 crime reporters and editors responded readily to direct and unambiguous police requests to bring the growth of drug-taking to the public's notice (Traini 1971)[4]. As the months passed the stereotypical image of the hippie began to change from the harmless flower child to the far more sordid image of the dirty, drug-crazed parasite. Similar transformations were quickly accomplished with regard to student militancy and other manifestations of extra-parliamentary opposition after the events in Paris in May 1968. In France, student agitation had brought a 'democratically elected government' to the verge of collapse and, in Britain, bewilderment rapidly became tinged with anxiety. The dissidents of the New Left did not confine their protest to single issues as had the CND protesters. They couched their dissent in the rhetoric of total revolution, completely disassociating themselves from any form of conventional social democratic politics, but at the same time rejecting equally the fascist and communist wings of totalitarian authoritarianism. The whole development was profoundly confusing and worrying to politicians and leader writers steeped in the British political culture with its stress on tradition, due process, and appropriate channels. Why should privileged and intelligent young people be drawn towards such curiously un-British conduct? Why should people with so many 'advantages' and 'prospects' turn against 'respectable society' and voluntarily embrace the stigmata of the poor and deviant? The contradiction was too profound for journalists to explain it away by common-sense notions of 'too much permissiveness' or 'natural youthful high spirits and idealism'. At the same time, the new leftist libertarian ideology itself was too dense and impenetrable to furnish journalists with effective explanations of the phenomenon. Readers could not be expected to make sense of explanations which explicated student alienation from the purposes and functioning of the state by means of unfamiliar and subjectively meaningless neo-marxist and situationist concepts[5]. Such ideologizing would hardly fit everyday definitions of news. If any acceptable resolutions were to be found for the contradiction embodied in student militancy they had to be simple and direct. And if that explanation had to draw upon ideological positions they had better be those with which readers were familiar (so familiar that, for many, they ceased to be ideological).

The resolutions which did finally materialize in the press have already been documented elsewhere (Halloran 1970; Murdoch 1973; Slater 1971; Willis 1971; Hall 1974). Briefly, the press drew on statements of politicians (mainly of the Right) which identified the disruptive influence of foreign students and conceptualized the situation in terms of small cliques of militant wreckers and large bodies of moderate opinion. The obvious inferences to be drawn were perfectly in line with a newspaper ideology informed by journalistic news imperatives: in the assumed absence of the type of basic structural inequalities and conflicts which might supply a genuine reason for militant activity, student militancy is to be understood as the result of agitation by a small number of mainly foreign subversives who have undermined the 'good sense' of normally moderate students and persuaded them to act in irresponsible ways. This explanation successfully met the criterion of simplicity and facilitated a concentration on personalities such as Tariq Ali and Daniel Cohn-Bendit. It formed an inferential structure for the reporting of the major anti-Vietnam War demonstration in London in October 1968 and other expressions of political deviance which followed it[6].

But, although the corruption model has been a pervasive one in the reporting of political deviance it has functioned as an explanation of events rather than an immediate image of the event in action. An action image is, of course, essential to the event orientation of news. It cures the ambiguity of behavioural forms by supplying instant meaning. It was not difficult for the press to find a suitable action image for the developing forms of extra-parliamentary opposition in the late sixties, an image which would adequately convey the drama and immediacy of protest and yet which, at the same time, could be relied upon to brand the events with the stamp of illegitimacy. The image adopted was that of 'violence'. Paul Hirst (1973:239) expressed its function well when he argued:

> ' "Violence" as a negative symbol applied to others' political actions enables one to raise the spectre of irresponsibility without making oneself responsible for countering that action at the level of its goals and rationale. It is the ideological term which evades the problem of ideology.'

But the image of violence was not selected and applied as a result of any Fleet Street conspiracy. It was an image dictated by the very perceptual apparatus of popular journalism which filters and codes reality according to news imperatives, and which identifies as the same those phenomena whose surface appearance is similar. This latter predisposition is crucial to the emergence of 'The Violent Society' as a focal concern of newspaper discourse.

The Vietnam demonstrations in London in October 1967 and March 1968 and the events in Paris in May 1968 were instrumental in the formation of the violence image. The press saw representatives of the New Left fighting running battles with the police in the streets and it was this, rather than the reasons behind the protests, that made an imprint on the news. Stripped of any real motivational or behavioural context the remaining image of violence in the streets was in no fundamental respect different from that evoked by the Shepherds Bush police killings. In both the police, as representatives of order and normalcy, were menaced by the forces of anarchy and chaos. In a situation of gathering law-and-order crisis it was understandable that qualitatively different events should come to be subsumed under one overarching image. As we have seen, the late sixties was a time of acute uncertainty and confusion when stable expectations were constantly disrupted and a whole plethora of moral systems were asserting themselves. It was a period of disillusionment when expectations of universal affluence and limitless technological progress nurtured in the fifties and early sixties ceased to be realistic and the meaning of 'progress' became problematic. Most of all it was a time when Left wing fantasies and expectations seized the opportunity to assert themselves, bringing in their wake a Right wing reaction which was to help the Conservative Party back into power in 1970[7]. As that reaction materialized, 'Youth' which had been the pre-eminent metaphor of social change in the post war years became increasingly inappropriate to the deepening anomie engendered by the cultural fragmentation of the late sixties. 'Violence' quickly replaced 'Youth' as a metaphor of change and the deepening anomie eventually began to find expression in the reassertion of the rule of law and the necessity of order in the face of impending chaos. During the 1966 General Election the Conservative Party leadership had resisted pressure from the party in the country to make law and order an issue, believing that voters did not regard crime control as a suitable subject for party politics (Butler and King 1966). Over the next four years, however, the 'law and order campaign' gathered considerable momentum. The Shepherds Bush killings marked the beginning of this moral panic about generalized lawlessness and it was kept alive by a sequence of events over the next few years. In 1967 the trial of the Richardsons revealed a particularly 'ugly and unacceptable face of capitalism'. Reports of the sentences in the 'Torture Trial' were accompanied by news of the discovery of the body of 'Scotch Jack' Buggy, a Soho gangster who had disappeared a few weeks earlier. When these events were coupled with the increasingly public activities of the Kray brothers, the escape of 'public enemy No 1', John McVicar, from

Durham Prison the following year, and a vast increase in armed robberies, there was more than enough material to stoke the fires of a moral panic about organized crime in the late sixties (Hebdige 1974). But in the generalized anxiety of the law and order campaign, organized crime was taken by the press as just one symptom of the 'disease of wanton violence' which was 'sweeping through the whole of society like a plague', threatening the survival of 'the British way of life'. In the press the term 'Thug' became a label with wider application than ever before. London protection racketeers and the skinheads who became the premier folk devils of 1969 were obvious candidates for the label, but, in February of that year Edward Short, the Education Secretary, received enthusiastic newspaper support for his denouncement of activists at the London School of Economics as 'academic thugs', while in September the *People* newspaper felt justified in labelling squatters in Piccadilly as 'hippy thugs' (21.9.69). At the same time, the rioting in Ulster which brought the intervention of British troops in August 1969 provided a vivid scenario of the breakdown of order.

In February 1970 Cambridge students broke up a dinner promoted by the Greek Government at the Garden House Hotel and two students at Essex University petrol bombed a branch of Barclays Bank. The Shadow Home Secretary, Quentin Hogg accused the Labour Government of presiding complacently over the largest crime wave in history. While the statistical basis of his claim may have been dubious[8], the coverage his statement was given in the media ensured that law and order would remain an issue at the June election. The Tory leadership had in any case decided to make it one of the main planks of their platform. As the election approached Quintin Hogg again drew attention to the issue in criticizing the labour administration's decision to call off the South African cricket tour, condemning the Government's inability 'to preserve freedom in this country or to maintain law and order'. A few days before the election Enoch Powell took up a similar theme in attacking 'the enemy within', the tiny minority of wreckers and infiltrators who were brainwashing decent people into accepting the collapse of an ordered society.

The Angry Brigade

Upon taking office the new Conservative government set about their task of re-establishing the Rule of Law in the spheres of both social and economic relations. Their first few months of office appeared to coincide with a fairly successful and promising phase of the war against crime and disruption. In July Justice Melford Stevenson handed out heavy sentences to the 'ringleaders' of the Garden House demonstration, and in November 'public-enemy No 1', John McVicar, was recaptured after some enterprising investigative work by *Daily Mail* crime reporter, Owen Summers. But the progress of order was largely superficial. Beneath the surface a series of political attacks on property was taking place. In September two New Left activists, Joe Keith and Tony Swash, were charged with six petrol bombings of 'ruling class' targets such as Conservative Clubs and Army Recruiting Offices, but these were only the exposed tip of an iceberg of unreported bombings. Most significant among these were the attacks (later associated with the Angry Brigade) on the homes of the Metropolitan Commissioner, Sir John Waldron and the Attorney General, Sir Peter Rawlinson [9]. The reporting of both attacks was prevented by Scotland Yard by issuing confidential memoranda to news editors via the Press Association asking them not to publish until inquiries were complete[10]. But despite the news blackout, a new form of political opposition was developing. Data from the USA, often used by both the press and policy-makers as an indicator of future developments in Britain, pointed to a similar emergent pattern of activity: 546 acts of guerrilla sabotage and terrorism were recorded in the first nine months of 1970, compared with only 16 in 1965[11]. Clearly, 'the enemy within' was beginning to bare his teeth. It was an occasion for renewed vigilance. In November, Edward Heath included a discussion of violence in his address to the United Nations: 'Increasingly, the use of violence has become not the last resort of the desperate, but the first resort of those whole simple, unconstructive aim is anarchy'. In December, the Home Secretary, Reginald Maudling, addressed the Jubilee dinner of the Crime Reporters Association. He identified a decline in parental authority and a growing willingness to accept and

tolerate violence as root causes of much crime, and declared his
intention to strengthen the police force. A few weeks later the
Guardian (4.1.71) reported that:

> 'The police are reconsidering their attitude to anarchists and
> underground organisations. What they regard as a fairly
> tolerant approach which they have adopted in the past, may
> have to be changed, many detectives believe, and replaced by
> a ''no-nonsense stand''.'

The existence of urban guerrilla activity in Britain, already
revealed in the underground press, was beginning to leak out
through the blanket of secrecy, but on the evening of January
12th an event took place which rendered further concealment
impossible. After a day of massive TUC demonstrations against
the new *Industrial Relations Bill*[12], two bombs exploded at the
Hertfordshire home of the Bill's architect. Robert Carr, the
Secretary of State for Employment. Early callers to the Scotland
Yard Press Bureau were told that the explosions had been caused
by a gas main, but their real cause was immediately apparent
when journalists arrived at the scene. Since by this time it was
almost midnight there was little opportunity for reporters to do
more than phone through the bare outline of the events to catch
the later editions of the next day's papers. By the time the
following day's papers appeared, however, leader writers had had
the opportunity of interpreting the meaning of the outrage and
crime reporters had been given the chance of talking with police
contacts and speculating on who might be responsible.

Robert Carr had already introduced themes for media
elaboration in an interview for BBC radio on the morning of the
13th:

> 'This streak of violence which has appeared in Northern Ireland
> and in other parts of the world is a very worrying phenomenon
> ... I believe it creates outrage in British society and will not
> become part of our national life ... What I am sure of is that the
> overwhelming majority of trade unionists, including the
> minority who I believe are opposed to my Bill, will share the

public outrage about this sort of incident, and if it were done
by anybody as part of a protest I am sure they are extremists
and a tiny minority indeed.'

Carr's interpretation of the event was amplified by other
politicians such as William Whitelaw who condemned the act as
cowardly 'and surely alien to every concept of democracy'. He
went on:

> 'But just because it is so alien to our British way of life, and so
> condemned by our British people as a whole, we tend to believe
> that it cannot happen here. The truth is that there are people,
> certainly in the world, and even apparently in this country who
> are prepared to use methods of this kind for their own ends.'

The theme of 'imported terrorism' was immediately taken up by a
number of newspapers. The *Daily Mirror* devoted its entire front
page to an editorial offering a £10,000 reward for information
leading to the arrest and conviction of those who had delivered 'a
sinister invitation to the British people to endure or condone the
sick society which has afflicted the United States'. The paper went
on to note the nation's shock and bewilderment that such a thing
could happen in Britain but warned: 'It can happen here, it
happened here on Tuesday night'. Its recommendation was that
the confusion engendered by the sudden disruption of stable
expectations should quickly give way to united resistance to any
threat to subvert the nation's traditional way of doing things:

> 'EVERYBODY is united in denouncing the bomb outrage.
> EVERYBODY ought also to be deeply concerned about the
> growing drift towards intolerance and hysteria in the British
> way of life ... The threat is ominously clear. The writing on
> the wall is there for all to see and heed. The people of Britain
> are mature enough, balanced enough, and decent enough to
> make sure that the drift is abruptly halted.'   (14.1.71)

The Times described the explosion as 'an attack on democracy'.
The *Guardian* talked about 'the disease of violence' taking root in
Britain and pointed out what was almost 'too obvious to need

stating' that politically-motivated violence can never be justified in a liberal democracy. The *Daily Mail* spelt out ' The Threat to Us All' (14.1.71):

> 'If a leading minister who is the very example of the British tradition of fairness and good humour is not safe, who is? Has the epidemic of political violence finally infected this country? ... Can we still afford our easy-going traditions? Can we still take it for granted that in Britain at least, in Ibsen's famous words, "People don't do such things"? Clearly this country is not immune from the attacks of madmen eaten up with unreasoning hatred of our way of life ...'

The *Sun*, too, referred to the impossibility of Britain being 'immune from such hideous attacks' ... 'in an age of globe-trotting graduates in ruthless violence'. Most of the newspapers were careful to follow the example of Robert Carr in disassociating the bombings from the 'legitimate' demonstrations against the *Industrial Relations Bill*. Only the *Daily Express* chose to link the attack to the developing tradition of confrontationist demonstrations over the previous few years which the paper claimed had 'created the climate of political violence which a few wicked individuals are now exploiting in an attempt to disrupt society'. The bombs were 'terrible forewarnings of what happens when respect for the rule of law is eroded'.

In attributing significance to the Robert Carr bombing, then, the leader writers of the national dailies (the *Morning Star* excepted) were unanimous in identifying the attack as something alien to the British way of life, a threat to the freedom we all enjoy under the rule of law, a threat deriving from an unquarantined foreign infection. The remedy prescribed was what the *Mail* described as 'a cool head and a firm hand', a calm public recognition of the threat, a reassertion of the rule of law, and the apprehension and punishment of the offenders without the curtailment of basic freedoms. As the *Daily Telegraph* put it: 'Let us show ... that order can be maintained, justice enforced, the nation governed and, not least, offenders punished without the disciplines of the police state'. When it came to the ascription of motive for the attack, however, there was far more uncertainty and confusion. Here the leader writers drew primarily on police statements rather than those of politicians. The officer in charge of the investigations, Detective Chief Superintendent Habershon was quoted as saying: 'It would seem quite evident that it was done as a form of protest, but just what they were protesting about I really don't know ... The people who did this must clearly be lunatics'. The statement contained a line of contradiction which was reproduced in most of the press coverage. It is a contradiction which, it can be argued, constitutes a 'deep structure'* of media representations of political deviance. We might term it the rationality contradiction. For an example of its operation we can return to the *Daily Mail* editorial in which it is claimed that the bomb attack was the work of both 'professionals hell-bent on murder' (the connotations being of rational behaviour e.g., in pursuit of economic gain) and 'madmen eaten up with unreasoning hatred of our way of life'. The leader goes on to suggest that the 'fanatics' responsible may be suffering from 'persecution mania' but apparently sees no inconsistency in recommending deterrence by firm action, a response which one would expect to be based on a model of political deviance as rational behaviour. The *Daily Mirror* also recommended deterrence although it could not identify any probable motive for the act. However it assumed that the motive must be 'twisted'. It would have been stretching coincidence too far to say that Robert Carr had been a victim chosen at random, he was obviously the target of a political attack, but who but a lunatic could hope to achieve anything by attacking a democratically elected government minister? The act was therefore 'senseless' (*The Times*) and 'futile' (*Sun*), the work of 'an unbalanced individual' (*Guardian*), 'a mad bomber' (*Sun*). Both the *Daily Telegraph* and the *Guardian* went so far as to suggest that the bomber was probably 'a tool of people more sinister'[13]. The *Telegraph* referred to 'professors, secure in the groves of academe' who give 'prim little

---

* 'Deep structure' here refers to a particular way of understanding and perceiving reality which lies (usually unnoticed) at the root of representations and accounts. The concept is drawn from the repertoire of semiological analysis.

lectures in ''institutionalised violence'' or ''repressive tolerance'' while in the shadows some immature devotee puts their theories into effect with a petrol bomb or gelignite'. The corruption model provides one means of resolving the rationality contradiction. Under its application political deviants are seen as formally rational but weak-willed individuals whose reason has been subverted by malevolent individuals who are rationally pursuing their own sinister ends. But the most effective means of transcending the contradiction was provided by Harold Wilson's comment on the Carr bombing: 'Use of violence, whatever the motive may be, if there is a motive, must be treated as a major crime.' The application of the master label of 'criminal' to an act renders the rationality contradiction obsolete because the act is to be understood as neither political nor lunatic. The act is instead relocated in a new domain of understanding and surrounded with connotations which call forth a condemnatory and punitive response. It thus evades the problem of rationality in the same way that the 'violence' label evades the problem of ideology. In the case of the Angry Brigade the imposition of the master status of criminal was successfully accomplished during the protracted police search for members.

The theorizing of the editorials was reflected in the news reports which followed over the next few days. The suggestion expounded in the early *Guardian* leader that the bombings had been carried out by a 'lonely madman' was quickly discarded as unworkable when an Angry Brigade communique arrived at selected newspaper offices and crime correspondents began to sound out their police contacts. The theme of 'imported terrorism', however, was utilized. On the day the £10,000 reward was offered, *Daily Mirror* reporters claimed that police were exploring the possibility that 'a foreign agitator who is expert at making a simple but effective bomb' was responsible for the explosions. On the same day, the *Daily Express* correspondents revealed the 'provisional conclusion' of their expert police sources that 'a communist ''cell'' inspired and financed from abroad' was responsible The following day *The Times* (15.1.71) floated the theory of a team of professional 'hit men' acting for foreign terrorists:

'Police ... are searching for a small team of freelance saboteurs who it is believed carried out the attack on a "contract" basis for an international group of political extremists. The men are known to be experts in the use of explosives and hire out their services for cash fees. They are thought to have been behind a number of bomb incidents last year, most of which were blamed on the IRA and anarchists. One man thought to be a member of the freelance bomb squad was being sought by police yesterday ... Special Branch detectives during intensive inquiries in the past four days have discovered that a large number of militant political extremists have been staying in London and the Home Counties supported by liberal funds brought in from abroad ...'

Perhaps not surprisingly, this extravagant theory has received very little support from subsequent investigations into Angry Brigade activities (Carr 1975). But it remains a classic example of the elaboration and, perhaps, the elevation of police speculation. As I have already suggested, stories of this type tend to be filed in situations where reporters are anxious to discover fresh news angles. They may find themselves under pressure to build unrelated fragments of information into a presentable story. This is a common pressure familiar to journalists in most fields of news processing. As one crime reporter put it, 'When there is no information forthcoming one is tempted to use one's journalistic licence'. He went on to assure me that members of the Crime Reporters Association are responsible enough to confine the exercise of their 'licence' to making reasonable assumptions, adding 'but the non-CRA boys do tend to let their imagination run riot'. When fresh angles are scarce but desperately sought is, of course, the time when the careful 'planting' of stories by informants is easiest (see chapter 6).

Returning to *The Times* report on the police hunt for Robert Carr's attackers, it is illuminating to trace the origins and development of a small part of it: 'One man thought to be a member of the freelance bomb squad was being sought by police yesterday'. Soon after the attack the crime correspondents of the

Evening Standard were tipped off that the police suspected Stuart Christie, a leading British anarchist who was later acquitted of complicity in the Angry Brigade conspiracy. The tip-off, which almost certainly came through unofficial police contacts, was speedily turned into a story for the *Standard*:

'A huge hunt is going on throughout London for a self-confessed anarchist who, detectives believe, is behind the double-bomb outrage ... special branch men are almost certain they know the identity of the man who planted the bombs. He is an anarchist in his twenties, who was strongly suspected of plotting other bomb attacks in London. Almost 300 Special Branch men based in London were trying to find the man today. He has vanished from all his normal haunts. They believe he is head of a team of about six highly organised and competent men who will stop at nothing to spread violence and terror throughout Britain ...' [14]

In fact, the Police were well aware of Christie's whereabouts but chose to take no action (*Private Eye* 1971). But the rumour of his disappearance quickly began to take on an independent life, serving as a convenient crutch for journalistic speculation. The day after the *Standard* report the *Daily Express* revealed that police were trying to 'flush out' the young anarchist who was now identified as a Scot. The *Mirror* assured its readers that an arrest was expected 'within 36 hours' and that the young anarchist's team of plotters had been successfully infiltrated by the Yard. When no arrest was forthcoming the *Express* suggested that since 'suspect No 1' was 'known to have a lot of ready cash' he would attempt to escape to anarchist accomplices on the Continent. In case of such an eventuality 'a number of rarely used private airfields were under surveillance'. When the weekend still brought no arrest, the *Standard* was obliged to report that their 'bomb man' was probably in Paris (18.1.71). Ten days later, the Police put a stop to most of the speculation by once more imposing a news blackout. The reasons for the official silence were spelt out by Clive Borrell in *The Times* (29.1.71):

'Scotland Yard ... want to safe-guard "certain facts which we do not want published". These "certain facts", I understand, point directly to the group responsible. Yard men are anxious that their present lines of inquiry should not be clouded by imitators who may try to gain publicity for a variety of causes.'[15]

Between the explosions at Robert Carr's home and the arrest in August 1971 of four libertarian revolutionaries who were eventually convicted of conspiracy to cause explosions, the Angry Brigade claimed responsibility for five further bomb attacks. Each was accompanied by a communiqué which, taken as a set, provides an explicit rationale for the explosions. The ideology of the Brigade was anarcho-marxist, heavily overlaid by Debord's situationism. In its communiques it argued that the bombings were a response to what it saw as the continuous violence of everyday life by which the mass of people are oppressed and exploited in the interests of a ruling class:

'We have sat quietly and suffered the violence of the system far too long. We are being attacked daily. Violence does not only exist in the army, the police, and the prisons. It exists in the shoddy alienating culture pushed out by T.V. films and magazines, it exists in the ugly sterility of urban life. It exists in the daily exploitation of our labour, which gives big bosses the power to control our lives and run the system for their own ends.'   (Communiqué 6)

The bombings were intended as symbolic attacks through which they hoped to direct attention to their critique of contemporary capitalism and its inherently repressive culture, and to shake the working class from its attitude of apathetic acceptance and channel its alienation into revolutionary but autonomous rank and file action:

'The politicians, the leaders, the rich, the big bosses are in command ... THEY control. WE, THE PEOPLE, SUFFER ... Slowly we started understanding the BIG CON. We saw that they had defined our "possibilities". They said: You can

demonstrate ... between police lines. You can have sex ... in
the normal position as a commodity; commodities are good.
You can rally in defence of the T.U.C. ... the T.U.C. "leadership" is wise. They used confusing works like "public" or the
"national interest". Is the public some kind of "dignified
body" which we belong to, only until we go on strike? Why are
we reduced then to dreaded scroungers, ruining the country's
economy? Is the "National Interest" anything more than
THEIR interest? Lately we started seeing through another kind
of con: There is a certain kind of professional who claims to
represent us ... M.P.'s, the Communist Party, the Union
leaders, the Social Workers, the old-old left ... All these
people presumed to act on our behalf. All these people have
certain things in common ... THEY always sell us out ... THEY
are all afraid of us ... THEY'LL preach towards keeping the
peace ... and we are bored ... poor ... and mainly very tired of
keeping the peace. THE ANGRY BRIGADE BECAME A
REALITY when we knew that every moment of badly paid
boredom in a production line was a violent crime. We had
rejected all the senile hierarchies and ALL the structures, the
liars, the poverty pimps ... to believe our struggle could be
restricted to the channels provided to us by the pigs, WAS THE
GREATEST CON. And we started hitting them.'

(Communiqué 7)

This was the rhetoric of the revolutionary vanguard designed to
exploit the 'propaganda of the deed', but, in fact, little of it
reached the ears of the 'apathetic millions' because it failed to
meet the criteria of selection applied by Fleet Street. Publicity was
clearly considered crucial by the Brigade, as it said in
Communique 6 the Robert Carr bomb was important because it
'shattered the blackouts of the Yellow Press', but it was caught up
in the same 'Catch 22' situation that the student demonstrators of
the sixties had experienced: The only way to attract media
attention to a cause was to commit sensational acts, but once
appropriated by the media nothing could prevent the form and
style of the protest being used as a criterion for the evaluation of

both the cause and its promoters. At the same time, the Angry Brigade, like other oppositional movements before it, was powerless to prevent its activities becoming part of the spectacle it sought to shatter. Even with the issuing of communique's explaining the significance of the act, a bombing could be easily extracted from its ideological basis and signified as simply a dangerous piece of criminal lunacy. Once the apparently irrelevant ideas had been successfully swept aside, the whole thing could be simplified into a variation of a conventional crime news format. 'Cops and Robbers' could be transformed into the new spectacle of 'Cops and Bombers', Good vs Evil in a fresh guise. This moulding of the emergent phenomenon to fit a pre-existing news genre was directed by newspaper ideology and facilitated by the organization of specialist reporting in Fleet Street.

As we saw in Chapter 2, newspaper ideology identifies as politics only those activities which take place within the formal parameters of conventional democratic processes. Activities which claim political status but which lie outside those parameters constitute a *threat* to politics. This ideological classification is buttressed by the structural organization of specialist journalism. Although in recent years, Fleet Street's lines of specialization have become more blurred[16], the everyday business of information-collection is still organized around the routine institutional sources which supply the specialist correspondent with his 'beat' — financial journalists are based in the city, defense, industrial, aviation, and education correspondents at the relevant Government Departments, and so on. Political correspondents have Westminster as their beat. Crime correspondents have Scotland Yard. This means that, to a large extent, it is the institutional sources that define the relevancies of a particular specialist field. Thus, crime reporters will generally cover any affairs which engage the attention of Scotland Yard: they do not independently define the boundaries of their specialization, but rather allow those boundaries to be defined primarily by their routine sources. This may seem, at first sight, a mundane observation, but it should become increasingly clear during the course of this study that the influence exerted by sources over the selection and construction of news stories is a fundamental and far-reaching one. I would suggest that crime reporters (and many other specialists) not only allow sources to determine their sphere of journalistic competence, they also trade off and take over source interpretations of phenomena within that sphere. Turning once again to the phenomenon of urban guerrilla activity we can see that the immediate responsibility for its repression was taken up by the Metropolitan Police and was therefore automatically included within the crime correspondent's sphere of competence; its situation there being entirely consonant with a newspaper ideology which viewed it as an essentially criminal phenomenon. The reporters themselves, possessing little experience in the interpretation of this type of political deviance, generally adopted the perspectives and understandings of their police sources. Police perspectives and understandings are closely tied to the practical concerns of their occupation. These relate to the apprehension of miscreants rather than to the understanding of their motivations or the political contexts of their acts. To the British policeman, the urban guerrilla is not so much a political actor as a particularly nasty and weird kind of villain who must be stopped before he can do any more damage. For the practical purposes of the policeman, the guerrilla's cause and ideological convictions are not merely difficult to comprehend but largely irrelevant to the task of catching him. As numerous studies of the police have noted, the detective sees himself, first and foremost as a 'thief-taker'; the core of his role is the control of property crime which he sees as essentially rational behaviour — the pursuit of economic gain by illegal means. At the same time, he generally finds it difficult to see crime which does not have an economic motivation as rational.

Even the policeman in charge of the investigation into the Angry Brigade's activities, ex-Deputy Assistant Commissioner Ernest Bond, has said: 'I reckon I have a fair understanding of villains' minds. They commit crimes for gain. But I will never understand the Angry Brigade who put their liberty at stake — and lost it — in a cause which, in my book, never existed' ('Bond versus the Bombers', *Sunday Mirror* 4.4.76). The law-breaker who is motivated by ideology is thus easily seen as 'a dangerous nutter' or 'a mad bomber', someone who is basically sick but who arouses no sympathy. One journalist I interviewed who had considerable experience of reporting in Northern Ireland found the typical perspective of English policemen on terrorist activities particularly disturbing:

> 'The policemen I've talked to tend to get very irrational about bombs. They tend to try to fit bombers into the category of "normal criminals", which doesn't work, and they're looking for some other motive. To the people who manufacture and place bombs, as far as they're concerned, they're at war. As far as the police are concerned they're not at war because war only exists when both sides are trying to kill each other.'

In the absence of pecuniary motives, many policemen find the behaviour of political deviants profoundly bewildering. It is even more bewildering when the deviants are young women. Colin Smith in his *Observer* article (18.11.73) on the Price sisters (convicted of the bombing of the Old Bailey in 1973) reports the reaction of provincial policemen to watching the two women in the dock at Winchester:

> '[They] somehow unsettled the country coppers of Winchester who, without the big city experience of their Special Branch brethren, shook their heads in disbelief that beauty could ever be so dangerous. "When I look at those girls", said a senior officer of the Hampshire force with a daughter of the same age, "I keep asking myself what on earth got them into something that should land them in that dock, and I couldn't find any answers".'

But this lack of reciprocity of perspective can also extend to the Special Branch. In his biography of a Special Branch Superintendent, George Smith, Norman Lucas recounts Smith's comments on Klaus Fuchs, the Atom Bomb spy:

> 'Fuchs lived in a world of his own. His idea that the powers of East and West should share atomic secrets was really the product of pacificism. Even when he stood in the dock he

really felt no sense of guilt. He was convinced that he was not guilty of any offence. The guilty were the statesmen of the West who had offended against humanity. *It was impossible for me, with my simple typically English background, to understand the strange views held by the arch traitor.'* (my italics.)

(Lucas 1973:77)

It could be argued that failure to understand the political deviant facilitates the repressive aspects of the policeman's task because it makes any identification with the deviant difficult. However, if that failure of understanding is taken over by the journalist during his absorbtion of source perspectives and interpretations it becomes more difficult to align with role demands unless they too involve the repression of crime.

Thus, the denial of a rational ideology to political deviants is not so much evidence of the machiavellianism of newspaper editors as a function of Fleet Street's inability to look beyond the stereotypes and interpretations which have been absorbed and constituted into its conventional wisdom. Very few papers on Fleet Street seem to employ journalists who are seriously prepared to acquaint themselves with fringe politics in Britain, to transcend the perceptual and cognitive constraints of newspaper ideology and to understand deviant views of the world. The degree to which many reporters on the Angry Brigade story remained locked within the conventional world view was apparent well before the background pieces on the main trial were written in December 1972. Many papers apparently found it difficult to follow the logic behind the Brigade's selection of targets. An article in the *Daily Mail* (28.1.71), for instance, expressed bewilderment at the attack on the Attorney General, Sir Peter Rawlinson: 'The Attorney General's quasi-political role almost puts him above controversy ...'. But the failure of understanding became increasingly obvious as the trial drew to a close. After the first week of a trial that was to last six months, the press benches had remained virtually empty. In recent years, as major trials have become more protracted, and Fleet Street's resources more stretched it has become standard practice for newspapers to rely on agency copy to keep them in touch with developments. The crime reporter will usually only arrive in time for the summing-up and verdicts, having already prepared a background piece anticipating the outcome — 'It's no good going too early because you get fogged by a mass of irrelevant information'. Court reporting is a declining specialization which has now lost most of its leading practitioners. The Association of Central Criminal Court Journalists remains an enclave of conservatism. The determination of its members to resist challenges to their shared values, perceptions, and understandings was evidenced in their indignant reaction to the *Evening Standard*'s decision to ask underground journalist, Richard Neville, to cover the first Angry Brigade trial (Regina vs Prescott and Purdie)[17]. By the time the second Angry Brigade trial approached its final week most court reporters were engaged elsewhere and the *Guardian* and the *Morning Star* were the only nationals regularly represented, but as the judge's summing-up began the trial once again attracted the attention of Fleet Street. Having missed so many days of evidence many of the journalists dispatched to cover the case must have found it difficult to pick up the threads of the trial:

'Journalists from the whole of Fleet Street began ringing Time Out as the summing-up drew to a close, and after the verdicts were announced. The questions they asked were born not of malice or active right-wing sentiments, but of ignorance, not just of anarchist of libertarian politics, but of the politics of the left and the working class in general ... After her acquittal, Kate Maclean talked on a TV programme about her politics and the issue of ''violence''. ''I don't think you can pick out a group of people and say that they are violent when this society is so violent all the way through and the state is violent ... the homeless and the unemployed are directly suffering because of the way in which this economy works.'' Those words were carried on the PA Service to all national newspapers. Not one used them. The sentiments are so unfamiliar to Fleet Street that they were not recognised as part of the explanation which we were being asked for at the same time.' (*Time Out* 15.12.72)

It is in no way surprising that Kate Maclean's words should be ignored by journalists guided by the imperative of conventionalism. It is this reliance on, and belief in, ready-made interpretations which filters out unfamiliar ideas from explanations of deviance and, in this case, cleared the way for the wholesale denial of rational ideology by the press in its post-trial coverage. When communiqués were quoted it was generally to ridicule the ideas they contained. Their claim to be serious political documents was effectively negated by the popular press in a series of dismissive statements: 'looney plots' (*Sun*), 'revolutionary clap-trap' (*News of the World*), 'violent philosophy' (*Daily Express*). The *Sun* (7.12.72) derided the scope of their critique: 'Pretty well anything might be considered a cause for revolution in the woolly-minded world of the communes ... Blow it up. Burn it down. Revolution. Their ideas were half-baked ...' In other papers the rationality contradiction was again evident. The *News of the World* referred to 'these sick people' and declared 'it is a terrifying yet sad story of mis-applied talent and demented minds' (10.12.72). The *Sunday Mirror* called them 'madly misguided'. But if their violence was not necessarily born of insanity, it was essentially negative and meaningless. The Angry Brigade were the forces of chaos personified. The *Express* described them as 'bomb-happy destructionists' with 'nothing constructive to offer to replace the trail of rubble left behind by their home-made bombs'. The *Sun* characterized them as, 'the people who tried to throw Britain into bloody chaos', and was clearly concerned that no considerations of ideology should obscure the criminality of their acts:

> '... there was the risk that the criminal issues would be fogged by politics. Right from the beginning the judge made it clear this was no "political trial". The people in the dock were not accused of having the wrong views. They were accused of bombing, shooting and burning.'   (7.12.72)

The popular press, in particular, did its best to locate the Angry Brigade in the same blood and terror scenario as the Krays and Richardsons. They were not simply an affront to the rule of law, they were an urgent threat to the entire democratic way of life.

The general orientation was reflected in headlines like the *Mirror's* 'BOMB PLOT GANG'S REIGN OF TERROR' and the *Express's* 'THE TRIBES WHO AIM TO SMASH OUR SOCIETY', as well as in textual references such as: 'terror campaign', 'plot to replace law and order in Britain with violence and revolution' and 'terror in the name of social justice'. Applauding the ten year sentences of the four found guilty, the *Daily Mail* declared, 'There is no room for sentiment in dealing with those who openly vow to destroy our society', while the *Express* echoed its words with, 'Spare no sympathy for the jailed Angry Brigaders. Because they sought to destroy our democratic way of life by bombs and terror.' The rhetoric of consensual denunciation was pervasive. The Angry Brigade's self-projected image of an agitational group within a nascent mass movement, a spark in a revolutionary powder keg, was ignored and the Brigade was cast as a tiny outlaw clique without any popular support, the archetypal outsiders sinisterly plotting the end of civilization. As the *Daily Mail* put it, 'The Angry Brigade do not enjoy any great backing even among the rebellious young'. Given the majesty of the consensus massed against it, it was clear to newspapers that the Brigade's activities had been doomed to failure from the start. With the conviction of four of its key members that failure became embarrassingly obvious. Since those convicted apparently had no aim except the destruction of society as we know it, failure was the only conclusion in the face of the obvious survival of society. The forces of order were getting the last laugh on 'the great new protesters who knew better than any of us'. Moral indignation was the order of the day and was effectively captured in the *Sun's* banner headline: 'DOWNFALL OF THE BIGHEAD BRIGADE' (7.12.72). A year before, after the conviction of Prescott, the *Mirror* had written of the Brigade:

> 'Their aim was appallingly simple. To overthrow the Government. Their strategy is equally simple. Create panic by terrorist acts. The authorities then react with repressive policies, and the workers rise in rebellion against this repression.
> *Simple but doomed to failure*

For the Angry Brigade could not understand that the people it was trying to provoke into rebellion have a deep-seated hatred of political violence.
Jack Prescott was caught by the things he despised most. A hard-working middle-class copper and a public which, far from flocking to the banner of political violence, rejected him.'

(2.12.71)

Twelve months later, the *Express* (7.12.72) made the same point: 'The bombers boasted: ''We are getting closer to final victory. We are slowly destroying the long tentacles of the oppressive state machine''. But they were wrong. They had no chance of winning. Not in this country.' The *Telegraph* (7.12.72) was surprised that they could ever believe that they were engaging in a serious political struggle: 'How could they ever delude themselves that these plottings were more than a self-indulgent, theatrical, *ultimately futile* flirting with nihilistic wickedness.' Futile it may have been but the threat of lunatic political violence was recognized as important enough to require continued vigilance. The police warning that some members of the Brigade were still at liberty was accompanied by speculation about possible future targets. A *Daily Mirror* crime correspondent revealed that 'Special Branch chiefs' expected an attempt to kidnap the Home Secretary and another minister. *The Times* carried the headline, 'ANGRIER BRIGADE IS FEARED' and reported police fears that 'A new wave of bombings will break out in protest at the convictions of the Brigade's ''lieutenants'' ' (7.12.72). Opposite the sub-heading, '200 At Large Still Have a Chance to Kill', the *News of the World* reported, 'Commander Bond's band brought some of them to justice. There are many more. One saw them at the trial — hairy ones, watching, scribbling, plotting'.[18] The *Express* spelt out the warning: 'Dedicated revolutionaries do not surrender easily ... the aim remains the same. To smash our society.'

Having signified the Angry Brigade's activities as simultaneously arrogant, meaningless, destructive, and dangerous, newspapers were still left with a nagging obligation to provide something that might pass as an explanation of the affair. For many newsmen, the natural response to the problem of why four intelligent youngsters should completely reject a society which would appear to have offered them so much was to take out and dust down the faithful but well-worn corruption model. Quite simply, the youngsters had been 'interfered with'.

As a 'self-confessed' anarchist with a previous conviction for attempting to blow up General Franco, Stuart Christie would have fitted the corruptor role admirably — had he not been acquitted. Indeed the design of the *Sun*'s post-trial coverage suggests that Christie might well have featured prominently in at least one paper's explanation of the conspiracy. But in the absence of any obvious candidate for personalization, blame for the four's conversion into revolutionaries tended to be attributed to evil influences within universities. The *Daily Telegraph* (7.12.72) quoted a senior Special Branch officer as saying:

'... it seems that once at a university, they are subjected to corrupting influences by certain academics in influential positions forcing their extremist views on them. Fortunately for the country only a minority of students become indoctrinated. But these influences at universities are a nursery of anarchy. They are a dangerous influence.'

His views were supported (with reservations) in the *Telegraph*'s leader column and in that of the *Express* (7.12.72):

'What will shock most people is how two highly intelligent young women from respectable families can get involved in anarchistic cells. Perhaps the answer is that they met at a university ... It is high time to take a look at what is going on in our Universities. Instead of being centres of academic learning many of them have become breeding grounds for malcontents and drop-outs.'

The idea of the sudden and sinister transformation at university was one reflected in the newspapers' biographies of the two women convicted. The *Daily Mail* (7.12.72) wrote of Anna Mendleson: 'Within a few weeks of going to Essex University the clever, fun-loving schoolgirl changed to a bomb-planting revolutionary who slept with a machine-gun in her room.' Her friend, Hilary Creek, apparently underwent a similar transformation from 'an outdoor girl and leader of the Sea Rangers', from saint to devil. According to the *Sun* both girls became the kind of beings who 'went in for wild sex and drug orgies and sickening blood-soaked ritual slaughter' (7.12.72). For the *Sun*, in particular, this moral metamorphosis provided the opportunity for the composition of titillating copy, for the description of commune life in 'crash pads' where: 'Sex was free and easy. Very free. Very easy. A man who fancied a girl resident could readily have her favours. The same went for a girl who fancied a man. Or a girl who fancied a girl ...' (7.12.72). In most other papers, titillation remained an undercurrent, emerging only in the dangerously romantic image of the agressive female, 'the girl who slept with a machine gun by her bed'. Both the *Mirror* and the *Express* chose the 'intriguing' contradiction between violence and femininity for their lead headlines after the trial: 'THE BOMB GIRLS: Both jailed for 10 years then Anna says thanks to two jurors' (*Daily Mirror* 7.12.72). 'ANGRY GIRLS — TEN YEARS: Kisses in the dock as four others set free' (*Daily Express* 7.12.72). If we compare the space devoted to photographs of the four convicted we find that in the seven highest circulation nationals on the day after the trial photographs of Anna Mendleson and Hilary Creek occupied almost twice as much newspaper space as those of John Barker and James Greenfield, the discrepancy being considerably larger if we take only the four top-selling 'popular' papers (Table 3).

Press reaction to the Angry Brigade has been examined in some detail for its illustrative value and because it marks a significant moment in the elaboration of the 'violent society' theme, the recognition of a new form of violence which emerged in the early seventies to pose a new challenge to the State's apparatuses of control. It was a challenge that threatened the hegemony of the dominant ideological system by attacking the assumptions, typifications, and interpretative models through which it is maintained, and seeking to exploit and deepen the contradiction

Table 3 Newspaper space (in square inches) devoted to photographs of Anna Mendleson, Hilary Creek, John Barker, and James Greenfield on 7.12.72.

Newspaper		Mendleson & Creek	Barker & Greenfield
Mirror		34.03	3.38
Express		50.92	16.80
Sun		15.68	3.98
Mail		21.28	21.28
	Sub total	121.91	45.44
Telegraph		8.28	8.28
Times		14.80	14.80
Guardian		47.01	32.64
	Sub total	70.09	55.72
	Total	192.00	101.16

between dominant ideology and the everyday realities of conflict and power which it obscures. In analyzing the reaction of the Press˒ we have not only explored the relationship between newspapers and the major apparatus of face-to-face control (i.e., the police), we have also glimpsed the Press in its role as defender of the dominant ideology, indignantly deriding the pretentions of alternative definitions of reality, and casually appropriating their expressive forms as part of the spectacle of the peculiar present. This neutralization of potentially problematic phenomena is habitually accomplished through the articulation of an ideological discourse which I have termed 'law-and-order news'. Law-and-order news neutralizes deviant world views by either denying their status as beliefs which should be taken seriously by sensible people[19], or condemning them as manifestations of wickedness or corruption. It locates them outside the commonsense, consensual domain of reasonable opinions ('extremist', 'criminal', 'violent', 'lunatic' etc.), explaining them away by means of concepts and mythologies of dominant ideology ('corruption', 'criminal infection', 'foreign agitation' etc.). This, as I have tried to show, is not a product of editorial conspiracy, but a reflection of the social organization of reporting, and the professional imperatives and commercial interests which underlie it.

In reacting to the Angry Brigade, the Press reawakened a dormant tradition of fear which can be traced back beyond the protocols of the elders of Zion, the Gunpowder plot, and the Witchhunts of the Seventeenth Century: the fear of the secret and malevolent conspiracy. In doing so, they supplied the law-and-order crisis with two of its most potent images: the Conspiracy and the Bomber. These were images with threatening and sinister connotations which were to be amplified over the next few years by events in Northern Ireland and the IRA campaigns in Britain culminating in the grisly public house bombings at Guildford, Woolwich, Birmingham, and Caterham[20]. But the crisis was yet to find an ultimate image of lawlessness. To trace its eventual emergence we must move away from political deviance back to the explicitly criminal, to the first echoes of the Shepherd's Bush shootings.

III *Criminal and political violence: the convergence of themes*

'The great silent majority who are on the side of law and order must stand up and be counted. We must become more and more vocal in our defence of those virtues and standards of behaviour which once made this nation great.'

Rt. Rev. A.L.E. Hoskins, Anglican Bishop of Lancaster at the funeral of Superintendent Gerald Richardson.

The Blackpool police killing

Five years after the Shepherds Bush Killings in the summer of 1971, the headlines again indexed the same pattern of murder. In June, the month that saw the Angry Brigade become 'Public Enemy No 1' with the formation of the bomb squad, Detective Constable Ian Coward was shot dead in Reading by two men in a stolen car. The men, Arthur Skingle and Peter Sparrow had been released from prison on parole. Then on August 23, three days after the arrest of those convicted in the second Angry Brigade trial, a Blackpool police Superintendent, Gerald Richardson was shot by Frederick Sewell after a jewel robbery. The impact on the press of this second shooting was enormous, coming as it did at a time of renewed anxiety about the violent society. On the day following the shooting *The Times* published an interview with two anonymous senior Scotland Yard officers attacking liberal policies towards violent offenders. Despite Yard denials there can be little doubt that the interview was a political move by the two officers, who, it soon emerged, were Assistant Commissioner Peter Brodie, the Head of the C.I.D., and Deputy Assistant Commissioner Richard Chitty, the officer who had been in charge of the investigation into the Shepherd's Bush murders. It was seen by many as an attempt to mobilize public opinion against the inactivity and continuing 'soft-line' approach of the Home Office, a move given increased significance by the unfortunate events in Blackpool and by the fact that it had come, in part, from Assistant Commissioner Brodie, an officer who was then being widely tipped to succeed Sir John Waldron as the next Metropolitan Commissioner. The *Daily Mirror* launched a major front page editorial under the simple, emotive headline: 'THUGS'. The leader, like others of the time, was impregnated with 'backs-to-the-wall' rhetoric and scenarios of disaster:

'... This newspaper has no intention of advocating a return to the obscenity of the noose and the cat. But the Mirror recognises that the modern wave of violence is in a different category from any other crime. The answer cannot be found in an extension of do-goodery and penal reform on behalf of the violent criminal. Let there be no doubt about what will happen if violence escalates at the present catastrophic rate. The streets of London and other major British cities will become as deadly for peaceful citizens and for policemen as the streets of New York. In those circumstances, society and the police would loose heart. Britain would become a battle ground. Mindless thuggery in the streets would be frontally opposed by coppers with guns ...

Somewhere a stand has to be made. The time is now ...'

(25.8.71)

The leader went on to advocate longer and more severe prison sentences for the violent criminal and more vocal support for the police. The *Sun* supported the same remedies to make sure that 'the thin blue line' is protected and 'victory in the war against violence' is assured. The *Mail* had already offered its own diagnosis of society's ills. It identified violence as 'the drug that poisons the Western World' and criticized the role models offered in popular films, books, and television drama as well as the intellectual apologists of the cult of violence:

> 'What can we do to stop this country going the way of the United States? ... We are dealing with a chronic sickness, not just a passing epidemic ... Today's obsession with violence reaches from the high priests of culture in Paris and New York — the Norman Mailers and the Jean-Paul Sartres — down to the mindless street-corner yobbo. It is a far worse drug than marijuana. It is poisoning the Western World ... The only antidote is some form of censorship. Distasteful yes ... But something has to be done if our children are to inherit a world worth living in.' (24.8.71)

The following day, the *Mail* (15.8.71) was recommending further measures to pump the toxicity out of society's blood steam:

> '... We have got to bring back that old fellow-feeling between the policeman and the public — and at the same time give him the tools to catch the high-speed villain. We have got to make it clear that crime does not pay — without at the same time condemning the criminal to rot.
> *For a start, sentences should be tougher, remissions for good behaviour more difficult to win, and there should be no parole for those convicted of violence ...*
> WE WANT TO SEE THE POLICE FORCE RESTORED TO ITS RIGHTFUL PLACE AS A RESPECTED PILLAR OF SOCIETY — NO LONGER NEGLECTED AS AN OUTPOST FIGHTING AGAINST HOPELESS ODDS.'

The editorial was accompanied by the launching of a major inquiry into 'The Police and Our Violent Society' which, for the most part, reflected the sentiments expressed by Brodie and Chitty in their *Times* interview and went on to air police grievances about pay and conditions, the end of the beat-bobby system, the general lack of public support, and the theories of 'pseudo-intellectuals'. The *Express* rejoiced to hear 'The Voice of the Yard' and its criticisms of the 'misconceived' parole and remission systems which have given 'namby-pamby treatment' to 'violent thugs' and allowed them to 'walk out free after serving only a derisory portion of their sentence'. It assured its readers that, 'do-gooders' and 'soft-liners' apart, 'the great majority of law-abiding citizens applaud the Scotland Yard men' and hoped that their 'splendid declaration' would bring the politicians 'up with a jerk'. A feature article by Donald Seaman which accompanied the editorial asserted that 'the temper of this country of ours, the most dutiful and law-abiding nation in the world, is at white-heat' and berated the prevailing penal policies towards 'trigger-happy thugs':

> 'I truly believe that if our present conduct continues, whereby we pay policemen less than dustmen for guarding our lives and property — and give the criminals we catch radio and TV and weekends at home — we will wake up one day and find we have no police force left.'

The Times, itself, when it came to assess the policemen's views, was less hysterical, taking issue with the policemen over the question of recidivism rates and the concept of prison as punishment but criticizing the suspended sentence system, excessive variations in sentencing policy, and inadequate provision for prisons. Brodie and Chitty were given least support by the *Guardian* who attacked the assumption that harsher punishments are necessarily an effective deterrent and suggested the policemen had presented a romanticized picture of crime and punishment 'in the old days'. The *Guardian*'s, however, was a minority view. Most of the papers were in the fevered grip of a moral panic that was to bring a continuous stream of proclamations from retired police officers and the indignant spokesmen of the authoritarian Right. The heartbeat of the panic could be monitored in the gigantic manhunt mounted to trace Sewell, a hunt which paralleled that for Harry Roberts five years before. By the second week in September the *Daily Mirror* was again offering a £10,000 reward, this time for information leading to the arrest and conviction of Sewell. Newspaper artists were invited to sketch impressions of how the wanted man might disguise himself. Sewell was eventually captured on October 7th as a direct result of the *Mirror's* reward. The arrest took place at the same time as the trial of Skingle and Sparrow which reached its climax a week later when Skingle was sentenced to life imprisonment with the then unique recommendation from the judge that he should stay in jail until he dies. The entire *Mirror* front page the following day was taken up with a photograph of Skingle, a quotation from the judge's sentencing and the gigantic headline 'STAY IN JAIL TILL YOU DIE' (16.10.71). The sentence came just a few days after the Tory party had once again debated the capital punishment issue and the discovery had been made that the murder statistics concealed an enormous increase in manslaughter since the abolition of hanging. Spurred on by this revelation the *Express* once again took up the law and order banner with a feature headlined: 'POLITICIANS DODGE THE ISSUE — BUT ITS THE POLICE WHO HAVE TO DODGE THE BULLETS!' (13.10.71) and a cartoon of Home Secretary, Maudling, literally 'cooking' the murder statistics.

The doom-laden images of anarchy projected in the leader columns and feature acticles were reinforced by a succession of images from Ulster where the IRA appeared rampant on the streets and even 'tough measures' like internment were apparently incapable of preventing the 'jungle law' of the catholic no-go areas with their beatings and tarring and feathering. Headlines attacking 'THESE BARBARIANS OF THE BOGSIDE' were more than enough to offset *Sunday Times'* allegations concerning the use of torture techniques by the British Army. But the essential characteristic of the law-and-order crisis of the seventies has been its generality, not simply the depth but the breadth of its anxiety. The murder of policemen, the bombing of cabinet ministers, the tarring and feathering of young girls in the

Bogside are not so much separate causes as varied occasion
expression. Its roots stretch much deeper than the top so
violence which sustains its perennial flowering in our newspapers.
It springs from an historical vein of 'long-suffering righteousness'
which E.P. Thompson (1970) has so brilliantly exposed in his
article on working class militancy and *The Times* correspondence
column. The Gunman, the Bomber, and the Thug are symbols,
not just of the disorganized present, but ultimately of an
historical discontinuity. They do not simply affront the moral
conscience of the community, they threaten both the stable world
view of the bourgeoisie and, more fundamentally, the social
stability on which bourgeois power and prosperity depends. They
are the personifications of a violent social change which darkly
threatens the destruction of established morality and profitable
relationships of exchange. In Gunman, Bomber, and Thug are
the shadowy and half-recognized spectres of anomie, the chaos of
expectation, the disruption of the taken-for-granted. This is the
key to understanding the peculiar generality of the law-and-order
crisis, the reason why, as I will go on to argue, it becomes
inseparable from the anxiety engendered when gasmen, miners,
and electricity workers withdraw their labour, behaviour which,
although perfectly legal, carries the connotations of lawlessness
('holding the country to ransom' etc.). In the autumn of 1972 this
non-specific anxiety was provided at last with a generalized
symbol of lawlessness, an image which effectively incorporated the
alien and imported character of the threat and the horror of
sudden and violent disruption: the Mugger. This latent function
of mugging as a focus for anxiety has also been noted by the
mugging research team at Birmingham University:

> 'The manufacturing of a mugging scare and the social reaction
> to it may be understood as the displacement of anxiety which
> has other sources onto a clearly illegitimate activity. The
> "mugger" who stands in the dock may be treated less as a
> socially located individual and more as a symbolic devil figure.
> He may then become the focus of our discontents, the recipient
> of unarticulated resentment. In such a context, the attempt to

...viour is perverted into a ritualistic restate-
...acy of the social order and the original sin
[21]

...ion of the mugger as 'a symbolic devil figure'
...nites can be overstated, just as the well-founded
...lone at night on certain city streets may be
...., but the power of the 'mugger' image and the
sudden ...pment of concern are undeniable.

The mugging panic

The British mugging scare began abruptly on August 17, 1972 when newspapers carried reports of the killing of 68 year-old Graham Hills at Waterloo Station 36 hours previously. In the *Daily Express*, senior crime reporter, Percy Hoskins informed his readers:

> 'Muggings, a rapidly growing crime particularly among teenage criminals, are causing grave concern to Scotland Yard. London's "black-spots" are the West End tube stations and side streets of Kennington, Notting Hill and Brixton. Peak hours for attacks are 11 p.m. on Friday and Saturday. Average strength of the gangs is four or five and the "favoured" weapon is the flick knife. CID Commanders in all London districts have been asked to start special patrols to meet this menace.'

The introduction of the new term of mugging into the vocabulary of law-and-order news was accomplished with ease because readers had already been exposed to the term in its American context. As the *Daily Mirror* expressed it in an introduction to a feature on the crime (17.8.72): 'As crimes of violence escalate, a word common in the United States enters the British headlines: Mugging.' The suddenness of the scare was made possible by the sensitization of the public that had already taken place. This meant that the initial stages of moral panic (Cohen 1972) could be skipped. The police, for their part, were well aware of the 'menace' and had already initiated plans to counter it (Hall 1975; Jefferson *et al.* 1975).

The identification of mugging as the latest and most urgent social problem represented the first confirmation of media prophecies about the growth of the Violent Society. Foreign patterns of criminality had apparently finally infected Britain, the nightmare scenarios of anarchy and gun law could no longer be dismissed as mere fantasy. The *Daily Express* described mugging as 'an American import that must not be accepted here' (17.8.72) and the *Daily Mail* warned that 'we would be blinded by complacency if we did not see that as each month passes the shadow of the mugger and the thug falls more darkly on our enviable way of life' (26.9.72). In the *Sun*, Ann Buchanan described the fear evoked by mugging in the United States, advising the British public to 'stop thinking of the police as "fuzz" and "pigs"' because 'it will be too late to scream for their help when we are afraid, as New Yorkers are, to walk down our own streets in broad daylight' (18.8.72). But while the mugging label itself effectively signified the alien character of the crime, newspapers were noticeably reluctant to associate the wave of attacks directly with mounting unrest and frustration within the West Indian population. For the most part, the only clues to the link were provided by the identification of mugging-prone areas — Kennington, Notting Hill, Brixton etc. The press were being careful not to offend liberal sensibilities and bring accusations of racialist reporting upon themselves[22]. This inhibition and failure to define race as a relevant variable made early attempts to account for the mugging phenomenon impossibly handicapped. But, by the end of September the West Indian connection was becoming increasingly explicit as cases began to come to court. At the same time, judges began to declare their intention of passing deterrent sentences on muggers. The newspapers took up such declarations enthusiastically but were immediately distracted from the core of the mugging problem — social deprivation and unemployment experienced most acutely in West Indian neighbourhoods (Jefferson and Clark 1973) — by the appearance of the atypical in the shape of female violence. Once again, the press' propensity to identify as the same those phenomena which appear superficially similar was evident, this time in stories such as: 'THE GIRL MUGGERS: One owns a car and a horse and lives in a £25,000 house' (*Daily Mail* 29.9.72). The case was that of three schoolgirls who had attacked a teacher the previous April, but in the climate of heightened sensitivity to violence it received front page treatment. The coverage tended to give the impression that mugging was a violent but classless teenage craze, an idea reinforced later by such references as: 'this fashionable craze among hooligans' (*Sunday Mirror* 25.3.73) and 'this trendy term for a crime as old as sin itself' (*Daily Mail* 20.3.73). This obfuscation of the structural bases of mugging was compounded by police spokesmen who refused to acknowledge the message of their own statistics. The *Sunday Times* was one of the first papers to find its way to the core of the problem at the beginning of October (1.10.72):

> 'The attackers are mostly British-born West Indians. Although the police take great pains to explain they do not view the muggings as a colour problem, community workers in the area (Brixton) admit that something over 80 per cent of the attackers are coloured youths.'

The article went on to quote a black ILEA community Warden:

> '... The reason for these attacks is basically social. There are usually strict regimes in West Indian family structures. But boys born here are exposed to outside influences that their parents are either unaware of or cannot understand. This usually ends up with the boy, even as young as 14, being shown the door, and literally he is on the streets with nobody to look after him and no money. He drifts and in no time at all he sleeps on the floor of rooms crowded with boys in the same plight. Going mugging becomes their accepted way of life.'

Few papers attempted to elaborate on this explanation by discussing the role of unemployment and the confrontationist stance of black power. Colin McGlashan's article in the *New Statesman* (13.10.72) and Richard Sears article in the *Daily Mail* (23.10.72) were two notable pieces among a handful of exceptions. For the most part, newspapers appeared obsessed with the violent image and the scope of the phenomenon, any attempts to account for mugging were drowned in a torrent of demands for repression. The general orientation of the press, is effectively conveyed by this *Sun* leader:

'TAMING THE MUGGERS
What are the British people most concerned about today? Wages? Prices? Immigration? Pornography? People are talking about all these things.
But the Sun believes there is another issue which has everyone deeply worried and angry: VIOLENCE IN OUR STREETS.
Every day innocent people are beaten up and robbed.
A new, distasteful word has been brought into our language — Mugging.
Nothing could be more utterly against our way of life, based on a common sense regard for law and order.
It is inevitable that we should now be seeing the heavy sentences that have been handed out at the Old Bailey in the past two days ...
If punitive jail sentences help to stop the violence — and nothing else has done — then they will not only prove to be the only way.
They will, regrettably, be the RIGHT way.
And the judges will have the backing of the public.' (13.10.72)

Even the *Daily Mail*, a paper which apparently recognized and understood the connection between the racial situation and mugging looked first to repression as a solution: 'The answer to mugging by anyone, black or white, is clear enough — catch them and punish them severely' (Editorial 23.10.72). The message was one with which most crime reporters readily concurred, eagerly embracing a role in the apparatus of control. As one reporter described it to me, the period was one in which 'the judges slapped mugging down and we reported what they said and the sentences they gave. If we hadn't made a fuss their sentences would have had no effect.'

By the end of October the menace of the mugger had been firmly established in the popular press as the most pressing social problem of the time. This definition of the situation received powerful reinforcement from first, the new Chief Inspector of Constabulary for England and Wales, John Maxwell Hill, who expressed his fear of 'a New York situation arising in this country', and then the Home Secretary, Robert Carr, who called for a national survey of mugging, defining the crime for the first time as 'robberies by gangs of two or more on people walking alone in the open'. Even Prince Philip publicly expressed his concern about the new crime wave. By mid-November, the *Daily Express* was finding support for its views in the results of a Harris public opinion poll which revealed that mugging 'evoked a significant new dimension of public anger and concern' reflected in large majorities in favour of tougher punishments, increased victim compensation, and urgent Government action (*Daily Express* 10.11.72)[23]. Throughout the late Autumn and early Winter more and more voices joined the newspaper chorus of judges and magistrates calling for more and more severe sentences, corporal punishment, and even bread and water diets for offenders.

There is no need to go on to describe the complete course of the mugging panic beyond saying that it reached a second peak in March 1973 with the Handsworth case[24], before tailing off in the summer of the same year. The significance of mugging in the law-and-order crisis of the last decade should now be evident. Mugging provided a supremely potent symbol of lawlessness to swell the repertoire of law-and-order campaigners, a vivid scenario of the chaos awaiting the breakdown of the rule of law, and a powerful image of the violent society. Much of the power of the image derived from the apparently random way in which victims and venues for the crime were selected. Unlike the wave of 'Paki-bashing' and 'Queer-bashing' of a few years before, victims were not chosen from any specific section of the population. There was a sense in which anyone almost anywhere was a potential victim. There was little in the way the crime was presented to contain or limit anxiety. Thus in many ways it was an ideal focus for non-specific feelings of tension and unease in society. As the Birmingham research team have expressed it (Jefferson *et al.*

1975:19), 'The moral panic about mugging was a moment when the suppressed and distorted responses to thirty years of accumulated social change surfaced.' However, it would be a mistake to isolate the mugging panic as a unique example of the way in which societal anxiety can be displaced and focussed. It has to be understood within the context of contemporary trends in the signification of other 'controversial' phenomena — notably industrial militancy. The period concerned, the Summer and Autumn of 1972, was one which saw not only the concentration of the violence label on the figure of the mugger, but also its simultaneous extention to other challenges to the Rule of Law.

Industrial bully-boys
Throughout 1972 the Tory Government's industrial wages policy had been under attack, first from the National Union of Mineworkers and then from the Railwaymen (Barnett 1973), but the first open defiance of the *Industrial Relations Act* did not come until the docks dispute in the summer. Five dockers were jailed for refusing to appear before the Industrial Relations Court and by the end of July the General Council of the TUC had called for a national strike if the 'Pentonville Five' were not released. It was at this point that violence emerged as a focal concern in the press coverage of the dispute. On August 1, as the first news of picket line disturbances was filtering through, the *Sun* ran an editorial calling for moderate trades unionists to stand firm against the industrial 'wreckers', fanatical Trotskyists, and Communists. A week later all the papers were carrying accounts of 'the battle of Neap House Wharf'. The headlines in the *Sun* over the next few days convey the extent to which, in the popular press, the image of violence came to dominate the reporting of the dock strike and the concurrent building workers strike:

8.8.72 page 2	'PUNCH-UP DOCKERS SEIZED AFTER BID TO STOP PORT'
9.8.72 page 2	'DOCKS DAY OF SHAME: Four Policemen injured as strike pickets battle over a tiny private wharf'

Illustration 1

"Why can't you see all

Reproduced by kind permission of the *Sun* newspaper

nt is peace on the docks?"

10.8.72 page 1	'22 HELD IN DOCK RIOT'
inside page	'POLICE SQUADS GRAB DOCK WAR "ARSENAL" '
11.8.72 inside page	' "TERROR GANGS" IN BUILDING STRIKE'
14.8.72 page 2	'6,000 MASS AT SIEGE WHARF'
15.8.72 inside page	'THE WAR OF THE WHARF: Nine policemen hurt as jeering dockers storm "peace line" fence'

The signification of the events was neatly summarized by a Rigby cartoon of wild-eyed, muscular dockers armed with tomahawks, pitchforks, and hooks savaging unarmed policemen (see *Illustration* 1). The concentration on violence shifted an essentially political challenge to what was perceived as a piece of class legislation firmly into the domain of law-and-order crisis with all its connotations of criminality. The docks dispute became yet another manifestation of 'The Violent Society', a conceptualization made increasingly available to the public through the media, a conceptualization capable of transforming a wide variety of political phenomena into evidence of an underlying disease of criminality.

On the day the *Sun* ran Ann Buchanan's page 6 article on the arrival of 'American style' mugging in Britain entitled 'Will We Be Scared to Walk in The Streets?', page 5 contained the following piece by Roger Carroll (18.8.72):

'UNION BULLIES MAKE CRIME PAY
Crime can pay. The dockland bully-boys have proved it. They have terrorised other workers. Fought the police. Roughed up union leader Jack Jones. And they have won ... This new menacing kind of violence is fast becoming the rule, not the exception ... And, though some sort of docks peace has been bought by surrendering to violence, worse could come. Moderate leaders of unions next in the pay queue have had the ground cut from under them. What arguments can they use now, to discourage their own militants from copying the violent pit and dock pickets? Militancy is pushing up the claims

too ... Electricity workers who accepted seven per cent last year are asking for 40 per cent next time. So are the miners. Union leaders know as well as anyone that claims of this size are totally unrealistic. But they are being swept up on a rising tide of militancy...'

It is a piece in which the themes of militancy, collective bargaining, violence, and criminality are inextricably twisted and knotted together in such a way that militant trades unionists came to increasingly resemble the muggers who were the epitome of lawlessness and The Violent Society. Two days after the *Sun* article, the *News of the World* (20.8.72) supplied a platform for Conservative M.P., Sir Tufton Beamish to demand, 'END THIS AGE OF VIOLENCE':

'... The present eruption of lawlessness has several disturbing features, not least its scale.

Crimes of violence against the person rose from 18,000 in 1962 to well over double that figure last year.

Normally peaceful citizens are persuaded to join a picketing line that turns into a disorderly mob, stoning lorries and attacking the police.

Attempts are made to murder Cabinet Ministers.

Bodies that should represent moderate opinion defy the law and are openly encouraged to do so by the politically motivated, in and out of Parliament.

It all adds up to a serious sickness that must be diagnosed and cured ...'

In September the *Daily Mirror* produced its 'Shock Issue' on Violence which, despite a genuine attempt at the explanation of some forms of violence, collapsed together the disparate phenomena of professional crime, murder, mugging, child beating, soccer hooliganism, conflict in Ulster, and industrial militancy. The following day, the same paper featured an interview with Reginald Maudling entitled 'DEMOCRACY IN DANGER? REGINALD MAUDLING speaks out on this age of

violence'. Maudling expressed his concern about political
violence, particularly in the sphere of industrial disputes. He went
on to point out two 'disturbing features' in the recent history of
industrial relations: 'First, the use of strikes which affect the
public as a whole. Second, the apparent wish of some people — a
minority I'm pleased to say — to defy the law as a whole (*Daily
Mirror* 20.9.72). Early in October the Home Secretary, Robert
Carr, addressed a conference of the Magistrates' Association in
London, encouraging them to 'deal firmly' with violent offences.
He selected soccer hooliganism, political and industrial violence
for special treatment. The following week (11.10.72) he returned
to the theme at the Tory Party Conference. He promised a tough
response to 'marauding bullyboys' who transform the right to
picket into 'a licence to intimidate'. Special police squads were to
be set up to counter 'flying pickets'. The underlying message of
his speech was spelt out the next day by Sir Desmond Heap, the
President of the Law Society, who warned his members that law
and order in Britain was being seriously endangered by 'a sizeable
minority' of destructionists. As evidence he pointed to increasing
disorder in the streets, violence during picketing, and successive
declarations of intent to ignore the *Industrial Relations Act*. The
Daily Mail carried a report of his speech, headlined 'BRITAIN
STANDING ON THE BRINK OF CHAOS', below a legend
proclaiming 'THE VIOLENT SOCIETY' which linked it to
reports of three muggings and an armed robbery (see *Illustration
2*). Strikes and militant opposition to the *Industrial Relations Act*
were increasingly acquiring the stigma of illegitimacy through
their constant association with violence. It was a process begun by
the press, in reaction to picketing disturbances, and reinforced by
Conservative politicians, and it found its eventual fulfilment in
the Gas-workers strike of February 1973. This was a dispute,
perhaps more than any other in recent years, to which the popular
press immediately applied an interpretive structure stressing
danger, illegitimacy, and irresponsibility. This interpretation was
most marked in the *Mail* and the *Express*. on February 12, the
front page of the *Daily Mail* proclaimed: 'Vital talks in gas dispute
as millions face peril THIS STRIKE COULD KILL.' The *Mail*'s

Illustration 2

THE VIOLENT SOCIETY

Knife gang stole wives' shopping money, jury told

A GANG of four toured London markets and Tube stations picking pockets and robbing people at knife point, it was alleged yesterday.

They worked to a system, three jostling the victim while the fourth picked his pocket.

And they did it regularly. One of the four was said to have told police that he usually 'worked' the Oval Tube station on Thursdays.

At the Old Bailey Winston Trew, 21, of Purley Road, Peckham, S.E., Constantine Boucher, 25, of Thouxombe Road, East Dulwich, S.E., George Griffiths, 19, of Grove Hill Road, Camberwell, S.E.,

Daily Mail Reporter

and Sterling Christie, 21, of Ermine Road, Lewisham, S.E. pleaded not guilty to charges alleging conspiracy to rob or steal on the trains, stealing purses and cash from unknown people and assaulting policemen.

Mr John Bogers, prosecuting, said that police went to arrest the four after seeing them try to pick the pockets of two old men at the Oval station.

Snatches

The gang tried to get away and a fight developed in which several policemen were hurt.

At Kennington police station, Trew burst into tears and was alleged to have said :

'I have done lots of jobs since Christmas, not only at Underground stations but at markets, shops and bus stops. I work the Oval usually on Thursdays.

'It was my idea because I was out of work and I have a wife and three children. Tonight while the others jostled I tried to steal three wallets from white guys on the platform.

'Thursday is the best day for nicking from women because they go shopping.'

Christie was alleged to have said in a statement : 'We have done a lot of handbag snatches on the Underground and also robberies. On Wednesday this week at the Oval with Griffiths and Boucher we stopped a coloured woman at the emergency exit and held a knife near her. I snatched her bag and she screamed. There was £10 in her purse.'

The trial continues today.

THE VIOLENT SOCIETY

3 YEARS for kicking a tourist

A 19-YEAR-OLD youth who mugged a German student, collapsed in the dock of the Old Bailey yesterday when he was jailed for three years.

Anthony Blunnie of Brocklesmead, Harlow, Essex, was unconscious for 10 minutes after he heard the sentence.

The court was told that Blunnie and two other youths had demanded money from Mr Christian Schaefer, a tourist, in St. James's Park, London. Blunnie punched and kicked him.

The judge sent one of the other youths—Robert Cohen, 17, of Epping—to Borstal and imposed a supervision order on the third, Raymond Cridland, 15, of Epping.

3 YEARS for alley ambush

TWO youths who robbed a man of 50p after kicking him in a dark alley, were both jailed for three years at the Old Bailey yesterday.

And Judge Edward Sutcliffe, QC, asked the public to report all suspicious circumstances to the police so that officers could catch muggers redhanded.

He said that in this case a policeman walked to Lewisham station by late-night passengers, saw youths kicking 'a bundle in an alley.'

The 'bundle' was Mr Ian Keelan, an insurance clerk.

Eugene St. John, 18, and James Hosten, 17, both of Lewisham, were jailed. Robert Howe, 19, was sent to Borstal.

12 YEARS for two 'gunmen'

TWO men who held up a taxi-driver and a shop assistant with imitation guns, were both jailed for 12 years at Maidstone Crown Court, Kent, yesterday.

Vincent Foxall, 25, and Allan Paterson, 22, both of no fixed address, robbed the shop assistant at Pwllheli, Carnarvonshire, of clothes and money and the taxi-driver at Hastings, Sussex of his cab and money.

Both victims were bound and gagged.

Mr Justice Theuger told the men, both of whom had previous convictions : 'I have to consider this case against the general background of criminal activity in the country.'

'Britain standing on the brink of chaos'

By PETER BURDEN

LAW and order in Britain are in serious danger, a leader of the legal profession warned yesterday.

A sizeable minority was poised to topple the country into a state of disorder, Sir Desmond Heap told solicitors in his presidential address to the Law Society national conference at Harrogate.

During the year there had been increasing disorder in the streets, violence during picketing and successive declarations of intent to ignore the law of the Industrial Relations Act.

Sir Desmond called for a bigger demonstration of public support for the police.

'Today policemen are really quite up against it,' he said. 'They are having a difficult, not to say a bad, time being pushed around, kicked around,

Warning by solicitors' leader

bashed around and shot around, and for what — for merely doing a job.

'We live in an age when carping at authority and denigration of those who carry responsibility is the order of the day and the world is a chillier and uglier place because of it.'

Sir Desmond's advice : Gather rosebuds while you may.

'Enjoy the environment of this country while it lasts, because when the 40 ton Continental road juggernauts begin racing across the face of this small country, heaven help us all.

The price that is being paid in the destruction of the environment by road transportation of bulk cargoes must be simply incalculable.

'It is merely a con man's tricky gimmick to suggest that door-to-door transport by road has ever brought down the price of the article. What price are we talking about ? The price of dear old cornflakes themselves ?

'That price is cluckenfed compared with the misery of noise, vibration, stink and catastrophic collision which has followed the destruction of a Victorian railway system, the most complete in the world.

He continued 'Today everything about John Citizen is becoming computerised, pigeonholed, dehumanised with the result that the little man himself is becoming mesmerised.'

Reproduced by kind permission of the *Daily Mail* newspaper (printed October 13, 1972).

Illustration 3

Reproduced by kind permission of the *Daily Express*
newspaper (printed February 16, 1973)

Illustration 4

DAILY EXPRESS

SOCCER HOOLIFAN

MUGGERS

RAPIS

"The Government won't cage the man-eating tigers beca

Reproduced by kind permission of the *Daily Express* newspaper.

SEPTEMBER 15, 1975

Cummings

"...ve signed a social contract promising to be vegetarians..."

London Express Service.

Illustration 5

DAILY EXPRESS

" You're right, gentlemen! The noise of the collapse of law ...

Reproduced by kind permission of the *Daily Express* newspaper.

er is intolerable! I'm going to soundproof my room immediately

hostility was spelled out in an editorial on the same day:

'... Phase Two of the Government's prices and incomes legislation has not yet passed through Parliament. So to that extent,
a gas strike is still "legal". But it is very far from being "all
right".
*This week's planned action by the gasmen is dangerous,
irresponsible and totally unjustifiable.'*

By February 15 the *Mail* was reporting deaths and injuries among
old people preparing for gas cuts and delivering a warning on
picketing:

'The vast mobs of dockers, miners and roving agitators were
able to intimidate lorry-drivers with iron bars last year because
the police had only vague instructions to play it cool.
If trouble threatens this year — be it caused by gasmen, miners
or anybody else — the police should be able to "snatch"
troublemakers, and also keep the picket lines down to the
minimum needed to perform the legitimate task of "peaceful
persuasion".'

The following day, the dominant meaning of the strike was
effectively conveyed by the *Express* in a 'photonews' feature
depicting 'The Human Side of the Gas Crisis'. Beneath the
headline: 'The Defenceless Victims', the *Express* reproduced a
photograph of an ambulance filled with old people (see
Illustration 3). The caption below pin-pointed the message: 'THE
EVACUEES: There's no place like home ... old folk leaving theirs
because of the gas dispute. "Why can't they sort out their
differences and leave us alone?" ' The whole layout was an
outstanding example of newspaper mobilization of pathos and
sentiments of sympathy and nostalgia as weapons of propaganda.
Every element in the layout combined perfectly to signify the
criminal inhumanity of the strike — surely, it seemed to say, these
sad old ladies were no less victims of criminality than those
attacked by muggers, surely there could be no more commanding
evidence of the threat to civilization and the breakdown of law
and order.

When the *Sunday Times* called 1972 'the year of violence' it chose a very apt phrase, if not for the most appropriate of reasons. It was, indeed, a year of violence rather than a violent year: not necessarily a period in which a larger proportion of people in Britain were wounded or killed but certainly one in which the concept of violence was given an extraordinarily salient position in media discourse. It was a year in which the threads of illegitimacy connecting delinquency, professional crime, political deviance and, finally, militant industrial action were drawn into a tight and twisted knot and labelled 'violence'. It was, as we have seen, an achievement of popular journalism and its institutional sources, a massive exercise in the transference and extention of ideologically-based interpretations and significations.

In their treatment of a whole range of diverse phenomena, from political and industrial dissent to mugging, popular newspapers in the early seventies continually selected and mixed together the elements of illegality, extremism, destruction, and violence into a cocktail of dangerous illegitimacy (see *Illustrations 4* and *5*). Newspapers, however, were not simply offering a prospect of unrelieved gloom, a scintilla of hope remained. In their scenarios of chaos the police have invariably been cast as the hope of salvation. If the police are to play that part convincingly and supply an element of reassurance, their reputation must remain relatively untarnished. The next chapter will examine the degree to which newspapers protect the police image from the subversive challenge of scandal and the ideological and relational foundations on which press representations of the Force rest.

5 Black sheep and rotten apples: the press and police deviance

> 'The defaulting policeman, like the defaulting parson or school teacher, "is news"; and stories of the prosecution and conviction of policemen are frequently given prominence in the press. We do not think that the reputation of the police service stands or falls by the occasional sensational reporting of allegations against a particular policeman. Sensible people realise that there are black sheep in most families.'
>
> *Report of the Royal Commission on the Police* 1962: para.399

Upholding law and order

The primary significance of the police in newspaper ideology lies in their physical and symbolic role as representatives and defenders of the established consensus and its institutions. The police stand for 'us' in the struggle against 'them'. They are entrusted with the task of doing battle with the forces of chaos, of patrolling the margins of the anarchic jungle at society's edges. As symbolic defenders of consensual values and institutions, the police earn the attribution of those qualities most closely associated with the consensus — righteousness, moderation, peacefulness, honesty, rationality, humanity etc. Thus, the police regularly receive praise from newspapers for their bravery and efficiency in bringing dangerous criminals to justice, for their remarkable restraint in the face of provocation, for their high standards of honesty and integrity. The *Daily Mail* captured the essential newspaper image of the police when it referred to 'the routine courage and reticent dedication to duty of those who man society's front line against violent crime' (15.11.72). The qualities of the Force are never more apparent than when contrasted with the brutality and dishonesty of many foreign police forces. As one *Daily Express* editorial put it: 'Just how lucky we are in our police force is emphasised in a report from America. There, it is revealed, New York police steal from the dead, accept bribes, cover up for dope dealers and may even commit murder.' The leader goes on to suggest that we should give '… a massive vote of thanks to, and confidence in the police, who above all others, make sure that Britain enjoys the rule of law, instead of gun law' (29.12.72). The boost to morale which this would provide would presumably have been especially important at a time when, according to another *Express* editorial, '… it is a fashionable pastime by a vociferous yet tiny minority to complain and denigrate the police at any opportunity' (18.5.72)[1].

Newspapers invariably identify the interests of the police and the public as complementary — protecting and being protected. Given that the notion of 'responsible reporting' entails the promotion of the public interest it follows that it also entails the promotion of police interests. Leader writers generally adhere to the broad guidelines of this doctrine but would wish to impose significant qualifications. They tend to be highly conscious of the role of the press as public watchdog and the need to warn their readers of abuses within the system. I interviewed a leader writer on a popular paper who described his paper's general policy towards the police as one of 'suspicious support':

'We are on the side of law and order, obviously, we think the vast majority of the police have a hell of a job and need all the backing they can get, but equally we are acutely aware, that there are occasional cases of corruption in the police and occasional investigations which are not prosecuted as hard as they should be for one reason or another and perhaps occasional ones which are prosecuted too hard by the wrong methods. And we do feel quite strongly that one of the functions of the press is to be a watchdog on the police for these things, exposing them if possible. But it would be quite wrong to say that we were anti-police. We are anti-corruption in the police, that's a very different thing.'

He admitted, though, that the need for these qualifications to the general doctrine of support for the police was unlikely to be perceived as quite so urgent by the men responsible for the day-to-day reporting of police activities, the specialist crime reporters. As he expressed it, 'being in close daily touch with the police you can get too close ... being good reporters their first interest is keeping their contacts sweet'. The crime reporters, themselves, rarely attribute their shared orientation towards the police quite so directly to self-interest. They prefer to emphasize their moral responsibilities as professional journalists, which make it impossible for them to remain uncommitted in 'the fight for law and order'. More often than not they are wedded to an absolutist ethic: they tend to conceptualize the world in strictly black and white terms, their attitude towards crime being as uncompromising as their beliefs about law-enforcement. While some reporters may allow themselves 'a grudging admiration for some of the old fraudsmen and conmen' or acknowledge the part played by environmental factors in criminal careers[2] they still maintain an attitude of condemnation towards the law-breaker and support for the law-enforcer:

'Crime is anti-society, anti-social and newspapers can't possibly line themselves up with something like that ... Everybody is anti-crime, except criminals. You can't be neutral, you've got to put yourself on one side or the other. I can never be detached on this sort of thing — I hate violence. When it happens I can't help but think in terms of my own family.'

(Crime Correspondent)

'In the main, one is on the side of law and order, but I can see things wrong with it, and I can see the unfortunate side of criminals, and I can also see the criminal who is deserving of no mercy.'   (Crime Correspondent)

'If you always accept that the police are right that is dangerous and can encourage abuses [but on the other hand] what you don't want to do is to make the police's job harder — you want to make it easier because that is the way to improve society as a whole. Newspapers are firmly on the side of law and order, you've got to have that or society would collapse.'

(Crime Correspondent)

'If I've got to come down on one side or the other, either the goodies or the badies, then obviously I'd come down on the side of the goodies, in the interests of law and order.'

(Crime Correspondent)

'I feel a responsibility to help the police in their job. I don't want to put crime in people's minds. I won't encourage crime ... naturally I'm against it and feel it's wrong, just like anybody else.'

(Crime Correspondent)

'I think the do-gooders have had a field day in recent years and have perhaps gone too far in that they sometimes forget the suffering of the victim when dealing with a criminal who perhaps has had a bad environment or perhaps came from a bad home ... If people who say, "let's molly-coddle the criminals", could see some of the injuries inflicted by violent young muggers on an elderly woman to steal her purse with a couple of shillings in it they might take the view that, while not going as far as wanting flogging brought back, there should be some salutary punishment imposed to try and prevent that sort of crime ... My sympathies will always be towards the police and the tough job they do in catching criminals. I think the police in this country do a magnificent job because of the limitations placed upon them by the law. I mean, the law ties one hand behind the policeman's back. He has to obey Judges' Rules and so many regulations that the criminal has every chance of defeating the ends of justice ... I think, to be fair, one does have a bias towards the police.'   (Crime Correspondent)

'It's important to support the police and make sure that public confidence in the force is not damaged ... They must have public support or they can't do their job properly.'

(Crime Correspondent)

Most crime reporters see their professional responsibilities towards the public as entailing support for the police in the 'crime war'.

This support work typically takes the form of stories and features which polish the public image of the force, reviving its shine when it begins to tarnish. Stories which might dull the shine are generally viewed as a regrettable and embarrassing nuisance. They are seen as inevitable occupational hazards or obstacles which have to be negotiated. Rather like a golfer, the crime reporter tries to keep to the fairway, avoiding the sand traps of police deviance. But if he becomes bunkered he just has to recognize his predicament and play out of it as best he can:

'I don't go around looking for trouble in the police force. I'm not looking for that kind of bother, but if I find it I'll report it. Fortunately, it doesn't happen very often. We do not make it our business to criticise the police — there are plenty of other people in Fleet Street who do that sort of thing.'

(Crime Correspondent)

To understand why crime reporters do not make it their business to criticize the police we need to examine, more closely, the foundations of their occupational ideology. In particular we need to be aware of the instrumental and affective bonds which bind together the crime reporter and his police informants.

Crime reporters and police sources: the mechanics of symbiosis[3]

In chapter 3 we looked at the dependence of the crime reporter on the police as a source of routine information and at the expansion of the Scotland Yard Press Bureau. That expansion, however, has been insufficient to meet the needs of the specialist reporter. First, the Bureau still lacks the full co-operation of senior detectives who control the information journalists seek. Many are content to sit back and wait to be asked for information and often regard such requests as an annoying complication to their investigations. One senior officer has been quoted as saying: 'Often I've had to fight the Bureau to prevent them getting stuff I knew but didn't want to get out. They are often a hindrance to us' (Deeley and Walker 1971:183). One of the Bureau's own press officers assured me that 'the police do not like giving information ''on the record'' to the

Press'. Part of the problem is that the Bureau's civilian staff lack the authority to demand the release of information, and must be careful not to offend senior officers:

'We do not have a high enough status to deal with senior policemen on an equal basis ... so we err on the side of caution; we are most circumspect when asked if certain police officers are being investigated, because we are at the behest of senior officers.'   (Scotland Yard Press Officer)

It is not surprising that this circumspection often appears to harrassed crime reporters as 'prevarication or downright obstruct-tion' on the part of officials who seem to lack any incentive to obtain stories. By the time information is released it is probably too late to be of use to the journalist — either because his publication deadline has passed, or because the police investiga-tion to which it refers has passed the point where legal constraints on newspaper reports become operative:

'A lot of stuff we could use comes out too late. The important thing for us is to get the job in the situation where we can write most about it, and that is when it's just happened, no one is caught, or if anyone is caught, no one is charged. You are then free to write screeds about it.'   (Crime Correspondent)

'At times it can be frustratingly difficult to drag information out of the Press Bureau. The long delays you have to suffer for even simple information can drive you to drink. You can ask them a simple question at, say, midday and there will probably be no answer by six or seven at night when it's coming up to the first edition deadline and you've got to explain to your news desk why you haven't got a story ... so you say, "right, if they won't give me anything, fuck it", and you write a "flyer".'*

(Crime Correspondent)

Second, despite the fact that some of the press officers have had experience in journalism, some crime reporters still doubt their ability to identify news. They feel that much of the Bureau's

*A 'flyer' is a story based on informed guess work.

'apparent censorship' boils down to a simple deficiency of news-sense: 'Some of these chaps can tell a good story and some of them just can't. It's a thing you learn and they've not really got much chance to learn it down there if they've never been out on the street working' (Crime Correspondent). Finally, the values of universalism which the Bureau has institutionalized mitigate against the interests of crime reporters who are seeking information which is relatively exclusive. And, although the familiar and trusted crime correspondent usually benefits from what little discretion the press officer is able to exercise, the extra tit-bits of information he does receive from that source are insufficient to prevent him seeking alternative sources who can provide more detailed and exclusive accounts[4]. Increasingly he uses the Bureau mainly as a source of *routine* information and as a means of checking information acquired elsewhere. As one press officer lamented:

'Typically we are confirming information put to us rather than us initiating information. Competition being what it is, the press learn information before we do ... crime reporters all tend to discount this place and use it only as an occasional source of reference.'

In Fleet Street circles the Bureau retains a reputation for censorship — it is jokingly referred to as the *Sup*press Bureau, and its mobile representatives — Divisional Liaison officers — are sometimes known as the Don't Let Ons. I was told of one DLO at the scene of the Shepherds Bush killings who, when questioned by crime reporters about the murders, refused to say anything except, 'Foul play cannot be ruled out'.

Thus, more often than not, the crime correspondent is obliged to go directly to the men who control the information he requires, and comes to rely on the cultivation of close personal contacts, particularly within the CID:

'The Press Bureau is all right for piddling little things, and it's useful for checking information, but when it comes to big stories you need help and guidance and this is where the Press

Bureau falls down ... As a privileged crime man I can by-pass the Press Bureau more or less whenever I like ... Personal contacts are vital.'   (Crime Correspondent)

'The information you get with police contacts is so much more important and interesting and penetrating.'
(Crime Correspondent)

'Official sources are virtually useless to someone who operates the way I do. Personal contacts are absolutely essential.'
(Crime Correspondent)

The cultivation of informal personal contacts, then, is vital to the professional survival of the crime correspondent, and the number and quality of these relationships are criteria for the allocation of status within the field. But the necessity of their cultivation also protects the territory of the crime specialist from attack by non-specialists. Thus, there may be a vested interest in the inadequacy of official sources:

'The traditional crime reporter welcomes police secrecy because it gives him a special position in the news organisation, because it gives him a chance to get information which other reporters cannot get hold of, information which is not available any other way.'   (Crime Correspondent)

Journalists on the fringe of the specialization, especially those working for the more 'liberal' or 'progressive' Fleet Street papers, often experience serious problems because they lack the right type of contacts. I was told of one such journalist who was obliged to take a bottle of whisky with him every time he visited a policeman: A second complained:

'I'm in a moral dilemma — I will not pay policemen for information (although I'm prepared to buy them a beer or a meal) and I do not have the regular contacts which most crime reporters have. So what do you do when you want information? Well, the best sources are either bent policemen who want money for stories, or disgruntled policemen who don't usually want payment. These disgruntled policemen are usually the most useful but, of course, they are not easy to find.'

If the reporter on the fringes of the crime field has to put a good deal of effort into *finding* suitable sources the crime specialist has to invest effort in *cultivating* suitable sources. As one reporter put it, the development of friendships with detectives requires 'a great deal of hard work and hard drinking', but it is invariably 'time well spent'. Over drinks or a meal, usually at a pub or restaurant but often in one another's homes, the crime reporter and the detective will exchange information, comment, and advice:

'Over the years you get to know a copper ... They're not just business contacts, they're friends — you meet them socially, you go out for dinner, you meet them for a drink, not to discuss business but just to meet them, like you meet your pals.'

(Crime Correspondent)

Reporter and policeman often develop an intimate knowledge of each other's family life — their summer holidays, the education of their children, and so on. Police biographies and autobiographies occasionally reveal something of the quality of these relationships. The biographer of Deputy Commander Reginald Spooner, for instance, produces this anecdote:

'Tom Tullett, crime reporter of the Daily Mirror, but once a CID officer himself, recalls that one evening he was having a drink with Spooner in a public house near Scotland Yard when Spooner suddenly said, "Here, what are you doing here drinking with me tonight? It's your wedding anniversary". "It was too", says Tullett.' (Adamson 1966:46)[6]

The pursuit of information provides a growth of friendship which is reinforced by a reciprocation of help and co-operation. The cultivation of contacts requires the investment of a considerable amount of time, but expectations are generally of long-term rather than short-term gain. As a senior correspondent on a popular daily paper commented: 'I'm having lunch with a contact today. I'm not expecting any information, but we'll have lunch and a chat and at the end of that I shall know him a bit better and he will be more likely to tell me things in the future.' Reporter and detective usually get to know each other through working on the same cases. Sometimes the original contact will be by telephone but the detective may want to meet the journalist privately to discuss a particularly delicate piece of information. A system of sponsorship also exists by which senior specialists introduce contacts to new recruits to the field, but this is not as significant as we might expect because most journalists establish a number of basic contacts as general reporters and apply for specialized posts on the basis of their contacts. But, while he may know a great many policemen, the crime reporter works essentially with a small core of reliable contacts: 'I could count on the fingers of one hand the number of good coppers who you could phone up and get a straight answer to a straight question. They're the ones you deal with, and they're the ones you respect' (Crime correspondent). Before being accepted by a policeman the crime reporter must usually undergo a lengthy period of probation:

'In the old days, a policeman would try you out over a period — sometimes it might be a couple of years — he'd feed you stories to see how you wrote them up, to see if you could be trusted. They tried you out for a long time before they trusted you and that's still true today really.'   (Crime Correspondent)

As relationships with individual policemen are steadily built up, the journalist acquires a more generalized reputation for dependability among policemen which helps him obtain information from unfamiliar sources. Membership of the exclusive Crime Reporters Association (see chapter 3) provides him with a metaphorical badge of trustworthiness which can be especially useful in overcoming the suspicion of sources in provincial forces:

'The CRA is quite useful in many ways, you can get to certain people and, if they choose to they can ask you for your membership number. If you are talking to a chief constable somewhere and he wants to be absolutely certain who you are you would give him your number and he would have it on a list in front of him.'   (Crime Correspondent)

But the trust and co-operation won by CRA membership numbers does not really compare with that won by years of patient source cultivation. It would be a mistake, however, to regard the relationship between the powerful senior detective and the crime specialist as one of patronage, they normally interact on a basis of equality and recognize mutual obligations. The crime reporter has much to offer the detective and can be a useful professional asset. To quote a former Metropolitan Police Commander:

> 'Often the man from the Yard can stand in real need of a crime reporter's help and good will. Sometimes the crime reporter, because of his greater freedom to question people, can actually help to uncover evidence which would be difficult for a police-man to obtain.'   (Millen 1972:221)

I have been told of a number of cases in which crime reporters have obtained murder confessions and of many in which reporters contributed in less spectacular ways.[7] The experienced crime correspondent is usually highly respected in police circles and will find himself regularly cast in the roles of friend, adviser, and partner in the fight against crime. Retiring detectives may seek his assistance when they write their memoirs. One detective had this to say of a crime reporter whose help and friendship he had found valuable:

> 'Throughout my years of police service I have on many occasions had good reason to be grateful for help I have received from senior newspapermen during my investigations. One journalist, Norman Lucas, Chief crime reporter of the Sunday Mirror, was at my side during almost all the investigations I led. In the 24 years he has been a Fleet Street crime reporter and author he has deservedly gained the respect of all ranks of the police forces throughout Britain.'   (Forbes 1973:1)

Thus, to a large extent, the relationship between detective and crime reporter is characterized by exchange. But this exchange is rarely formal or overt. Reciprocal obligations are implicit in the relationship, it is taken for granted that favours will be returned and friends will be helped:

'We don't expect them to tell us anything, there's no reason why they should, but under the "Old Pals Act" which works in other businesses as well as ours you do expect a little bit. It's not a question of buying drinks to curry favour, it's a question of having drinks with them to be sociable.' (Crime Correspondent)

'I would urge my editor not to publish a story if I knew that if it were published a criminal would get away or it would cause three or four weeks extra police work. But, in return, I'd hope that the policeman would make sure I had the tip-off about the arrest when it happened. I think this is quid pro quo, we can help each other. Similarly, I would hope that if you have know-ledge of a crime you can favour a police contact.'

(Crime reporter)

Clearly, then, the quantity and the quality of informal source accounts is influenced to some degree by what the reporter can offer in exchange.

The most obvious exchange resource the journalist has at his disposal is money. But, although direct payment of certain types of sources is recognized as legitimate, it is generally considered an inappropriate (although not unknown) method of obtaining information from the police. It is far too crass and unsubtle and defines the reporter/source relationship as one of business rather than friendship. The offer of food and drink, on the other hand, carries connotations of sociability rather than commerce or corruption:

'I never give them money. I'll take them out for a meal, something like that. That's legitimate entertaining. Mind you, taking a couple of coppers out usually costs as much as bunging them twenty quid. Still, the paper pays the expenses of course.'

(Crime Correspondent)

The purchase of food and drink is used merely as a means of lubricating social interaction, but the crime reporter controls other, more powerful, exchange resources. These derive from his position within an organization offering the possibility of instant com-munication with the public. For the police, such communication makes the task of crime prevention and investigation considerably easier than it would otherwise be. Moreover, mass communication creates the opportunity for members of an organization to promote their interests and disseminate their ideas on a large scale. The crime reporter is able to act as intermediary between the press and the police, offering the police both informational and promotional assistance. He can facilitate the launching of formal public appeals for information about crimes but he can also help the police to communicate with specific individuals or minority groups. This private communication may take the form of threats directed at the criminal underworld to the effect that homes of known offenders will be raided until someone informs on a wanted man; or it may involve the strategic 'leaking' of information designed to panic or mislead their quarry (see chapter 6). The crime reporter also has his own underworld contacts who are more likely to give information to a journalist than to a policeman. Here again, the crime reporter can fulfil an important intermediary function, facilitating 'the anonymous tip-off':

> 'Joe Smith might know a lot of details about a certain robbery and, for whatever reasons, he wants to tell ... He won't go to a policeman and tell him direct, but he'll tell me in the full knowledge that I would tell whoever is investigating the job. But he wouldn't want to be revealed as the man giving the information.' (Crime Correspondent)

The role of the crime reporter in police promotional activities is again as intermediary and facilitator, interviewing policemen and liaising between newspaper and Scotland Yard; but it is also as copy writer — he is the man who makes public police activities, and he can portray those activities in a favourable or unfavourable light. Thus, an important exchange resource for the crime reporter are his accounts themselves. Although explicit bargains are rarely negotiated he can still exchange favourable comment for source co-operation by means of tacit mutual understandings.[8]

Assimilation

Crime reporters, then, control valuable exchange resources in their relationships with sources. Those relationships are essentially symbiotic — reporter and policeman depend on each other's good will and trade information and ideas. But, in the final analysis the relationships are asymmetrical because the journalist is always in an inferior negotiating position — the reporter who cannot get information is out of a job, whereas the policeman who retains it is not. Therefore, it is usually the crime reporter who initiates interaction, and actively cultivates the relationship. Thus, as the relationship develops, it is the reporter's world which is drawn towards that of the policeman rather than vice versa. Gieber and Johnson (1961) in their study of reporter and source roles call this process 'assimilation'. It is, in fact, a complex process of socialization by which the journalist's frame of reference, methods of working, and personal system of perceptions and understandings are brought into line with the expectations of his sources. The importance of mutual trust, confidence, and understanding is emphasized and the journalist is encouraged to conform to his source's model of the 'good reporter' — he exercises and values 'responsibility', he does not pester for information at inconvenient times, he sympathizes with his source's problems, he identifies with his source's interests, he accepts what he is told and reports it faithfully. As one crime reporter said of his police contacts: 'You get to know them. You understand how they think, how they are likely to act. You talk the same language.' By fulfilling his sources' expectations the reporter, not only receives good copy, he also earns the respect of his sources. He becomes a confidant and drinking companion. Obviously the degree of assimilation varies, but no crime reporter remains entirely unaffected by his relationships with his police informants.[9] As a general rule, he is obliged to make his stories acceptable to his personal contacts without ignoring the news imperatives of his profession:

'I'm not bothered about upsetting people, but you have to be a bit careful about upsetting coppers because they're my bread and butter. Officially they can't influence me at all, but in practice I try very hard to play it their way, providing there is a story in it. But what is a news point is often not what they want me to include. But, having got a news point and a basic story, I'll co-operate as much as I can in putting over what they want.'   (Crime Correspondent)

It is, of course, difficult for the reporters, themselves, to admit that their accounts are significantly constrained by source relationships. Their professional ethic of integrity and detachment continues to exert a powerful influence over their public statements and private perceptions. When asked if they feel that their close association with police informants could perhaps impair their ability to criticize the police, they usually evoke the rhetoric of this same professional ethic:

'As a crime man working closely with the police over a long period you inevitably become sympathetic to their problems. But this does not mean that you cannot criticise them when they deserve it.'   (Crime Correspondent)

'I am a reporter, not a policeman, nor a civil servant, nor a copper's nark ... After 20 years of dealing with this subject you should have enough experience to know when to criticise.'
(Crime Correspondent)

'If it came to the crunch, I would rather ditch a contact than suppress information it would be in the public interest to know.'   (Crime Correspondent)

However, some crime specialists are prepared to admit that the reporter's critical faculty can be undermined:

'I think, to be fair, to some degree one tends to admire policemen because you know what they're doing and how they're doing it and they're co-operative and friendly with you and I think one does have a bias towards the police. I think one tends to be able to produce for the newspaper the police version of some particular event.'   (Crime Correspondent)

'There are some crime reporters of the old school ... who have been in the game so long that they have completely sold out to the police.' (Crime Correspondent)

'I wouldn't get myself involved in commenting on jobs that involved people I know — I don't particularly want to stick my bloody neck out, I'd loose all the friends I've ever made.' (Crime Correspondent)

But it is not usually a case of inability to criticize when the occasion demands it, it is rather a general reluctance to criticize, a desire not to offend those whose help and friendship one values, the ready acceptance of the police version of the story, the undermining of the *will* to criticize. All this is a consequence of long association and common experience, shared perspectives, values and interests:

'Inevitably you do get close to policemen and become very good friends, and when the point comes to criticise or even attack it's a difficult decision to make. I think I would do it, although in certain circumstances ... that would be a test of friendship or contact.' (Crime Correspondent)

It is not that crime reporters actively promote the interests of the police to the detriment of others, or that they deliberately ignore conflicts in their role; it is rather that they often simply do not perceive these conflicts. As one informant put it, the crime reporter may sometimes be 'the guy in the middle', but usually 'everybody is marching in the same direction' and consequently 'there aren't generally many crises of loyalty'. Other comments emphasized the same point: 'Generally, what we write is parallel with and complementary to what the police are saying; but this is not a deliberate policy, it just happens that so often the interests of the press, the police and the public are complementary' (Crime Correspondent). The major exception to this generalization is, of course, the case of police deviance which may not only bring news imperatives into conflict with police interests but may also severely embarrass the crime reporter. The routine reporting of internal police 'rubber heels' investigations would be unlikely to disturb stable source relationships, but any direct association with investigative journalism in the area of police deviance puts even well-established relationships in Jeopardy. Newspaper exposés of police deviance are the kiss of death to the specialist crime correspondent. Three options are usually open to a crime reporter who has information about police deviancy and who wishes to avoid a 'freeze out':

    i.   He can write the story up anonymously.
    ii. He can pass the information to a colleague who is able to write the story because he does not rely on the police for information.
    iii. He can suppress the information.

One reporter on a Sunday paper with a reputation for running exposés of police deviancy favoured the second option:

> 'I, probably more than anybody else on this paper, have quite a number of police contacts and it would completely destroy my role to have my by-line on a story knocking the police ... If such a story does come my way I hand it over to my colleagues to handle, I wash my hands of it ... Quite frankly, I think it's hypocritical, but I've got to live a long time in Fleet Street doing this kind of work. What alternative is there for me?'

A little later in the interview I asked if crime reporters on other papers ever offered him stories they were unable to handle:

> 'It does happen in other fields ... but I can never remember a crime reporter offering me a story and I don't think that any crime reporter would do this. You see, if it's a good story about the police they'd have it in their papers, if it's a bad story they'd tend to forget it.' [10]

Ostracism is a powerful sanction and suppression is usually the safest course. But the crime reporter does not necessarily see the non-publication of this type of information as suppression. Often the process of assimilation means that definitions of situations and codes of conduct derived from sources replace those of journalism. The informal ethics of police work dominate the formal ethics of journalism. The process may result in police deviancy being seen by a few crime reporters as an essentially private affair, unsuitable for public scrutiny. But this does not mean that the reporter takes no action when cases of police deviancy come to his notice, it means that he allows his response to be governed by the expectations and codes of his unofficial sources — he 'sorts out' the situation:

'I've had two or three cases ... where the guy [an informant] has ended up saying, "Look, I've arranged to meet this copper at such and such a pub tomorrow and I'm going to get him to accept this bribe''. And, in that case, I've got straight on to a pal in that particular division to say to him, ''Look, one of your chums has got a meet tomorrow at 6.30 — no need for me to tell you who or where it is, you find out who it is and perhaps you'd make other arrangements for him''. In other words, make sure he doesn't keep the meet. And, in this way, the guy who is *allegedly* going to accept a bribe will not keep the meet. His boss has got no proof of what he has done before and the guy who was allegedly going to take the bribe has got the wind put up him because he knows that somebody else knows about it. So everything's hunky dory in the end, or at least I like to think it is.
Author: You wouldn't go to A10?
What me? No, not at all — that's grassing going to A10. I haven't been a good boy all my life, I'm sure you haven't.'
(Crime Correspondent)

'If I know a copper who's bent, it depends on how bent he is. If it came to my notice that one of my contacts was really bent I would feel obliged to do something about it. I wouldn't write about it in the paper, I'd talk to my mates in the police force ... But it's never happened. It has been found out that two of my contacts were bent, but I didn't find them out. They're in jail at the moment and it's proved expensive cultivating new contacts.' (Crime Correspondent)

Exposing corruption

Exposés of police deviance may embarrass crime correspondents, but this has not prevented newspapers from running stories of this type. Indeed, since the mid-sixties, one Sunday newspaper has almost specialized in the exposure of police malpractice. The development of this type of exposé journalism has accompanied the decline of cheque-book journalism. It is part of a more general trend towards investigative reporting which received its impetus from the scandals of the early sixties (Vassall, Profumo, Rachman, Sheffield, Challenor), but may also be seen as a strategy for dealing with the competitive threat posed to Fleet Street by the expansion of television news and current affairs coverage. Unlike pressmen, broadcasters were handicapped in the investigative field by their statutory obligations of impartiality and objectivity and by the problem of obtaining suitable film material, difficulties countered most successfully, of course, by 'World in Action'. Investigative journalism may invite praise from Fleet Street colleagues but, in the particular case of exposures of police deviance, investigations are invariably (a) carried out in violation of perceived audience preferences, and (b) result in severe disruption of relationships between the newspaper and the police.

(a) Readers' expectations
Journalists often justify newspaper content in terms of 'giving the readers what they want'. They generally recognize that they are in the business of producing *commercial* knowledge, a product which is necessarily responsive to the apparent demands of the market. Even specialists on the quality Sunday papers subscribe to this view. As a crime reporter on one of these papers put it: 'A paper is an economic concern, it's got to pay, it's got to be successful. Any journalist who says his only job is serving the public interest is not telling the truth.' But, the recognition of news as commercial knowledge is characterized by a certain ambivalence, and the reporting of police deviance is one area in which ideas of serving 'the public interest' rather than the public's appetite may assert themselves. When newspapers run

stories about police malpractices they are showing their readers what they think they ought to see, not what they think their readers want to see. There exists a widespread belief (even on papers that run them) that exposés of police deviance do not help circulation because readers do not like to have their apparently complacent image of the Force threatened. A journalist working on the *Observer* suggested to me that people reading crime news in mass-circulation papers 'don't want a critical approach', rather, 'they want to be reassured that all is well'. A reporter on the *Sunday People* expressed the idea more graphically:

> 'Police exposés are not normally very good for sales. The thing is, the average reader likes to feel he's safe in his bed at night and this gentleman in size 13 boots pounding up and down the street is the only line of protection he has against the ravaging hoards of vicious thugs, drug pushers and negroes who want to rape his sixteen-year-old daughter (who has had it so many times she's forgotten anyway). Therefore, they don't like their peace disturbed and, therefore, they tend to react to stories against the police ... I think the public at large, outside of central London where they're relatively sophisticated, do not like the peace of their lives shattered by the thought that their friendly local bobby might be getting a turkey out the back of a local butcher's at Christmas or something. They just don't want to know about it, and I can understand why they don't ... it makes them worry, they don't like to worry.'

Like many other exponents of the craft of popular journalism, he saw his readers as conservative 'mums and dads', living snugly within the illusion that all is well with the world as long as they are protected from the 'wreckers in their midst'. But unlike some he saw it as his professional responsibility to give their complacent world views an occasional shake, for their own good: 'In a democratic society you must have a check on the police. The only check you can have is your free press ... We're not anti-police, we're anti-rotten police.' To an important extent, then, exposés of police corruption or brutality give journalists the sense that they are autonomous actors in touch with the finest traditions of their craft — crusaders in the cause of truth, protectors of the people's freedoms rather than mere functionaries of a production process which panders to consumer wants. This sense of autonomy and significance is reinforced by the indignant police response to exposés.

(b) *Police responses*
In November 1955 the trial of a West End Central detective sergeant, Robert Robertson, took place at the Old Bailey. He was accused with Ben Canter, a solicitor, and Morris Page, a West End 'fixer', of conspiring to defeat the course of justice by fabricating evidence at the trial of Joseph Grech, a notorious 'vice baron'. It was alleged that Grech had bribed Robertson to secure his acquittal on a housebreaking charge, but also that Robertson and a West End Central Inspector had been extorting money from him to prevent them raiding his brothels. The trial was conducted against a background of newspaper speculation and public controversy sparked off by a story by Arthur Tietjen in the *Daily Mail* which reported that a 5,000 word report on corruption had been delivered to Metropolitan Commissioner, Sir John Nott-Bower. According to Tietjen, the report revealed 'a vast amount of bribery and corruption among certain uniformed police officers attached to West End Central police station' after an investigation involving 'club proprietors, prostitutes, gaming-house owners, brothel-keepers and men living on immoral earnings' (*Daily Mail* 17.11.55). The article went on to publicize numerous details from the confidential report by Superintendent Hannam. Police reaction to the article was immediate. On the day of publication, Sir John Nott-Bower delivered a 'pep-talk' to his beleaguered troops in 'C' division and issued a statement refuting most of Tietjen's information and any suggestions that ' "the Metropolitan Police as a body is corrupt — suggestions which are grossly unfair, have no foundation in fact, and can do untold harm to the morale of the London police" ' (Wilkinson 1957:134). The following day the article was further attacked by Sir Laurence Dunne, the Chief Magistrate and by the Joint Under-Secretary at the Home Office who described the piece variously as: 'misleading', 'mischievous',

'unwarranted', and 'unsubstantiated', and condemned its probable effect on public confidence in the Force. In fact, there is every reason to believe that, with the exception of one or two sentences, the article was substantially accurate, but the reaction to stories of this type is not necessarily dependent on their accuracy. The interests of police morale are often seen as more important than the public's right to know. In 1963, when the *Sheffield Telegraph* exposed the brutal methods used by certain local detectives to extract confessions from suspects, the city's Chief Constable accused the paper of running a 'malicious campaign' against the police. But public statements by senior officers are generally only the tip of an iceberg of hostility and indignation which cools relationships between policemen and journalists. In exceptional cases, there may be a blanket ostracism of all the reporters of a paper. *Sunday People* reporters assured me that the paper's exposés of police deviance in the late sixties and early seventies had 'killed completely' relationships between policemen and the paper's journalists: 'It became known that if any one policeman had a journalist on this paper as a friend he was dead; so we were dead.' I have also been told that one reporter associated with the investigations became afraid to enter a police station alone and heard that the number of his car had been circulated within the Force who were reputedly 'out to get him for absolutely anything'. This is obviously a dramatic example, but it underlines the instability and fragility of the police/press symbiosis.

In 1969 *The Times* published an exposé of police corruption in London which was to become a milestone in police/press relations. Investigations were carried out by a special team of reporters working independently of the paper's crime staff, but the repercussions of the story were wide-ranging. A crime specialist on the paper told me:

'I did not work on the inquiry, but the mere fact that I work for the Times was enough for CID to think I was tarred with the same brush ... It created more indifference than actual antagonism: people were just not as available as before. At one time they said, "Christ, I don't want to be seen talking to you" ... We burnt our fingers badly over the bribery case. We don't want to do more stories like that, we want to live it down — it brought us into a direct head-on clash with the police.'

The Times exposé is significant because it appears to have led to a re-negotiation of terms in the informal contract which binds together police and press. The trial of the two detectives prosecuted as a consequence of *The Times* investigations ended just six weeks before Sir Robert Mark became Commissioner of the Metropolitan Police in April 1972. During and around this period Mark seems to have spent a considerable amount of time visiting and lunching with Fleet Street Editors, news editors, and crime correspondents and negotiating a new set of tacit rules and expectations for interaction between the police and the news media. Essentially, negotiations appear to have centred on a 'package deal' by which Sir Robert agreed to do his best to make his men more open and co-operative in their dealings with the press, and to reduce the level of corruption within the Metropolitan Force, in return for press co-operation in the publishing and withholding of information and an informal understanding that evidence of police malpractice would be passed to his new A10 branch at an early stage [11]. Most editors have now accepted the deal, but one obvious consequence is that it has now become less likely that evidence of police deviancy will be collected by newspapers. As one dissident news executive put it:

'Scotland Yard wants us to do the research on bent cops and then hand it over to them without printing it — but that means there is no incentive to do it, not if we can't print it — we're not a charitable organisation we're in business to sell papers.'

(Journalist: Popular Sunday paper)

Not surprisingly, most crime reporters are delighted by the new rules and expectations which one specialist described as 'an agreement to act like responsible citizens'. Their adoption will save the crime specialist a good deal of embarrassment and will mean that he will not need to play the awkward role of troubleshooter between police and press quite so often. A *Sunday People* reporter described the role in action:

'I've had experience on this paper of at least one crime reporter from another paper who acts more or less as an unpaid press agent for Scotland Yard, phoning up and saying, ''Oh, you're ruining all the relationships the press had with the police''. Or often deals where the police try to suppress a story of one of our reporters and are trying to extricate themselves and use this chap as an intermediary.'

The demise of exposé journalism focussing on the police is likely to be one effective means of resolving the contradiction between news imperatives and notions of responsible reporting, but it will not be the first resolution to be employed.

'Bent cops': explaining away police deviance

In the past, the impact of corruption and brutality exposés has been cushioned by the provision of an interpretive framework which reaffirms the favourable reputation of the Force as a whole by isolating the deviant policeman. During March 1972, at the height of the anxiety generated by *The Times'* exposé and the more recent *Sunday People* attack on the Commander of the Yard's Flying Squad, the following editorial appeared in the *Daily Mail* (6.3.72):

'PUTTING THE POLICE IN PERSPECTIVE
There is not much wrong with Britain's police force. And those who claim that policemen are being sucked into a great wave of corruption have not looked at the facts. Quite rightly, any allegation against the police gets the most rigorous investigation. That is the only way to maintain public confidence.
Commander Kenneth Drury, the head of the Flying Squad may or may not have been foolish to spend that holiday in Cyprus with a strip-club owner. But there is no doubt that it was right to suspend him from duty pending a full inquiry. Nearly 40 other Scotland Yard detectives are now under suspension for one reason or another. But remember — there are 21,000 officers at Scotland Yard. The case of the two detectives who were last week jailed for conspiracy and accepting bribes was a

shocking one. But look at the figures. In 1970 there were 1½ million crimes committed; 232,000 persons were convicted. How many were policemen? Just 88.

In a county the size of Derbyshire, in an average year, exactly ONE police officer is likely to be convicted of an offence — which may be only shoplifting.

While crime has been rising by leaps and bounds, the number of policemen who crack has changed little. And consider their temptations. Detectives, ill-paid and overworked, have to mingle with crooks flashing big bank-rolls. They are under constant pressure to "forget this one, inspector, and I'll see you right".

The first men on the beat, the Bow Street Runners, were themselves recruited from the underworld. Ever since, the police have striven to root out corruption from their own ranks. Their success is astounding when you look at other police forces around the world. The struggle continues. And the Daily Mail gives the police its unwavering support in that struggle.'

The piece illustrates clearly most of the dominant understandings which the press bring to bear on the problem of police deviance. The collective guilt of the Force is minimized by the stress on deviance as a minority activity which leaves the vast majority of policemen untouched and untainted. In this case attention is drawn to the proportion of suspensions and convictions relative to the number of men and women in the Force, an interpretation which derives its power from the implicit notion of 'the bent copper', the weak policeman who 'cracks' under pressure. This encourages the reader to view police deviancy in terms of individual pathology rather than an endemic feature of police work. 'The bent copper' is the stereotypical exception who proves the rule that cases of police malpractice are isolated and untypical incidents. He is the odd bad apple which even the Yard must find in its barrel; the policeman who cracks and succumbs to the temptation offered by affluent criminals as a result of conditions of service imposed by poor pay and long hours. The logical solution to the problem must be more policemen and better rates of pay, a policy supported by most papers. Finally, we have the notion of purging — the tireless rooting out of corrupt elements which can only enhance the good reputation of the Force. These interpretations reappear again and again in press representations of police deviance — take, for example, the *Sun*'s comments (4.3.72) on the *Times* exposé case:

'Britain's Police are a force to be proud of. Hold on to that. They are still wonderful. Now and then there is bound to be an odd bent copper. When a couple of them turn up at Scotland Yard people are bound to be disturbed and so they should be. But the point is that the law HAS purged itself of these two. Let's never forget the honest, steadfast hundreds of others.'

Of course, the effectiveness of this editorial in cancelling out the front-page headline — 'THE WICKED YARD MEN GO TO JAIL' must remain a matter of conjecture. The conflict between news imperatives and ideologically based notions of responsibility is, however, evident[12]. The *Sun*'s interpretation of the detectives' activities as exceptional was in direct opposition to that in the original *Times* story which suggested that the case was not as isolated one (29.11.69). But the interpretations of police deviance which appeared in March 1972 were by no means new to the press. If we return to the scandals of the sixties we can detect similar interpretive conventions at work. The *Daily Express* leader on the Sheffield brutality scandal, for instance, was titled 'Reassurance':

'... The public will be reassured by the extraordinary rarity of this sort of occurrence in Britain. Indeed its very rarity emphasises the generally high quality of the 159 police forces in this country. Their record in protecting and serving the public is unparalleled throughout the world.'   (7.11.63)

The *Daily Mirror* expressed similar sentiments (7.11.63): '... The vast majority of decent conscientious policemen are smeared by the rogue coppers. But this is very sad. For in general the British police are still the finest in the world.' Commenting on the Sheffield case and that of Detective Sergeant Challenor (the West

End Central policeman who was found to have planted half-bricks on demonstrators), Frederick Newman assured the readers of the *Daily Sketch* (25.6.64):

'These are isolated cases and the vast majority of Britain's 86,580 policemen are the honest-to-goodness sorts who are still symbolic of that pillar-like, massively avuncular rectitude that could always be guaranteed to tell you the right time and the right place ...'

These interpretations appear to me grossly misleading, not because I believe policemen to be typically brutal and corrupt, but because the interpretations distort reality by reducing the spectrum of police types to its two extremes. It is as if the Force was composed entirely of heroes and villains who stand either side of a line which divides good practice from malpractice, a line which is clear and identifiable to all. Moreover, the stereotype of the bent copper glosses over the complex strains and contradictions of police work in general and CID work in particular. It ignores completely the subtle situational moralities which policemen develop to cope with these strains and contradictions. Research on the police has consistently pointed to two co-existing but contradictory models of the criminal process, one based on the importance of 'due process' and the other on the salience of 'crime control' (Packer 1964). The classic statement of what is essentially a contradiction between ends and means is to be found in Skolnick's work on the American police. He writes:

'As workers in a democratic society, the police seek the opportunity to introduce the means necessary to carry out "production demands". The means used to achieve these ends, however, may frequently conflict with the conduct required of them as legal actors.'   (Skolnick 1966:243)

Similarly, a study of the British police force by Maureen Cain (1971; 1972) found that, 'policemen feel that they are forced to live on the fringes of the law'. The policemen she spoke to were 'cynical about the hypocrisy of society which paid lip service to one set of rules but put pressure on them to work by another'.

One summed up the situation by saying, 'You can't play it by the book. You'd never get anywhere in a job like this' (1971:88). The conflicts of due process and crime control are experienced most acutely by detectives, and their working resolutions are most clearly demonstrated in an informant system by which jealously-guarded 'snouts' are tied to individual detectives by friendship, blackmail, and exchange. Clandestine dealings with a network of valuable informants become the key to promotion in the CID but, at the same time represents the thin end of the corruption wedge. These insights are not exclusive to sociologists. They appear to form the basis of Sir Robert Mark's reorganization of CID work and his proposals for legal reform. They have been discovered by novelists such as G.F. Newman (1970; 1972; 1974) and Colin MacInnes (1960) and also by some journalists. In her book on the Challenor case, for instance, Mary Grigg observed:

'The public expects the police force to combat crime; and it also expects the police to do this successfully without the slightest impropriety. Police officers had discovered in practice, however, that they could either catch criminals or behave properly, but that it was very difficult to do both.' (Grigg 1965:114)

On the basis of his own research at Scotland Yard, freelance journalist, Peter Laurie (1973) has claimed that:

'Going by the book is the counsel of perfection, rather than reality. Although no policeman can publicly admit it, effective crime detection often entails less than immaculate methods ... When policemen are "bent" it is not just because of greed, but because they can see no other way to do the job.'

These arguments, however, find little representation in leader or feature columns which remain as rigidly governed by the imperative of simplification as the news columns. Paul Ferris (1973) is one of the few journalists to have set out the problem:

'The average detective is encouraged by his colleagues, by the Press and T.V. to feel he is fighting a holy war against crime. How holy a war it is and to what extent detectives are justified in bending the rules and endangering civil liberties, are matters rarely discussed in public with much honesty.'

Few newspapers appear to take seriously the ideas that 'law' may not be synonymous with 'order', that the 'good copper' may be regularly obliged to break the rules in order to get convictions, or that the 'bent copper' may still spend most of his time protecting some of society's members from their more predatory fellows. Ideas of this type are subversive in the most fundamental sense because they threaten, not only the conventional interpretive structures of newspaper ideology, but also the professional news imperatives on which those structures depend. Stories about bent cops obey the imperatives of dramatization,simplification, and personalization. Moreover, they reproduce the public definitions of those in powerful institutional positions, including the police themselves. During his period as Home Secretary, Robert Carr made frequent references to 'black sheep' or 'rotten apples' in the Force (e.g., *Guardian* 6.2.73), but perhaps the most influential statements in recent years have come from Robert Mark, who was particularly adept at exploiting news imperatives. When he introduced his organizational reforms he was aware that he had to ' "walk a tightrope between introducing the new measures and not destroying police morale and public confidence" ' (Cockerell 1975). He seems to have achieved this by exploiting the stereotype of the bent copper in explaining and justifying his reforms. He has stated that, in his first years as Commissioner he was probably more interested in catching corrupt detectives than in catching other criminals: ' "A bent detective is not only himself a wrongdoer ... he harms the whole fabric of public confidence in the courts and the police; and so far as I'm concerned he will always be a prime target' (Cockerell 1975)[13].

The notion of the odd black sheep who can be separated from the all-white flock, then, is a pervasive one, eagerly embraced by both police and press because it protects the general reputation of the Force while providing a focus of news interest. Crime reporters generally accept it without question because there is no practical reason to challenge it. It is incorporated in their private understandings as well as in their public accounts. Most of the crime reporters that I interviewed produced variations on the same basic theme:

> 'You have to accept that there are rotten policemen, just as there are rotten pressmen, just as there are rotten apples in every profession. But, make no mistake they are a minority, and the police want to root them out just as much as we do.'
>
> (Crime Correspondent)

Journalism is a 'habit of mind' which operates most often 'at the level of the specific concrete case' (Bensman and Lilienfield 1973:221), the level of drama and immediacy. The conditions which give rise to the concrete case are, at best, of only secondary interest. The ironic aspect of the situation, however, is that the meaning and significance of the concrete case is supplied by the conditions from which it emerges. By ignoring these conditions the journalist is creating a vacuum of meaning which can only be filled through the news imperatives. The event becomes understandable as the dramatic face of the peculiar present or by reference to familiar conventional interpretations or, perhaps still more disturbingly, explanation is left to those in powerful institutional positions with vested interests in the event. This brings us back once again to the control exerted by institutional sources over information and understandings in the domain of news. It reminds us, once again, that news is not just what newsmen want to tell us but also what powerful sources want us to hear. We have already seen how police sources can socialize specialist reporters into accepting their conventional wisdoms and characteristic patterns of perception and thought. The next chapter will examine the use of more direct and explicit techniques of news management by agencies of social control. At the completion of this examination, we should be in a position to assess the influence of professional news imperatives and source manipulation and management on the manufacture of news.

6 Yard man speak with forked tongue?: sources and the management of news

> 'In Britain we do not like the idea of a concerted publicity campaign directed against any particular class of society. But the criminal class is at war with society at large and it could not complain if society used all the weapons in its armoury to fight crime and these would include the weapons of knowledge, of ridicule and of contempt. The criminal would be shown up as the avaricious and malicious little rat that he often is ... The fight against crime is no longer a cold war. It is a desperately serious business and we shall have to employ propaganda against crime as we employed propaganda during the war.'
>
> Judge Gerald Sparrow 1969 : 184-85

A Permanent Undersecretary at the Foreign Office, is said to have once remarked to a journalist, 'You think we lie to you. But we don't lie, really we don't. However, when you discover that, you make an even greater error. You think we tell you the truth.' The remark directs our attention to one of the most significant and yet under-researched influences on media representations and accounts: the influence exerted by news sources in their control and management of information.

In this chapter I shall be looking at the role played by agencies of social control — particularly the police, but also the army — in determining the content of news by direct and indirect control and manipulation[1]. The goals of news management will first be identified and then the techniques appropriate to those goals will be examined in detail. Finally, a few case studies will be selected so that we may see how various techniques can be combined and used in the manipulation of an on-going news story.

The goals of news management by agencies of social control

Control agencies will usually recognize three broad goals in their dealings with the news media:

   i.   To protect the public reputation and image of the control agency.

   ii. To directly facilitate the work of the control agency in controlling and apprehending deviants.

  iii. To promote the particular aims, ideologies, and interests of members of the control agency.

To say that control agencies recognize these goals is not to say that they always declare or admit them openly. Their awareness of these goals, however, can be deduced from observation of the techniques appropriate to them which the agencies employ and develop. If we require further confirmation we can often discover the goals thinly-concealed between the lines of public statements by control agency personnel or clearly stated in more restricted material such as the army's 'Land Operations' manual which advises against muzzling the media because 'the press, properly handled, is potentially one of the government's strongest weapons' (quoted in *Time Out* 10.1.75). As far as Scotland Yard is concerned, Sir Robert Mark made no secret of his awareness of the importance of media representations and their potential as propaganda weapons. As long ago as 1966 he argued that 'police/public relations are not governed by the truth necessarily. They are governed by the appearance of the truth.' (*Listener* 25.8.66). As Deputy Commissioner in 1971, in a speech to the Institute of Journalists, he described the relationship between the police and the press as 'an enduring, if not ecstatically happy marriage. We help each other in difficulties, tolerate each other's faults and try to promote each other's interests without too much disregard of our own.' On becoming Metropolitan Commissioner he quickly instituted a new, more 'open', press relations policy, which included training for members of the Force in coping with press and television interviews, and expressed a new willingness to allow journalists to interview those policemen most closely associated with a case. Policemen (above the rank of sergeant) who speak to the press no longer face disciplinary action and some detectives are now co-operating so much with crime reporters that some stories might almost be classed as collaborative pieces.[2] But this was not necessarily Sir Robert's intention. In fact he expressed a desire to end what he saw as the 'improper relationship' between many older detectives and some crime reporters, replacing it with his more open system of press conferences and direct communication with editors and senior specialists. The new policy was set out in an internal Scotland Yard memorandum on May 24th, 1973. One passage reads:

'It is my firm belief that the Metropolitan Police have a great deal more to be proud of than the public know and that a little more openness with the news media, heightening trust, confidence and co-operation, is all that is required to correct that ignorance. In particular, there is convincing evidence that, given the opportunity to do so, the press ... will give a great deal of support to the Force.'

It is interesting to note that the justification of the new policy is not simply the public's right to know, but the advantages to the Force of letting the public have more information about certain areas of police work. Sir Robert, himself, however would argue that the various interests of press, police, and public are only analytically separable. As he put it in a recent interview, 'I believe that the interests of the press and our interests coincide with the public interest' (Mark 1975). In the same interview he expressed his satisfaction in the degree of success his new policy had achieved in its first thirty months of operation:

'We believe the press have such a high degree of trust in us that we expect them to believe us when we tell them the truth, and we are fully confident of a responsible attitude on their part. Any apprehensions are unnecessary, because it is an entirely voluntary arrangement ... There is such a degree of confidence and trust now between Fleet Street and the Metropolitan Police Force that you almost make a journalist uncomfortable if he disbelieves you.'

He accepted that the way he had used this heightened trust and co-operation could lead to 'a change of "news management"' but he emphasized the voluntary nature of press co-operation: 'In our dealings with the press we have never made demands, only requests. And we have made it clear that a denial of police requests would never lead to reprisals on our part.' But the situation Sir Robert has created is one in which the possibilities for successful news management have been maximized. Middle- as well as high-ranking officers have a considerable degree of autonomy in their dealings with journalists who, if Sir Robert was correct, are inclined to believe what they are told and accept the police interpretation of whether or not information is in the public interest. This means that journalists may be inclined to further over-assess definitions of the situation articulated by sources who are already in an enviable position with regard to the media's structure of access and hierarchy of credibility (see chapter 2). There is also the disturbing possibility that Mark's rhetoric will conceal the fact that the police are involved in a daily propaganda campaign against those 'they see as their adversaries who, themselves, are offered few opportunities to contest police definitions of the public interest. The police's first responsibility is to the interests of social control rather than those of accuracy and truth. They are primarily interested in disseminating news that is 'helpful' rather than news which is true. We have already seen Judge Gerald Sparrow's recommendations of how the media can be used by the police for propaganda purposes. In 1970 the Conservative Political Centre published a pamphlet by Tory MP and barrister, William Rees-Davies in which a more detailed strategy for the propaganda war on crime was spelt out:

'The Criminal Intelligence section has a great undercover role to play ... Rumour can be fostered that a particular colleague has informed, or has been a careless talker in public. Equally, if one colleague has not been invited to partake in a criminal enterprise, he can be informed that the reason was that he was regarded as unreliable or incompetent, so that his confidence is undermined. Convince such a man that he has become an

outlaw amongst his associates and he may turn informer by way
of revenge, in exchange for his own protection. When a robbery
has been committed and goods have been removed, advertise
inflated figures of the amounts stolen so that the organiser
believes he has been cheated by his underlings of the take;
thus subversion quickly spreads. Supply accurate information
regarding their girlfriends where they are involved with other
associates, whereby dissention is created. Play on known
weaknesses ... carry war into their own camp. In brief, employ
tactics effectively used in time of war by the Intelligence
Department and the Department of Economic Warfare.'

(Rees-Davies 1970)

Not surprisingly, the police are entirely familiar with techniques
of this type and well aware of their likely advantages. Although
they may not be a regular feature of investigations, there is ample
reason to believe that they are used in selected cases.   .

Most journalists in Northern Ireland soon come to realize that
they are involved in a propaganda war. As Simon Winchester of
the *Guardian* has put it:

'Propaganda is an essential part of a guerrilla war: and any
reporter who thought his interviews with Harry Tuzo [the army
GOC] or Sean MacStiofain [Provisional IRA Chief of Staff]
were a reflection on his brilliance as a journalist displayed a
total naiveté: both men gave interviews only if they felt their
propaganda was going to be printed. They assumed, then, that
the reporter to whom they talked was more gullible than
brilliant and often — too often — they were right.'

(Winchester 1975:173)

But the first realization of this propaganda war can often come as
a shock. Take, for example, Winchester's own experience at the
'Falls Curfew' fairly early in the troubles:

'The gunfire that began around 8.30 p.m. [3.7.70] went on
and on, and it invited inevitable reply by the army. To anyone
who experienced the battle it was perfectly obvious that
hundreds and hundreds of bullets were being fired by both

sides — and yet the army had the gall, when asked by reporters later in the weekend, to say that its soldiers had fired only 15 shots in sum. The official figures were to be published later: Soldiers in the Falls that weekend fired no less than 1457 rounds ... Ever since those later figures were quietly published, many reporters found it terribly hard to accept contemporary accounts of a serious disturbance by the army public relations' men. Never, since then, have I found myself able to take the army's explanation about any single incident with any less a pinch of salt than I would take any other explanation.'

(Winchester 1975:71)

After the initial realization the journalist generally comes to accept news management as inevitable; his awareness of its existence merely reinforces an incipient cynicism towards news. He knows that all his sources are 'selling him a line', that they are all to some degree unreliable. But it would be mistaken to assume that each side's propaganda will cancel out the other sides'. The IRA and the Protestant para-militaries may be able to win the occasional propaganda battle, but in the war as a whole they are heavily out-gunned by the security forces. First, as we have seen (chapter 2), journalists are under considerable pressure to demonstrate their responsibility by accepting the 'official' version of events. Army statements are backed by the authority of the State. Second, the security forces' PR machine is far larger and more efficient than its rivals. At the beginning of 1976 the army had over forty press officers in Ulster with a back-up staff of over 100, while the RUC had twelve full-time press officers. Beyond these the Government had another twenty civil servants briefed to deal with the media (Stephen 1976). This means that it is far more convenient to use the official sources than to attempt to find alternatives[3]. Another *Guardian* journalist, Simon Hoggart (1973) has testified to the way in which convenience can lead to dependence and the easy reproduction of the army definitions of reality:

'Most journalists working in Northern Ireland are almost completely dependent on [the army's] information service [and the smaller one run by the police], simply because there is no other source for news of day-to-day violence. This means that the army has the immense advantage of getting in the first word, and it is left up to the integrity of the journalist to check that word one. Some do, some don't. Most only check when there is time or the incident looks like becoming controversial and a few hardly bother at all. When the British press prints an account of an incident as if it were an established fact, and it is clear that the reporter himself was not on the spot, it is a 99 per cent certainty that it is the army's version that is being given.'

It is this dependency on control agency accounts that supplies the firm foundation of successful news management and facilitates the development and refinement of its techniques. We can now return to the general goals of news management and examine the various techniques appropriate to them.

Goal 1: protecting reputation and promoting image

The aim in this case is to ensure that the general tenor of journalists' accounts remains 'helpful' to the overall goals of the control agency by contributing towards a favourable public image. The techniques appropriate to this goal can be classified as either 'sticks' or 'carrots' designed to either coerce or persuade the reporter.

Techniques

(a) *'Freezing-out'* This is a punishment-centred response to stories critical of the control agency, by which further information is denied to the reporter or only minimal accommodation is made to his requests. More than any other technique, its success is grounded in the type of dependence on official sources we have already observed. In the relationship between crime reporter and detective it remains a background threat, potentially effective but rarely used because the process of assimilation makes its use unnecessary. But the Yard has also institutionalized the 'freeze-out' through its system of issuing press cards to approved journalists, a system which appears to have been considerably tightened up since 1971. Between 1971 and 1974 the number of cards issued appears to have been cut from over 8,000 to 2,000 (*Time Out* 24.5.74). The NUJ has protested that the same reporting facilities should be offered to all its members but card-holders continue to be given preferential treatment and cards continue to be withheld from representatives of the radical press who presumably cannot be trusted to report events responsibly.

In Ulster, too, the 'freeze-out' remains primarily a background threat, but there are at least two notable instances in which the tacit threat has been carried out. In August 1971, just after the Internment operation, Simon Winchester broke the informal rules governing the attribution of statements when he attributed fears about the likely long-term success of the operation to Harry Tuzo, the army's General Officer Commanding, rather than merely to 'a senior officer':

> 'The row that ensued went on for days. Signals went out to army units across the country to the effect that I ... was to be regarded with something bordering on contempt by all other press officers. I was told not to come up to Lisburn again for some long while. It was suggested that I write — and in fact I did later write — a letter of apology to the general. I felt like a naughty schoolboy; and I was being punished with the one weapon the army could use with effect against me — the denial of information.' (Winchester 1975:173-75)

Two years later, Robert Fisk of *The Times* refused to accept the army's interpretation of a confidential document which had come into his possession. Peter Boderick, the head of the army's PR team responded by sending a message to *The Times* describing Fisk as 'a hostile reporter'. To be frozen out by sources is embarrassing and inconvenient, but, in the last resort, the effectiveness of the technique is limited by journalists' willingness to share and exchange information among themselves. In Ulster the camaraderie among journalists tends to be fairly strong and the sharing of source accounts is commonplace. Moreover, the denial of information may merely serve to alienate the journalist and his paper and encourage hostile stories. The army have learnt, and the police are rapidly learning, that the carrot is generally more effective than the stick.

(b) *'Buttering-up'* This technique is essentially the converse of the 'freeze-out'. Its aim is to make a favourable impression on the journalist by affording him privileged or particularly hospitable treatment. It is still under-developed in Britain where journalists still invariably take the initiative in cultivating contacts within the control agencies through the process of wining and dining. But Mark's fresh press relations policy was evidence of a growing appreciation of the desirability of making a good impression on journalists. Newsmen with experience of reporting in Ulster, however, are far more familiar with the technique. *Observer* correspondent, Andrew Stephen tells us (Stephen 1976):

> '... the newspaperman newly arrived in Belfast finds himself courted from every quarter. As likely as not he will soon be whisked off to a genial alcholic lunch at the Officers' Mess in Lisburn; a Provisional IRA frontman will invite him home where his charming wife will produce hot buttered toast and coffee; and at the Ulster Defense Association headquarters in the Newtownards Road any visiting journalist is assured of ginger cake and a mug of strong tea.'

The testimony of other reporters also points to the army's increasing reliance on 'carrot' techniques. After a story suggesting that the army had been unnecessarily brutal in putting down a Protestant riot, Hoggart was invited to Lisburn for lunch and drinks and shown papers which suggested that the soldiers might have had some justification for their actions. 'I am sure the lunch and drinks had nothing to do with it, but if I am completely honest, I think the approach might have made me a little more cautious, when writing about the army' (Hoggart 1973). After another story critical of the army Hoggart expected hostility but instead,

> 'I was given an excellent exclusive story by an army major ... This is the smartest approach of all, for in spite of journalists'

reputations, any reporter would prefer a good story to a free drink. Drinks with informants, after all, come on expenses.'

(Hoggart 1973)

Army press officers are issued with a 'Manual of Public Relations' which advises them to establish rapport with journalists who '''should always be treated as guests of officer status''' and '''hospitality should be offered to them on suitable occasions''' (Stephen 1976).

The success of the technique is grounded in journalists' predisposition towards identifying with the control agency and is cemented by the development of affective bonds between the reporter and individual members of the control agency. The degree to which crime correspondents identify with the police has already been noted, but a good deal of empathy can also be found between journalists and the army in Ulster, especially in the case of those reporters with military experience. Simon Winchester has analyzed the reasons for the 'dreadful and inexplicable sense of loss and shock' he and other journalists experienced upon seeing the death of the first British soldier to be killed in the troubles (Winchester 1975:124):

'There was an indefinable feeing of being in a foreign country in Ireland, North or South — and, it must be admitted that there was some identification, some commonality between the ordinary British squaddie on the street and the ordinary British reporter ... who followed him around and wrote about him ... Often both would moan together about the ills of Ireland; often he would understand you and equally often you would understand and sympathise with him. Like us, he, the individual soldier was no real part of the trouble; like us he had been sent out from England to do a job.'

(Winchester 1975:124)

While the existence of this type of empathy does not mean that journalists will actively co-operate in the dissemination of army propaganda, it does contribute towards a predisposition among many reporters to accept army statements at their face value.

But however efficient the buttering-up process, the odd renegade or maverick reporter is still likely to remain to produce stories which might be detrimental to the control agency's interests. In these cases more severe methods may be employed to ensure compliance.

(c) *Harassment and repression* In occasional circumstances control agencies may threaten or employ legal sanctions or other techniques of intimidation designed to win a reporter's conformity to their expectations of the responsible journalist, and perhaps to deter other deviants. Robert Fisk has revealed that the army in Ulster has built up extensive (although not always accurate) files on British and Irish journalists in the province, sometimes by means of tapped telephones (*The Times* 25.3.75). Although I have no firm evidence, it would be surprising if there were not similar dossiers on London journalists at Scotland Yard. Certainly, there have been a number of cases in recent years in which journalists associated with stories the police would rather had been left unpublished have been harassed.

In May 1974 David May of *Time Out* bought a French temporary residence permit belonging to a kidnapped Spanish banker together with photographs of the banker in captivity. He then resold the photographs to the *Sunday Mirror*. When May was questioned by the police he refused to identify his contact and was charged with dishonestly handling the permit, a charge on which he was later acquitted. The prosecution, however, was the culmination of a series of frictional episodes between May, *Time Out*, and the police. May had been involved with the defense during the second 'Angry Brigade' trial, he had interviewed the escaped bank robber and 'British agent', Kenneth Littlejohn, while he was on the run and his magazine had published restricted material and adopted a generally critical attitude towards the police. The proprietor of a Fleet Street news agency, John Rodgers, who acted as a 'middle man' between May and the *Sunday Mirror* in the photographs deal, was cautioned twice concerning his possession of photographs which the police claimed had been stolen from their files, and his files of criminal 'mug shots' were confiscated. The action was apparently effective. As Rodgers put it:

'They effectively put you out of business, at least for a while. Your contacts are afraid to talk to you in case the police are watching and you think twice before handling a story which might land you in a lengthy legal battle.' (*Time Out* 19.9.75)

The case of freelance crime reporter, Thomas Bryant, provides another example of the use of 'dishonest handling' charges against journalists whose work has angered the police. In 1975 Bryant had no less than 47 charges — including dishonestly handling the *Police Gazette* and confidential police information and photographs and inducing a police officer to commit a breach of discipline — dismissed at committal hearings. He claimed afterwards that there had been a Yard vendetta against him for years because he had 'never been afraid to write stories which have often upset the police' (*Guardian* 2.8.75).

Harassment is a feature of police dealings with members of the fringe or radical press, but similar allegations are also occasionally made by journalists working for 'respectable' Fleet Street papers. *Guardian* reporters, for instance, have told me that they have always felt that their paper was unpopular with the police who have regarded it as a little too libertarian. Its journalists have rarely forged close ties with police contacts. Relations with the police became increasingly strained in 1971 when the paper began to interest itself in the civil liberties issues raised by the investigation into the Angry Brigade. During the Stoke Newington 8 trial, a female journalist from the paper's staff who tried to utilize the defense organization as a source experienced harassment from some police officers and was insulted by one reference to her as 'a little shit'. I am told that the Winchester bomb trial and the George Ince trials also produced frictional episodes and that one reporter who went to interview a senior officer in the Bomb Squad found himself being vigorously questioned about his Irish contacts.

But perhaps the most notable case of harassment by police of a Fleet Street journalist is that of *Sunday People* reporter, Trevor Aspinall. Aspinall was arrested near Dunstable in April 1974 during the course of an investigation into arms traffic in the Luton area. He was charged with conspiracy to obtain firearms and inciting others to sell firearms without a certificate. The conspiracy charge was eventually dropped and Aspinall was acquitted of the incitement charge in November 1974. Like the prosecution of David May, the episode was the culmination of a history of poor relations between the police and the paper, in this case centering on the *Sunday People's* exposés of police deviance. A few years before, the same reporter had been involved in a similar episode. While his paper was running an exposé of police deviance he had been involved in another investigation into arms smuggling — the illegal importation of firearms disguised as fountain pens. Aspinall had obtained one of the guns and had surrendered it to the police on the day before publication. Soon after his article and the exposé appeared two policemen had walked into his office and threatened prosecution for illegal possession of a firearm.

Buttering-up, freezing-out, and direct repression, then, may all be used by control agencies in seeking journalistic compliance with their wishes, but each of these techniques is controlling the *journalist* rather than the information he receives. When it comes to the second goal of news management, the direct facilitation of particular control projects the control of information becomes paramount.

Goal II: The direct facilitation of projects

The aim here is either to prevent the publication of information which might damage the progress of a control project or to use the news media to communicate selected information to the subject of a project. We can characterize these two aims and the techniques appropriate to them as, respectively, passive and active.

Techniques: passive

(a) *Secrecy* This is simply the withholding of information from the news media at the discretion of senior officers of the control agency. The release of almost all information from control agencies is the result of an operational decision about its possible effects on the success of ongoing control projects. Secrecy is the filter which holds back certain information and prevents it reaching waiting newsmen. It is, of course, a constant irritation to journalists who are rarely sure of what is being kept from them, but it only occasionally provokes much more than a mumble of discontent. One of these exceptional occasions came in 1973 when the Chief Constable of Thames Valley Police decided to withhold information about burglaries from the news media on the grounds that publicity might encourage further crimes. The news blackout provoked a wave of protest from both the local press and the NUJ. The success of the secrecy technique, however, is endangered by the existence of alternative sources of news or the willingness of some members of the control agency to leak information to favoured reporters. This can lead to embarassing disclosures as it did, for instance, during the investigation into the kidnapping of Mrs Muriel McKay early in 1970 (Deeley and Walker 1971), but ruptures in the fabric of secrecy can be hastily sealed by the use of 'denials' such as those issued by the army until 1976 concerning Special Air Service activities in Ireland. If information leaks out and denials are likely to be ineffective alternative techniques may be employed.

(b) *Suppression* Control agencies may exert pressure on editors permanently to drop a story which might be detrimental to their interests. Evidence, here, is thin but sufficient to suggest that suppresssion does command a place in the repertoire of news management techniques, although the degree of self-censorship exercised by 'responsible' newspapers makes the need to suppress stories rare. Two examples of apparent suppression can be cited.

In October 1973 *Red Weekly* reported that a detailed exposé of widespread illegal phone-tapping by the army in Northern Ireland had been dropped by *The Times* after pressure had been applied by senior members of the government. A *Times* reporter had apparently spent three months researching the story.

In March 1974 *Time Out* reported that senior members of the Bomb Squad had managed to prevent the publication in several papers (including the *Daily Express*) of articles critical of their early attempts to discover IRA bombers in England.

If these reports are accurate, they are likely to refer to fairly isolated cases in which the frustration or annoyance, experienced by particularly newspapers as a result of control agency activity or inactivity, was in danger of overcoming their usually 'responsible' news policies. More often, conflict between newspapers and control agencies arises from requests to hold back information.

(c) *'Stops'* This is a form of temporary suppression which involves the control agency taking the news media into its confidence and asking them to postpone the publication of certain information which might prejudice the progress of a control project. 'Stops' may be applied at the level of the specialist correspondent or the news executive. At the executive level they are generally communicated through informal briefings of editors by senior members of the control agency but some requests from the Metropolitan Police Commissioner are issued more formally as confidential memoranda delivered through the Press Association or even by hand.

In October 1973 the *Mirror* and *Telegraph* provoked a confidential memorandum by printing the address at which suspected IRA bombers McMorrow and Coyle were known to have stayed. The Yard suggested that it might be thought that the landlord had tipped off the police and his life might be endangered.

Another memorandum was issued in January 1974 when the *Observer* printed the code word used by IRA bombers. There are many other examples, but perhaps the most striking instance of voluntary and temporary suppression by news media is the 1975 kidnapping case involving Alio Kaloghirou in which a news blackout was maintained for ten days until the girl was returned to her family. Each day for a week 20 selected reporters attended a special Yard briefing on the case. They had mixed feelings about the blackout, some feeling that it was their duty to report the news and that publicity might help the hunt for the kidnappers, but all kept silent. In return, the police promised them 'everything' about the case when the girl was safe and they assumed that this meant an interview with the girl. There were even discussions about how long after her return this would be possible, but friction arose at the end of the case when police stopped all interviews despite Alio's willingness to give one. Eventually a compromise was reached by which she was recalled to Scotland Yard for a carefully controlled and monitored interview, but the episode did nothing to dispel journalists' suspicion of the police and encourage further co-operation.

The case is also remarkable for the light it sheds on newspaper executives' responses to news management. In their editorials most newspapers were anxious that their silence in this case should not be taken as an indication that they would automatically co-operate with all future police requests to withhold information from the public. It should rather be seen as an untypical exception to the rule of openness and exposure. Any future requests would have to be treated on their own particualr merits. [4]

Sir Robert Mark was delighted with the behaviour of the press in the case:

'We would never have believed it possible to achieve the voluntary participation of the press in an achievement of that kind ... If I had made these requests to the press in the first week I became Commissioner, I do not think for one moment that any newspaper would have taken notice.'   (Mark 1975)

There are questions, however, which remain unanswered. What would have been the reaction of the press if the operation had been unsuccessful? At what point would the voluntary blackout have been lifted? Is there need for a formal and public code of practice governing press responses to police requests for co-operation? Moreover, it is a mistake to see the 'stop' applied in the Kaloghirou case as exceptional. The only exceptional aspect was the extent of press co-operation. Crime reporters are continually making decisions about the publication of information which might prejudice inquiries:

'It's a continual tussle if you're a crime reporter and getting information in a backdoor way not to harm an inquiry by printing information that's given to you ... You've got to be careful of coppers shooting their mouths off and getting you into trouble. But we go into it with our eyes open. We've got a sort of built-in computer which tells us what we can and can't use. It's an automatic reaction. We make mistakes, of course, but usually the computer gets it right.' (Crime Correspondent)

Techniques: active
(d) *'Smoke screens'* When control agencies wish to confuse the news media or placate criticism or direct public attention away from a control project, they may set up 'smoke screens' in the form of statements or leaked stories of dubious veracity.

We have already seen this technique in use in Simon Winchester's account of the Falls Curfew and the army statement concerning the number of bullets fired. But perhaps the most striking example is provided by the case of Margaret McKearny, the girl described by the police in a sensational and unprecedented press release as 'the most dangerous and active woman terrorist operating here' (quoted in press 5.9.75). A massive public appeal for information about her was launched by Forces all over the country and co-ordinated by the Bomb Squad. Her picture dominated the front pages. There was speculation at the time that the appeal itself may have been an attempt to take pressure off the Northern Ireland office which had been under increasing criticism over government security policy (*Guardian* 9.9.75) although the primary motivations are more likely to have been those suggested later in this chapter (see p.203). But the essential smoke screening took place when the police attempted to account for their possession of McKearny's photograph. A Yard press officer originally stated that the photograph had been taken in Southern Ireland by an 'information source', which many papers assumed to be a member of the Yard's C11, criminal intelligence unit, but this information was probably intended only as 'guidance' (non-communicable background information) for the Press Association representative who received it.Certainly, the suggestion that a 'police spy' was operating in the Republic angered the Irish

Government and embarrassed the Yard. Soon after the publication of the photograph the Yard issued a statement dismissing the suggestion that a man from C11 was operating in the Republic as 'a complete fabrication' and claiming that the photograph had been discovered in Manchester during the search of a house.

(e) *Defamation* This is an essential component of a propaganda campaign, a 'dirty-tricks' technique designed to discredit control subjects and thus, often, to legitimate control projects and attract public support.

Defamation appears to have become a stock technique in the repertoire of the army in Northern Ireland. Eamon McCann (1971) has documented cases in which soldiers have shot Irish civilians who they have mistaken for terrorists, and shown that in these cases the army press office has invariably described the victims as petrol bombers or gunmen. After thirteen civilians were killed by the army on Bloody Sunday 1972, for instance, a senior officer is said to have informed the press that all thirteen were on the army's wanted list.[5]

This type of 'black propaganda' was also used to counter allegations of brutality against internees. On the day before the *Sunday Times* printed its exposé of the disorientation treatment suffered by an internee who had been recently released, the *Daily Express* ran a story, which could only have emanated from the army press office, that the *Sunday Times'* informant had, in fact, been beaten up by the IRA after his release. On the same day (23.10.71), the *Daily Mirror* ran another story planted by the army. It concerned the hiring of communist gunmen by the IRA. The story served to legitimate the shooting of a Polish-born man who turned out to be nothing more sinister than a free-lance photographer (*Private Eye* 5.11.71). The army continued to step up its defamation campaign until 1974 when some of the 'off-the-record intelligence briefing' began to become a little too fanciful for comfort. In particular, an army officer toured newspaper offices in Belfast suggesting that a prominent Protestant politician had been involved in the disappearance of

Thomas Niedermayer, the West German consul who was kidnapped from his Belfast home just after Christmas 1973 (*The Times* 25.3.73). Since this incident there has been a tightening of control by the Northern Ireland office over what press officers are allowed to say to journalists (Stephen 1976).

The most striking use of defamation by the police in Britain must surely be the co-operation between Special Branch and crime reporters in discrediting the London Vietnam War demonstration of October 1968. In their book 'Crime in Britain Today', two crime reporters associated with *The Times,* Clive Borrell and Brian Cashinella, reveal that before the demonstration Special Branch infiltrators had uncovered a plot to 'take over, on military lines, such institutions as the Bank of England, Lloyd's, the Stock Exchange, Ministry of Defence, major communication centres and even Scotland Yard itself' (Borrell and Cashinella 1975:19). Special Branch contacts leaked the information to Borrell and Cashinella who broke the story in *The Times* and saw it quickly taken up by the rest of Fleet Street. When *The Times*' story appeared, the Home Secretary, James Callaghan, called a secret meeting of newspaper editors and proprietors:

'At this gathering in the Home Office he privately voiced his fears that "something" would well happen on 28 October ... At the same time, Sir John Waldron called a meeting at Scotland Yard of senior Fleet Street editorial executives and spoke freely, but privately, of his fears ... It was essential, politically, that an "anti-demonstration feeling" should be fired in the public imagination. It was felt necessary that public opinion should be against the demonstration, with all its hidden threats, without alarming people generally that London was about to suffer like many other Continental Capitals.

The Special Branch then hatched up their own plot. They decided to "leak" their fears to the press and allow the situation to snowball. Public Antipathy would do the rest, they reasoned. Certain Fleet Street journalists, including ourselves were quite independently appraised of the situation through the "old boy" network. It was a story no one could refuse, coming from such an immaculate source ... and as article followed article, public reaction against the march quickly grew. It was a clear case of the media being manipulated by the Special Branch to serve their own ends. But in our view it was totally justifiable, because the consequences otherwise could have been devastating.' (Borrell and Cashinella 1975:20)

The response of Borrell and Cashinella to blatant news management by the police is one typical of many crime reporters. Once convinced that they are acting in the 'public interest' (which may be difficult for them to separate, operationally, from the police's interest) they will usually co-operate willingly in communicating stories that the police wish to see published:

'The police can use us with our knowledge. They can say, "Look, can you jolly this one along, stir things up a bit, get a bit of agitation going", and we can write along those lines without saying that the coppers said it. You'd be surprised, as well, the number of times it stirs up the old hornets' nest ... It's good fun — it's fun for us and it also does the job for the police.' (Crime Correspondent)

Ethical scruples may restrain the reporter from publishing information he knows to be untrue, but conflict with professional ethics is usually avoided by the ready acceptance of the veracity of police statements and the assertion of professional imperatives. In any case, crime reporting is a field in which it is extremely difficult to establish the 'truth' of a situation because of the restrictions placed by sources on the flow of information:

'You are not necessarily dealing with straight facts. A lot of it is speculation. You have to rely a lot on deduction ... You are not always given the information straight. Quite often you have to guess what the police are thinking.' (Crime Correspondent)

The paucity of alternative sources and the process of assimilation, then, supply ideal conditions for successful news management.

(f) *Deception* In using this technique, control agencies attempt to trick a control subject into error by issuing misleading information. Essentially, this involves utilizing news as a medium of private communication with either the conscious or unconscious help of journalists. This is the type of psychological warfare recommended by William Rees-Davies when he argued, for instance, that inflated figures of the amounts stolen in robberies should be advertised so that the thieves might fall out. The use of deception is well illustrated by the police search for the Black Panther, the Kidnapper of Lesley Whittle, early in 1975. Once detectives were satisfied that she had been kidnapped in the early hours of January 14th they confronted the double problem of returning Lesley safely to her family and trapping her kidnapper. But the achievement of these goals was severely jeopardized once the kidnapper became aware of police involvement. They decided on the devious strategy of trying to persuade the Panther that, although Lesley's brother, Ronald Whittle, had called in the police, he was still not co-operating fully with them. When interviewed, Booth and Ronald Whittle contrived to give the impression that they were operating with divergent priorities and strategies. By January 25th, having established that Ronald was ready to contact the kidnapper secretly and pay the ransom the officer in charge of the case, Chief Superintendent Robert Booth was publicly suggesting that important information was being kept from him: 'I believe that a member of that family has had some communication and has not seen fit, only in the interests of the child, to tell us'. The following day, Ronald Whittle was saying,

> 'The chances of getting Lesley back alive must be improved if the police are kept out of it ... It is not up to me to criticise them but there has been a conflict of priorities. They want to capture the kidnappers. I want Lesley back safely.'

Five weeks after the kidnap, Booth was directly imploring the kidnapper to 'dismiss from your mind that there is any collusion between the police and the family', but his words were apparently failing to reassure the Panther. A more elaborate hoax was instituted with the unwitting co-operation of the BBC. During an interview for a 'Midweek' feature of the case, Ronald Whittle 'let slip' information about an abortive rendezvous with the Panther at Kidsgrove two days after the kidnap. When questioned about this revelation Booth appeared totally taken by surprise and terminated the interview. But this ruse, designed to establish the fiction that Roanld Whittle was not co-operating fully with the police investigations, was immediately transparent to those journalists who consulted their cuttings of January 17th, some of which contained reports of what Booth called 'a cruel and wicked hoax' which had sent Ronald racing across country in an attempt to meet the kidnapper. But when two local papers had the audacity to imply that the 'Midweek' episode might be an elaborate charade, a furious Booth denounced them for 'irresponsible reporting'. However, this latest hiatus in police/press relations was quickly overtaken by events with the discovery of Lesley's body. Deception was now redundant and the police issued a statement about Ronald's visit to Kidsgrove: 'This visit was made with the full knowledge and under the operational control of the police. Any statements so made by Mr Whittle or the police were done in an attempt to instil confidence into the kidnapper.'

These hoax tactics are by no means unique to the Whittle case. In their book on the McKay kidnapping Deeley and Walker (1971) show how the police managed to convey an exaggerated impression of Mrs McKay's urgent need for special drugs in the hope that her captors would panic and attempt to buy the drugs from chemists alerted to just such a move. A similar ploy was probably used during the search for the kidnapped baby, Kristen Bullen, in 1973. Certainly, a baby who was apparently dependent on thrice-daily phenobarbitone injections managed to survive without any for over five days (much of which was spent in the open). During the 1974 investigations into the forging of Harold Wilson's signature by Ronald Milhench, news management was taken to extraordinary lengths by Chief Superintendent Alan Jones. A reporter on the case explained to me that he began by issuing journalists with sheets of prepared questions and answers which provided scripts for his news conferences, and then, as the investigation intensified, he called for the assistance of the press in misleading Milhench about the focus of police inquiries:

'There was a press conference three days before Milhench was pulled in at which we were told to write a story that the police were going to float round the North of England when they weren't at all. They were after Milhench and they wanted the heat off because they were advancing this story that he might shoot himself and his children ... Now that puts you in an extraordinarily difficult situation. You know you are writing a story which will make people think, ''Christ, this bloke's got no idea what's going on.'''

Here, unlike the Whittle case, the media were taken into the confidence of the police. Collusion is likely to achieve the more successful deception because the reporter will probably see the situation as one of co-operation rather than manipulation. Deception is closely related to another technique of psychological warefare: pressurization.

(g) *Pressurization* Rather than simply deceiving a control subject, agencies of social control may attempt to panic or intimidate him into error by leaking suitable information. This is a technique familiar to crime reporters:

'Often the police will issue information which makes a good story and say, ''Well, if you print this it may help us catch this guy''. Say if he's hiding and the police don't know where he is they may say, ''If you print this he may start running''. Usually it's a case of leaking information that the police are getting closer and that, say, an arrest is expected in the next 36 hours. Well, when he hears this the guy gets jumpy.'

(Crime Correspondent)

In his autobiography, Ex-Deputy Assistant Commissioner John du Rose describes how the media were used in the search for the killer of six London prostitutes in the mid-sixties. The investigators' aim was to harass the killer into making a blunder, and to this end, writes du Rose,

'I organised the release of a small but steady stream of hints that we were getting close to him. In this war of nerves important clues were leaked in day-to-day bulletins covering our activities in many areas. The original number of suspects was given at twenty but these were gradually scaled down until it was revealed that, of the three that remained, one was known to be the killer.' (du Rose 1973:120)

Du Rose claims that this pressurizing resulted in the killer's suicide. The same 'war of nerves' is evident in the police search for the Black Panther, especially after the discovery of Lesley's body on March 7th. After Booth's rather rash forecast on the following day that 'within 24 hours we will have him if it means pulling out every stop in creation', the Panther was steadily bombarded with hints that 'the net is closing around him'. By March 13th newspapers were reporting police speculations that the Panther's 'sick mind is fast deteriorating' and informing their readers that 'police now know almost everything about him — except his name' (*Daily Mail*). A few days later photographs of his handwriting were released and it was reported that the police 'are revealing step-by-step just how detailed a picture they have built up of ... the Black Panther' (*Guardian*). On March 21st we heard that the police had made 'the vital breakthrough', the discovery of a set of the Panther's fingerprints, and the new head of the investigation, Commander Morrison, was quoted as saying, 'The arrest may come today, or even in six months time, or even a year. But we will get this man.' Then, as media interest began to wane, the *Daily Express* revealed that 'even Britain's criminal underworld is joining the hunt ... Informers have been flooding a "hot line" with calls suggesting who the murderer might be' (22.3.75). But this type of pressurizing was fairly mild compared with an earlier report in the *News of the World* (16.2.75) which could perhaps best be classified as intimidation:

'CRACKSHOT TRAP FOR ENEMY No 1
A squad of police marksmen are standing by for a shootout with Public Enemy No 1, the ruthless killer who has kidnapped 17 year-old heiress Lesley Whittle. The detectives who are

closing in on Britain's most wanted man know their quarry will not hesitate to kill if he is cornered ... "We're geared for a shootout if it comes to that," I was told by a senior officer. "We have the men ready and they are top-class shots". The band of quiet professional men, who can shoot to kill or maim, sit in the police station at Dudley ... waiting for the call to arms. But they still hope that the cunning killer ... will see he is out-gunned and give himself up without a fight ... Police believe time is running out for the gunman ...'

Again, although an extreme form of 'psycho-warfare', the use of 'subtle' threats did not begin with the Black Panther case. A review of newspaper reports on the search for John McVicar, who escaped from Durham jail in 1960, and for the killer of the Unigate milkman, Frank Kidwell, in 1973 would reveal a similar pattern.

Before going on to examine the third goal of news management we can see how the techniques associated with the second goal can be operated in combination by selecting a few case studies.

Case study 1: the murder of Kenneth Lennon

On Easter Saturday, April 13 1974, the body of Kenneth Lennon was found in a ditch in Banstead, Surrey. He had been shot three times in the head and neck. It later transpired that Lennon had been a Special Branch informer and two days before his death had given an account of his recruitment and career to the National Council for Civil Liberties. He had been instrumental in the arrest of 'the Luton Three', a group of IRA sympathizers he had befriended and helped to stage an armed robbery. Both the case of the Luton Three and that of Lennon himself illuminate a number of police news management techniques.

1. On the day the Luton Three were arrested during their abortive and amateur attempt at a wages snatch, Special Branch sources leaked a story to the *Daily Mail* to the effect that they had foiled a plot to kidnap Brigadier Kitson, the army's counter-insurgency specialist. The Luton Three were described as a

'desperate "snatch squad"' whose members 'had studied Brigadier Kitson's own controversial book on guerrilla warfare, "Low Intensity Operations" as well as the kidnap operations of the Tupamaros' (*Daily Mail* 11.8.73). How and why this leak originated we can only speculate on, but, as Geoff Robertson in his analysis of the Lennon case points out, it must have been damaging to men who were tried only three months later (Robertson 1976:72-3).

2. At the end of the Luton Three's trial senior police officers held a press conference in the pub opposite the court. Here they suggested that the police had been tipped off about the Luton Three by a telephone call from a woman with a North country or Ulster accent who had warned of 'IRA action' in Luton on August 9. She named two of the three convicted and added that she was opposed to the operation because 'it might cause trouble for my man'. Smoke-screening was in operation. The informer in the Luton Three case was clearly being identified as the wife of the third defendant, Mrs Jeremiah Mealey, in order to protect Lennon. The *Daily Express* the following morning, left its readers in little doubt. It featured a photograph of Mrs Mealey and a quote from a senior police officer: '... we think it was one of the wives who turned them in'. As her husband argued at the Court of Appeal: 'In view of the fact that the police had at that time full knowledge of Lennon this would appear a deliberate and callous attempt to endanger my wife and cover the traces of a police agent' (Robertson 1976:80-1).

3. The discovery of Lennon's body was characterized first by secrecy and then by the tactical leaking of information. Two crime reporters I interviewed spent a whole day at the murder scene trying to locate a Yard DLO without success. Initial reports suggested that Lennon might have been the victim of a gangland feud but eventually reporters were able to deduce that it was being treated as a political killing from the presence of Special Branch officers. One reporter commented that it was:

'... one of the most difficult cases ever to get even the tiniest piece of information from anybody. That was where politics came into crime reporting. It was a clear attempt, in my mind, to suppress the true facts of the case. The most sensible thing to do would have been to take the press aside and explain the situation.' (Crime Correspondent)

Journalists, however, were soon reproducing a variety of police theories about the case. A death squad had been specially flown in from Ulster on a £250 Mafia-style contract to kill the informer who they had held and tortured for two days. The chief executioner was believed to have killed a dozen men in two years. By the time Lennon's NCCL statement was published it had been fairly well established in the press that Lennon had been the victim of an IRA execution by a group that was apparently known to the police.

4. After the publication of Lennon's statement the technique of defamation appears to have been used against the NCCL. *Daily Mail* reporters referred to the 'immediate reaction of senior officers that they were victims of a major plan by the IRA to discredit them by any means' (17.4.74), and reported that some officers 'believe Lennon was under IRA orders' when he made his statement 'designed to smear the Branch'. The *Daily Express* (18.4.74) quoted a Special Branch officer:

'Lennon's silliest move was to go to Civil Liberties. They are an organisation of known Left-Wing sympathisers and nothing would be easier than for the NCCL to get in touch with Sinn Fein. This need not be done officially, we are sure the IRA has its informants everywhere.'

The following day, the *Express* followed up the suggestion of IRA infiltration by focussing on NCCL's Northern Ireland expert, Catherine Scorer, whose office had been used to interview Lennon and who had typed his statement. The feature by John McCormick and Brian Cashinella began: 'An attractive redhead with IRA contacts denied last night that she put the finger on Kenneth Lennon' (19.4.74).

5. Soon after the publication of the NCCL statement, Home Secretary, Roy Jenkins, ordered an inquiry into the Lennon case

under the direction of Deputy Commissioner, James Starritt. The Starritt Report took only a week to complete but seven months to publish. Geoff Robertson has described the report as 'a Special Branch press release':

> 'It draws entirely upon police records and recollections, the accuracy of which is never questioned. No attempt is made to cross-check Lennon's statement with the civilians and organisations mentioned in it. Everything the police say is loyally accepted, no matter how improbable their story.'
>
> (Robertson 1976:160)

Even before completion the report's conclusions were leaked to favoured crime reporters who announced that Special Branch had been exonerated from blame[6]. The publication of the report, however, was delayed until just after the Birmingham pub bombings in November 1974 when, presumably, the climate of public opinion could be expected to be favourable to the report's findings.

Case study 2: The Angry Brigade

Some of the news management surrounding the Angry Brigade case has already been described in chapter 4: the way in which the first bombings were kept secret and the reaction of the police to the attack on Robert Carr, for instance. But the case also illustrates the use of other techniques. An examination of press reports at the time of the arrest at Amhurst Road of Barker, Creek, Greenfield and Mendleson is particularly illuminating. Certainly, the press were not taken into the confidence of the police who instead seem to have employed the smoke screen technique by putting out a story that threats had been made to blow up three London police stations, a story reproduced in *The Times* and the *Daily Mirror* the morning after the arrests (21.8.71). The story may, of course, have been a true one but it must certainly have served to account for bomb squad and general police activity the previous day. When details of that activity were released they were so inaccurate that it could only have been an exercise in deception and pressurization.

Inquiries by the radical press revealed that no more than three London houses were raided over that weekend but most newspaper reports suggested there had been 20 raids. Peter Harvey's account in the *Guardian* (23.8.71) indicates some of the content of the 'carefully-phrased, 87-word statement' issued by the Yard:

> 'Scotland Yard detectives hunting the Angry Brigade made dozens of raids throughout London and the Home Counties over the weekend. Last night the widespread operation, one of the biggest and most intensive for many years was continuing and investigations were also under way in a number of Provincial cities ... Planning for the weekend's raids began almost a week ago ... About 60 detectives ... were split into small teams. Each team was given a list of offices and homes ... Almost without exception, each raid proved successful ... etc.'

The information emanating from the Yard was almost certainly designed to panic members of the Angry Brigade still at large into contacting each other either by calling at houses under surveillance or by using tapped telephone lines.

Case study 3: The West End firebombings, August 1973

In the twelve months before August 1973 Scotland Yard received a number of warnings from Army Intelligence in Ulster that a major IRA bombing campaign in Britain was imminent. But when that campaign began, it was some time before IRA involvement was acknowledged.

The first incendiary attacks on West End stores began on August 18. The following day Republican journalist, Gery Lawless, received a statement from the Irish Republican Publicity Bureau claiming that the bombs were the responsibility of the Provisional IRA. Lawless rang Scotland Yard Press Bureau who first denied that there had been any fires in West End stores and then issued a statement saying that the incendiaries were the work of 'someone with a grudge against the firm' and that no political motive was suspected. A 'number of former employees of Harrod's' were apparently suspected and the *Evening News* even reported that some had been arrested.

When the bombings continued the Yard produced more theories. The *Daily Express* reported that an organization called the Irish Citizen Army might be responsible (22.8.73), the *Daily Mail* that the International Marxist Group were under close surveillance (23.8.73). The most widely reported theory was that the bombings had been carried out by an amateur IRA splinter group with the help of British anarchists, an idea which served to legitimate extensive raids on communes, squats, and the homes of political radicals. When no Irish bombers were discovered it was suggested that they must have fled after falling out 'with the Angry Brigade girls who had been sheltering them' (*News of the World* 30.9.73).

Goal III: The promotion of the aims, ideologies, and interests of members of the control agency

The aim here is to use the media for what may be broadly defined as 'political' purposes, particularly to influence policies which are beyond the immediate domain of the control agency.

Techniques

(a) The most basic technique is the simple and direct use of the media to promote and publicize views and policy objectives by the delivering of public speeches. The definitive example is the way in which Sir Robert Mark used the BBC Dimbleby Lecture in November 1973 to argue for changes in the administration of justice in the courts (Mark 1973).

(b) The media may also be used for propaganda purposes in less direct ways. The effectiveness of the second technique depends on the timing of public statements for maximum impact. We have already seen an example of this in the unsuccessful interview given to *The Times* by two senior officers during the leadership struggle at the Yard in 1971 (chapter 4). Another example of the timing of statements is the way in which some senior officers occasionally make damaging statements about prisoners when their parole may be imminent. At the time one prisoner (Walter Probyn) was applying for parole he was described by one of his arresting officers as a 'monster' and 'public enemy no 1' (*Sunday Mirror* 18.6.72). Other officers made similarly damaging comments at the time when some of the 'Great Train Robbers' were being released on parole (e.g., *News of the World* 6.4.75). As we might expect, Sir Robert Mark appears to have paid careful attention to the timing of his speeches. In an address to the Guernsey Chamber of Commerce in September 1974 he dismissed urban terrorism as a 'nuisance' which did not pose a fundamental threat to society, but added:

' "Of much greater impact on society as a whole is the modern tendancy for industrial disputes to be settled by strength rather than reason and the threat — or use — of force in expressing dissent at political demonstrations".' (Guardian 4.9.74)

Sir Robert's remarks coincided with the TUC Conference at Brighton and the second day of the inquiry into violence during a National Front march in Red Lion Square which resulted in the death of a Left-wing demonstrator.

In February 1976 Sir Robert made a major speech on his attempts to eradicate corruption in the Metropolitan Police to a group of Conservative Women at Caxton Hall, London. He told his audience that half of the 72 officers who had been tried by a jury in the previous four years had been acquitted although 'not more than a few of them could conceivably have been not guilty'. Two days after his comments were headlined in the press twelve serving and retired detectives, including two former Yard Commanders, were arrested on corruption charges. The early-morning arrests were accomplished in a welter of publicity. The arresting officers were accompanied by a battery of press photographers and a reporting team of six journalists from the *News of the World* who had been tipped-off beforehand. If Sir Robert was looking for maximum exposure of his anti-corruption campaign he must have been well satisfied. Crime reporters must have been embarrassed, but one at least managed to retrieve something from the debacle by exclusively reporting the allegations of one of the arrested detectives that the whole affair had been 'staged for TV' (*Daily Mail* 1.3.76).

(c) The third technique involves the direct exploitation of the media for the purposes of control agency propaganda. Again the most striking example is the Margaret McKearney case. It seems a likely that the launching of the McKearney appeal was an act approved at ministerial level and calculated to put pressure on the Irish government. Certainly it must have been partly designed to disrupt IRA lines of communication, but more fundamentally, when it became clear that McKearney was living openly in Eire, it functioned as a means of pressurizing the Dáil to pass the bill designed to expedite extradition between Britain and Eire. The bill's progress had been held up for five months since its introduction in May 1975.

Journalists who rely on powerful organizations for day-to-day information, then, face severe and possibly insoluble problems. They are at the receiving end of a constant trickle or flow of propaganda — sometimes open — sometimes disguised — which cannot simply be ignored because it is vital to their professional life. In coping with this situation many journalists develop either a cynicism which distances them from the propaganda they are obliged to communicate or an affinity with members of the source organization which makes the propaganda acceptable. When the source organization is a control agency, however, the need to produce stories which are acceptable to the source organization is intensified by the severity of sanctions which may be used against the recalcitrant or deviant journalist. It has now become apparent that even the most well-established specialist correspondents are not immune from disruptive currents flowing between control agencies and the press. In May 1976 the chief crime reporter of the London *Evening Standard,* John Ponder, was acquitted of charges of dishonestly handling three police photographs and inducing a member of the Metropolitan Police Force to commit a breach of discipline. Ponder's case was directly related to that of Thomas Bryant, the freelance journalist acquitted of similar charges nine months earlier. Ponder was alleged to have obtained photographs of three men charged with the murder of 'Ginger' Marks from a police officer whom he refused to name. He was then alleged to have given the photographs to Bryant because he felt sorry for him. Bryant, at the time was apparently penniless and recovering from illness. In court, Ponder's counsel had argued that the jury should not convict his client on the evidence of senior police officers who condemned the giving of information to the press, referring to one senior police witness who had not sought to hide his dislike of the press and his desire to make an example of John Ponder — possibly for the misdeeds of a police officer. After the case Ponder issued a statement in which he claimed that he had been a victim of changing police polices towards the press: 'I believe I was a scapegoat and that I was used to stop the long accepted system of individual police offices and journalists sharing a confidential relationship' ('Inside the Press' 26.1.75). He added:

> ' "The truth is that the police are trying to stop any exchange of information between individual policemen and journalists except through official channels; a move towards a flow of controlled information only from the police to the press, and in my view a move towards what I find abhorrent — a police state".'[7]

Ponder's was an emotional reaction to 16 months in fear of going to jail and, as such, might be considered alarmist; but his general assessment of the situation is probably an accurate one. Early in 1975, when the new press relations policy had been established, Sir Robert Mark was reported to desire an end to what he saw as the 'improper relationship' between many older detectives and some crime reporters, and to substitute a system more open to centralized control. This type of system minimizes the possibility of unwanted leaks and ensures compliance with news blackouts. A policy of tighter control over information is one which will inevitably find support among right-wing politicians and, indeed, is already being advocated as an emergency measure to deal with the crisis posed by urban terrorism. During the police siege of four IRA men and their hostages at Balcomb Street in December 1975, for instance, the Conservative MP for Brent North, Dr Rhodes

Boyson, called for a complete news blackout which, he argued, would enable the police to do their job 'without having to talk to TV and newspaper reporters'. He suggested that there had been similar measures in wartime, that the country was now fighting a war against the urban guerillas and that 'we should be able to rely on the public spirit of journalists and TV people to stay away until the police say all is well again'. Each time such a news blackout is used, however, and each time journalists exercise their discretion in 'staying away', the non-reportage of significant events becomes more familiar to the news media and familiarity breeds acceptance.

7 Conclusion

'In what manner opinion ... prevails over strength, or how power, which naturally belongs to superior force, is maintained in opposition to it; in other words, by what motives the many are induced to submit to the few, becomes an inquiry which lies at the root of almost every political speculation ...'

Archdeacon William Paley (1785)
Principles of Moral and Political Philosophy. Book VI Chapter 2.

'The first freedom of the press consists in its not being a trade.'
Karl Marx: *Rheinische Zeitung* 19.5.1842

In one of his essays, G.K. Chesterton said of popular journalism, 'it is popular mainly as fiction. Life is one world, and life seen in the newspapers another.' This study has sought an understanding of how part of that world of life-in-the-newspapers is fashioned and sustained, how journalists and their sources combine to create and recreate it daily. Chesterton is correct in saying that it is 'another' world, but we would be wrong to divorce it entirely from the world of 'life' and to dismiss it simply as 'fiction'. Newspaper fiction is not the antithesis of factual reality, it is a distortion of that reality, pulled and puckered out of shape by the interests and the everyday practices of newsmen and their informants. As a distortion of reality it is far more persuasive than mere fiction. Even, for the sceptic, with his commonsense caveats about not believing everything one reads in the newspapers it may still pass as an approximation to truth. His problem, and ours, is to know which parts of the approximation are inaccurate, to know in what ways our windows on the world are subject to flaws and imperfections and tricks of the light. Without this knowledge the worlds of life and life-in-the-newspapers begin to dissolve together. As Jock Young in his study of drug taking has shown, the impact of newspaper stereotypes and approximations on the real world has the effect of translating fantasy into reality — media representations create preconceptions and new situations are negotiated by their participants to fit them (Young 1971). What the previous chapters of this study have argued is that newspapers do not necessarily distort reality in random ways. They rather transform the world of life in a systematic fashion. It is a process which exhibits patterned regularities governed by a consistent set of interests, practices, and professional relationships. Any analysis which seeks to understand the process by which media representations are created must treat that set of interests, practices, and relationships as an integreated whole; and, as I indicated in chapter 1, this is precisely what the major research tradition of the social sciences has generally failed to do. It is only when we have completed such an analysis that we can begin to discover the wider political meaning of media representations, to explore linkages, for instance, between media institutions and the repressive agencies of the state, to draw out the implications of life-in-the-newspapers for life-in-the-real-world.

If we feel let down by the analyses of the social science tradition of theory and research we might feel tempted to turn to an alternative tradition. In particular, we might well expect that the literature of marxism would offer us a more substantial basis for the development of a coherent and integrated sociology of mass communications. On examination, however, we would find that it also suffers from a serious deficiency. Marxist analyses of mass communications tend to be bedevilled by a limited problematic in much the same way as social science analyses. We might say that the difference is that social science research often fails to see the wood for the trees while marxist approaches rarely give one the impression that the wood is composed of trees at all. The marxist perspectives provide a valuable counter to the type of *laissez-faire* model of mass communications (Young 1974) which we discussed in chapter 1, in that they successfully identify the overall political role of the media in the continuing hegemony of a capitalist class and assert the overriding importance of the media's structure of ownership and control in that process; but they generally fail to go beyond this insight. They fail to relate a political economy of mass communications to a *sociology* of mass *communicators*. For the most part, writers in the marxist tradition simply assert the crucial role of ownership and control in determining the production of a uni-dimensional representation of reality in the media and ensuring that it is a representation steeped in the legitimating ideology of the dominant economic class. They seem to settle for a crude determinism relating ownership and control to the maintenance of class relations thus:

only see rising class capitalism

| Control of mass media by capitalist interests | → | Production of dominant ideology | → | Mystification, false consciousness and the reproduction of class relations |

Marxist Model.

If we examine the immediately-relevant components of a marxist sociology of knowledge and mass communications we will be able to see that the question of the mechanisms by which political, social and economic interests come to be reflected in media representations of reality is rarely confronted. The relevant components have their roots in a passage from *The German Ideology* (Marx and Engels 1846:35):

work in favour prise, ruling idea

'The ideas of the ruling class are, in every epoch, the ruling ideas: i.e. the class which is the dominant *material* force in society is at the same time its dominant *intellectual* force. The class which has the means of material production at its disposal, has control at the same time over the means of mental production, so that in consequence the ideas of those who lack the means of mental production are, in general, subject to it ... The individuals composing the ruling class possess, among other things, consciousness, and therefore think. In so far, therefore, as they rule as a class and determine the whole extent of an epoch, it is self-evident that they do this in their whole range and thus, among other things, rule also as thinkers, as producers of ideas, and regulate the production and distribution of the ideas of their age.'   (Marx and Engels 1846:35)

The ruling class, then, is able to propagate its ideas by virtue of its control over 'the means of mental production'. It is, in turn, its dominant *material* position which enables it to gain and maintain control over these means of mental production which, as

Althusser and Gramsci were later to argue, are realized in various (ideological) apparatuses of the state — from schools and churches to the arts and the mass media — which are both the stake and the site of class struggle. The class which controls these apparatuses by virtue of its economic power is able to support its own professional ideologists 'who make it their chief source of livelihood to develop and perfect the illusions of the class about itself' (Marx and Engels 1846:36). The passage tells us little about the orientations and motivations of professional ideologists, themselves, but the term 'illusions' suggests that the ruling class does not cynically manipulate dominant ideology for the purposes of expediency. That is, it is not consciously used as a means of duping and persuading members of other classes into subserviency. This is a point so often missed by vulgar marxist interpretations of class dominance, but which is well brought out by Althusser when he argues that ideologies do *not* owe their existence to

> '... a small number of cynical men who base their domination and exploitation of the "people" on a falsified representation of the world which they have imagined in order to enslave other minds by dominating their imaginations.'   (Althusser 1971)

On the contrary, ideologies are born 'from the social classes at grips in the class struggle, from their conditions of existence, their practices, their experience of the struggle etc.' For Marx, both proletariat *and* bourgeoisie are subject to the power of ideologies and accept them as true because of their ongoing experiences of social life[1]. However, ideologies are not merely a product of experience, they are fundamentally a reflection of *interests*. Ideologies are world views grounded in the interests of particular social groups. The transformation of a sectional ideology into a dominant ideology involves, according to Marx and Engels (1846:36), the successful portrayal of particular sectional interests as general societal interests:

> 'For each new class which puts itself in the place of the one ruling before it, is compelled, simply in order to achieve its

aims, to represent its interest as the common interest of all members of society, i.e. employing an ideal formula, to give its ideas the form of universality and to represent them as the only rational and universally valid ones.' [2] *[handwritten: So ltz nake best way to do things]*

The phrase, 'in order to achieve its aims', appears to introduce an element of intentionality, of conscious action in pursuit of the goal of hegemony. We have then in this passage from *The German Ideology* the beginnings of a thread of ambiguity which runs right through marxist writings on domination to the present day. It is an ambiguity which is sustained by a consistent failure to analyze closely the process of knowledge production at a mundane level. This failure is particularly evident in the marxist perspective on the mass media which, in its repeated emphasis on structure and political effects, neglects the mundane, 'commonsense' construction of everyday reality by professional communicators. As Graham Murdock and Peter Golding (1974:207) have argued: 'It is not sufficient simply to assert that the mass media are part of the ideological apparatus of the state, it is also necessary to demonstrate how ideology is produced in concrete practice.' Marxist analysis only rarely operates at this level of concrete practice. It tends to ignore the kinds of routine operations, tacit assumptions, conceptual frameworks, and occupational constraints which systematically shape the everyday production of knowledge.

Marx, although himself a journalist with the *New York Tribune* for a time, wrote little specifically about the news media. At the time he was writing, the mass-circulation newspaper carrying a dominant ideology to the people was still a thing of the future, and the papers of his day were either large-circulation radical publications subject to continual state repression or small-circulation papers written exclusively for the wealthy ruling class about itself, and no doubt perfecting its illusions and myths about itself. Certainly, Marx appears to have been contemptuous of much of the reporting of his day. Atrocity stories in the British press during the Paris commune provoked the following comment in a letter of 18/1: 'The daily press and the telegraph, which in a *marx did not write about mass media* (handwritten)

moment spread inventions over the whole earth, fabricate more myths ... in one day than could have formally been done in a century.' He regarded his own association with the myth-fabricators as little more than intellectual prostitution. In a letter to Engels, he wrote of the *New York Tribune*: 'It is really loathsome to have to think oneself lucky that a filthy rag like that takes one on ... [but] for all the talk about independence one is tied to the newspaper and its public, especially if one gets paid in cash as I do.' Evidence here, surely, of an ambivalence towards the role which is still characteristic of journalists today. But these fragments of correspondence do not constitute a theory of the media or, really, a framework on which to construct such a theory. Nor do Marx's intellectual successors appear to have been particularly interested in elaborating an analysis of the production and reception media representations. With the exception of the critical theory of the 'Frankfurt school' and its focus on mass culture[3], the analysis of the mass communication process has been abandoned to the essentially empiricist approach of academic social scientists. It is not surprising, then, that, as recently as 1970, Hans Magnus Enzenberger was able to write in New Left Review, 'So far there is no marxist theory of the media'.

The 'second generation' of marxist theorists who did so much to refine, develop, and apply Marx's insights contributed relatively little to our understanding of the relationship between dominant ideology and the agencies of its reproduction under capitalism. In *What is to be Done?* Lenin's discussion of newspapers is confined to the radical press, to recommending the most appropriate type of paper for the revolutionary party (Lenin 1970). Gramsci's essay on 'the intellectuals' (Howe and Nowell-Smith 1971) takes us some way towards understanding the social position of journalists. Gramsci distinguishes two groups who perform the function of intellectuals, the 'traditional' professional intellectuals, administrators, scholars, scientists, theorists etc. who have their origins in an earlier historical moment, and the 'organic' intellectuals who accompany an emergent class formation, becoming functionaries in the bureaucracies of its superstructure and contributing towards its hegemony. He further distinguishes between two superstructural levels — 'civil society' and 'political society' — which correspond to two different modes of class domination, the engineering of spontaneous consent and the exercise of coercive power against deviants. For Gramsci, then, the intellectuals are "'the dominant group's 'deputies' exercising the subaltern functions of social hegemony and political government'" (Howe and Nowell-Smith 1971:12). We may assume that journalists are one of those groups engaged in performing the function of social hegemony, but the unanswered question must be 'how come?'.

Recently, Althusser (1971), in his attempt to articulate and advance a marxist theory of the state, has developed Gramsci's formulations. In the same way, he distinguishes two means by which the ruling class maintains its dominance — the Repressive State Apparatus (government, administration, army, police, courts, prisons etc.) and the Ideological State Apparatuses (of which the communications apparatus is one)[4]. The difference between these two means of domination is relative rather than absolute. Every control apparatus contains elements of coercion and consent in varying proportions:

> 'All the State Apparatuses function both by repression and by ideology, with the difference that the [repressive] State Apparatus functions massively and predominantly by repression, whereas the Ideological State Apparatuses function massively and predominantly by ideology.'

This refers to both internal and external control over, on the one hand, the functionaries of an apparatus, and on the other hand, its clients, audience, victims, or whatever the appropriate term might be. The nature of repressive control within the communications apparatus is not spelt out; we might speculate that it takes the form of censorship, or extensive sub-editing, or even blocked promotion, all aimed at fostering a uniformity of view. As far as the audience is concerned, Althusser does tell us that the communications ISA functions by 'cramming every "citizen" with daily doses of nationalism, chauvinism, liberalism, moralism etc'. But he really tells us very little about how those daily doses of 'isms' are concocted by the media's functionaries. The only insight we are given into the world of the functionary is when Althusser refers to the operators of the educational ISA (which he considers the most important of the ISAs), the teachers. In fact, he pauses to consider if his discussion of the ideological function of the school may have given offence to 'radical' teachers:

'I ask the pardon of those teachers who, in dreadful conditions, attempt to turn the few weapons they can find in the history and learning they "teach" against the ideology, the system, and the practices in which they are trapped. They are a kind of hero. But they are rare and how many (the majority) do not even begin to suspect the "work" the system (which is bigger than they are and crushes them) forces them to do, or worse, put all their heart and ingenuity into performing it with the most advanced awareness (the famous new methods!).'

We have, here, I suppose, the makings of a typology (albeit a fairly simplistic typology) of the people who operate the various apparatuses — the subversive resisters, the naive accomodators, and the willing collaborators. But, unfortunately, Althusser makes no attempt to develop it. In fact, throughout his essay, Althusser begs more questions than he poses or answers: what exactly are the motivations of the controllers of the ISAs?; how do they view their role?; what are the forms taken by the ideological struggle within the apparatuses to the dominant ideology?; how is their co-operation and conformity ensured?[5] Ralph Miliband's discussion of the mass media in *The State in Capitalist Society* is more sophisticated and takes us rather further along the road to understanding their political function. First, he qualifies the conceptualization of media output as an ideological monolith determined by ruling-class interest, but he argues that, despite its apparent diversity of opinions and perspectives, the output of media organizations is nevertheless a 'crucial element in the legitimation of capitalist society'. The media's freedom of expression

'... has to be set in the real economic and political context of these societies; and in that context the free expression of ideas

214 *Law-and-Order News*

and opinion *mainly* means the free expression of ideas and
opinions which are helpful to the prevailing system of power
and privilege ... they too are both the expression of a system
of domination and a means of reinforcing it.'

(Miliband 1973:197-98)

Whatever their differences of style and policy, the news media, for
instance, are united in a deep-seated commitment to the values
and institutions of the liberal-democratic consensus and a
'passionate hostility' to anything outside that consensus. They are
committed, in one way or another to an essentially conservative
ideology:

'At the core of the commitment lies a general acceptance of
prevailing modes of thought concerning the economic and
social order and a specific acceptance of the capitalist system,
even though sometimes qualified, as natural and desirable ...
[The] press may well claim to be "independent" and to fulfil
an important watchdog function. What the claim overlooks,
however, is the very large fact that it is the Left at which the
watchdogs generally bark with most ferocity and that what they
are above all protecting is the status quo.'

(Miliband 1973:198-200)

Miliband attributes this predominantly conservative stance
primarily to the fact that as large-scale capitalist business
enterprises have increased, media organizations have increasingly
'come under the ownership and control of a small and steadily
declining number of giant enterprises with combined interests in
different media and often also in other areas of capitalist
enterprise'. The ideological dispositions of the owners and
controllers inevitably reflect their economic interests and, in turn,
come to be reflected in editorial policies, either directly (as in the
case of the late Lord Beaverbrook who ran his newspapers
explicitly for propaganda purposes) or indirectly through the
informal socialization of communicators:

'Quite commonly, editors, journalists, producers, managers,
etc, are accorded a considerable degree of independence and

are even given a free hand. Even so, ideas do tend to "seep downwards", and provide an ideological and political framework which may well be broad but whose existence cannot be ignored by those who work for the commercial media. They may not be *required* to take care of the sacred cows that are to be found in the conservative stable. But it is at least *expected* that they will spare the conservative susceptibilities of the men whose employees they are, and that they will take a proper attitude to free enterprise, conflicts between capital and labour, trades unions, left-wing parties and movements, the Cold War, revolutionary movements, the role of the United States in the world, and much else besides. The existence of this framework does not require total conformity, general conformity will do. This assured, room will be found for a seasoning, sometimes even a generous seasoning, of dissent.'

(Miliband 1973:205-6)[6]

In the case of newspapers, this general conservative framework of interpretation is further reinforced by the influence of advertisers who largely finance the press. But we are still left with a number of problems concerning the framework — what exactly does the process of 'seeping downwards' entail?; how is the framework communicated and learnt?; how are communicators able to utilize its broad guidelines in specific interpretive situations?; how does it fit into the rest of their occupational ideology?; is it in conflict with other occupational imperatives such as 'objectivity' and 'detachment'?; does its use entail difficulties with important news sources?; how do communicators react to the framework — are they conscious of it and, if so, do they resent it? These are, of course, essentially specific empirical problems which are difficult to answer in a general analytical survey like Miliband's. However, he does at least show an awareness of them; particularly the last one concerning the reception of the ideological framework. He recognizes that the type of structural, mildly-deterministic explanation he offers

'... suggests that those who are actually responsible for the contents of the mass media ... are the unwilling tools of conservative and commercial forces, that they are suppressed rebels, cowed radicals and left-wingers, reluctant producers and disseminators of ideas and opinions which they detest, angry dissenters straining at the capitalist leash. This is not a realistic picture. There *are*, of course, a good many such people working in and for the mass media, who suffer various degrees of political frustration ... But there is little to suggest that they constitute more than a minority of the "cultural workmen" employed by the mass media. The cultural and political hegemony of the dominant classes could not be so pronounced if this was not the case.'   (Miliband 1973:210)

Miliband, in fact, offers us a typology of media personnel which is very similar to that implicit in Althusser's essay. There are the 'cultural workmen' of the Left, the cultural workmen of the Right, and a third group (who probably constitute the majority) 'whose political commitments are fairly blurred, and who wish to avoid "trouble" '.

All this is certainly a step in the right direction, but it is still well short of a fully-developed sociology of the news media. We are given the flavour of the mix of interpersonal and economic constraints which shape media representations, we receive the impression that representations are the product of conscious decisions made by thinking actors within a framework of imposed limitations. This is surely an improvement on the vague generalizations and obscure determinism of Althusser's analysis, but it remains an analytical sketch lacking in empirical colour, a skeleton without flesh on the bone, however skilful the sketch or sturdy the skeleton.

Perhaps the most sophisticated and comprehensive marxist analysis of one aspect of the news media is provided by Paul Hoch, an American academic, in his book *The Newspaper Game* (1974), which, despite its polemical style, genuinely begins to get to grips with the phenomenon of news.

Hoch identifies the newspaper as primarily a profit-oriented *business*, the offspring of monopoly capitalism.

'Once one sees a newspaper as a business, oriented to serving the advertising and other brainwashing needs of the rest of capitalist business, the door to understanding is open. It then becomes a matter of tracing the consequences of this right down the line ... news becomes a commodity to be slickly handled and brightly packaged ... advertisers must be deftly wooed (and not offended) ... and business considerations, both of the newspaper owners and their partners in capitalism generally, dictate the politics at every stage of the game.' (Hoch 1974:17)

The major newspaper corporations of the West share common class interests with the rest of the industrial elite, and the press, together with the state apparatus, 'acts as a kind of secretariat for those common ruling class interests'. Hoch begins his analysis by outlining a theory of the development of the popular press which, he argues, was a consequence of the transition from 'competitive' to 'monopoly' capitalism during the last third of the nineteenth century. The existence of the cheap mass newspaper was made possible by the development of the mass advertising characteristic of the monopoly stage of capitalism. During the earlier competitive stage, newspapers were dependent on revenue derived from circulation. This kept prices high and distribution restricted to a wealthy elite. However, comparatively little capital was required to set up a paper, which meant that small-circulation papers for 'radical' intellectuals were feasible:

'All this began to change with the gradual centralization of industry in mass-production monopolies. First of all, there was now an incredible mass of consumer goods to be disposed of. So there was a need to create a mass market. Mass advertising money would provide the power. Mass newspapers would be the vehicle. Mass production required mass consumption. Which required a mass advertising media. Which became the popular newspaper.' (Hoch 1974:15)

Hoch, then, in providing an historical dimension which is surprisingly lacking from most other marxist analyses of the media[7], focuses our attention on the importance of the popular press in the selling of commodities, in the stimulation of 'false needs' (Marcuse 1964) so vital to the survival of monopoly capitalism. But the mass newspaper is itself a commodity and thus also relies on the creation of false consumer needs. Hoch argues that the 'need' for the mass newspaper was stimulated by the very process of mass production it helps to sustain, as well as by the growing 'privatization' and break up of the working-class community which came with industrialization:

'With the coming of the mass advertising industry and its mass newspapers it became clearer and clearer that workers were producing, not only standardized mass-commodities, but that the profits of their labours were being poured into advertising to produce their own "needs" for these commodities as well. Robbed of any real creativity and decision-making power in production (which on the assembly line became an alienating, soul-destroying grind), workers could be encouraged after a fashion by their newspapers to look for creativity in consumption ... In earlier periods, such leisure as there was provided workers with a little time to do such creative things as they mightn't have time for in their jobs. But as the commodities piled up — including the new mass newspaper commodity — they began more and more to invade the sphere of leisure ... For most, leisure became more and more a time to sit back, doing more or less nothing, soaking up pre-packaged, mind-dulling "entertainment" ... Bored stiff and mentally abraded by their assembly line jobs or isolated in their home life, working class men and women could be induced to take in the trivilized, lowest common denominator sensationalism and bigotry of their popular newspaper. In a period in which capitalism's increased division of labour had destroyed all the old self-definitions and wrecked the old community, the new media offered everyone various subjects for discussion with their fellows, membership in the tribe of newspaper readers, the illusion of being part of "public opinion". Entertainment that didn't challenge the mind — and maybe even put it to sleep — but that at least take the mind off the constant

(atrocity of one's assembly line job. A bit of freshness. A bit of
/ bigotry. A bit of escape. The perfect opiate.' (Hoch 1974:15-17)

According to Hoch, then, the mass-circulation newspaper is a
commodity which creates the conditions for its reproduction by
selling other commodities. But the stimulation of false needs is, of
course, not its manifest purpose. It aims to supply news and
entertainment to the waiting public, and it is staffed by professional communicators who are committed to just this end. Thus
we have a potential contradiction which demands a resolution. For
Hoch, this resolution lies in the notion of news itself as a
commodity to be judged by the criteria of its consumers. The
editors become the barometer of its saleability for producers who
are in constant competition for scarce newspaper space: 'News
becomes a commodity to be judged by the standards of the
market. As dictated from the top down' (p.97). Journalists'
products are cast in a standardized form (like so much other mass-
merchandise), a form which reflects the prevailing 'top-down'
conceptions of what is newsworthy and what a 'responsible'
reporter should write about it. These conceptions gradually
become incorporated into the working reporter's frame of
reference and style of treatment in a largely unconscious fashion.
They become a taken-for-granted part of his professional
ideology. As such they are conveyed to the unsuspecting mass
consumer — ideology in the guise of news and entertainment, an
ideology which permeates the very language of the press:

'By the words they use, and the way these words are linked
together, capital's newspapers are presenting us with a certain
stereotyped view of reality. The top-down view of reality. And
the "facts", the "problems", the words that are used and the
way they are put together are not much more than ideological
props for the world view without which they would not be
"facts" "problems" or valid words.'   (Hoch 1974:38-9)

His polemic is persuasive, but we should beware of accepting all of
its arguments without qualification. First, his account of the
historical development of the popular press is, perhaps, a little

oversimplified, based as it is on a rather romanticized vision of life before monopoly capitalism, and on the assumption that assembly-line workers provided the audience for the new newspaper. We might point to the development of a mass schooling system as a precondition for the emergence of a mass newspaper; but this only qualifies Hoch's thesis, it does not nullify it. Similarly, the notion of news as a commodity should be treated with a certain amount of caution. Graham Murdock and Peter Golding also take the recognition that the mass media 'are first and foremost industrial and commercial organisations which produce and distribute commodities' as a starting point for their political economy of mass communications, but they point out that news is not necessarily perceived as a commodity by everyone involved in its production:

'The process of producing mass media output is a dual one. For the owners, investers and managers media products are commodities to be packaged, promoted and marketed in the same way as any other ... For many of the people who actually make them, however, media products are not simply commodities but media for creative expression. This balance between commodity production and creativity is a precarious one, however, and one which is ultimately framed and determined by the general economic context within which production takes place.'   (Murdock and Golding 1974a:223)

We have already seen (p.5-6) that Murdock and Golding argue that this general economic context defines the limits of creativity, the range of the autonomy of the communicator, and influences the organizational climate of cultural production. When combined with the routine, work-a-day nature of professional journalism, the endlessly-repeated procedures of 'newsgathering', concerns of profitability and financial shortages create a *tendency* among communicators to see news as a commodity. It remains essentially a tendency, however, rather than a permanent definition. Like most definitions of the situation, the definition of news as a commodity is probably evoked when it suits the particular practical purposes or mood of the definer, in this case the professional communicator. It will be one of a repertoire of definitions available to him which he will select to facilitate or justify a course of action, or state of mind, to himself or to others who might question him. As part of a repertoire, it is able to co-exist with apparently contradictory definitions of news — as a vital public service, a medium for creative expression, or whatever. The communicator, like any other actor, will juggle and substitute his definitions more-or-less as it suits him. Thus, one Sunday newspaper reporter I interviewed was able at one moment to impress upon me the validity of his paper's style and zeal in exposing the undesirable in society, as well as his own integrity and sense of professional responsibility in 'not writing stories I don't believe in'; yet at another moment in the same interview was able to produce this statement of purely instrumental commitment:

'I regard news as a commodity — it's there to buy, it's there to report, it's there to be processed, it's there to be packaged, it's there to be sold. That's to say, I'm in much the same position as the man who goes to work at Ford's at Dagenham — I do my work, how it's sold by the company is someone else's business. Do I like my paper? I don't think that's a fair question because I would say that if I go to work at Ford's do I have to buy a Cortina? ... I'm doing a job. Sometimes I may very well like what I'm producing, but I don't think the two things have to go together.'

These statements are not necessarily a reflection of a purely cynical commitment to his work, more likely, they are a genuine reflection of the essential ambiguity which surrounds both news and communicative work. News is, at once, a commodity, a creative enterprise, and a public service, but the appearance of its nature changes according to the perspective from which it is being viewed and its role in the current enterprise of the actor who is viewing it. The definition imposed on the phenomenon will generally be in accord with that enterprise. This applies as much to the consumer of news as to its producer. For the man who wishes to be entertained, news is predominantly entertainment.

For the man who wishes to be informed, news is predominantly information, but it may at the same time be entertainment. The process of defining, while largely utilitarian, is far from simple. Similarly, for the journalist involved in the everyday work of constructing the news from the raw material of source accounts (against the clock), it may be convenient to define the enterprise in terms of industrial commodity production because he knows his work will be open to criticism. He is probably not producing particularly penetrative or 'literary' journalism, but he may still be producing a subtly individualistic and painstaking piece of prose to which he has some kind of intellectual commitment. Thus, while he distances himself from his creation by defining it as a commodity, he may still take a pride in his mastery of the genre of popular journalism. He may argue that it is more intellectually taxing to produce a short account of an event using words of two syllables than it is to construct a longer account using longer words. Moreover, he realizes that he is providing the public with information which they could obtain in no other way.

News is different things at different times and many things at the same time. Its meaning as a cultural form, as well as the meaning of its substantive content, is ambiguous. As far as the defining and classifying procedures of the journalist are concerned, this ambiguity is echoed in his working conditions which are a peculiarly blended mixture of freedom and control. These, in turn, find their reflection in the journalists's general ambivalence towards his work. He may be able to exercise a good deal of autonomy in his choice of story or methods of investigation, but he is constrained by a set of audience expectations which circumscribe the form and content of his final product. The journalist is obliged to address himself to four distinct audiences:

    a. his editors
    b. his colleagues
    c. his sources
    d. the general readership.

Each of these imposes a significant constraint on the representations and accounts of reality he produces. It is not simply a matter
of pleasing the editors and operating within the conception of
'proper' reporting dictated from the top down. Many journalists,
as we have seen, are further obliged to maintain close and cordial
relationships with valuable news sources on whose goodwill they
rely in obtaining stories. Most journalists also value the good
opinions of their colleagues and feel a responsibility towards their
readers (or viewers) whose perceived interests they champion and
whose imagined sensibilities they do their best not to offend. But
the fact that their audience is so highly differentiated does not
necessarily imply that every journalist is faced with a set of
impossibly contradictory expectations — editors expecting him to
produce one type of story, sources another, readers another, and
so on. While it is true that a journalist cannot please *all* of the
people *all* of the time, he can, without too much difficulty, please
most of the people *most* of the time. The constraints which
operate on journalists' accounts are not generally contradictory.
They influence accounts in more or less the same direction,
circumscribing an area of common acceptability. Constraints
reinforce rather than nullify one another right the way through
the journalistic enterprise. The economic contexts within which
production takes place, the restricted time period within which
the newspaper must be reproduced, the conventional wisdoms of
professional journalism, the largely shared and complementary
expectations of editors, sources, colleagues, and readers all work
towards the creation of the same type of product, which, in turn,
recreates the conditions for its reproduction. Today's news is
processed according to the expectations moulded by yesterday's
news; a cycle of reproduction which Paul Rock (1973) has termed
'eternal recurrence' — the constant recreation and reinforcement
of the taken-for-granted frameworks of knowledge production.
The result is perhaps not so much a commodity with *all* the
connotations of alienation and reification which that term
generally carries in Marxist writing, but rather a species of what I
have already termed 'commercial knowledge' — a saleable
product designed with consumers in mind, yes, but still produced

by men who retain a certain kind of integrity, who generally 'believe' in their product and whose allegiances extend beyond their immediate paymasters.

Professional communicators are not simply puppets on strings pulled by capitalists. Nor do they necessarily feel oppressed by the power of the machine they serve. They are men and women who exercise choice and construct their own realities within the constraining parameters set by their ideal and material interests and their professional stock of knowledge. Generally speaking, these constraining parameters are rarely experienced as oppressive, and few are anxious to transcend them to any significant degree. They are usually tacitly-accepted 'facts of life' which impose an element of order on what might otherwise appear a confusing and chaotic world. Their acceptance serves to absolve the communicator from the necessity of continually reflecting upon, and theorizing about, the nature of his occupation and the society in which he works; it enables him to get on with the job of 'reporting the news'. While retaining a certain detachment and distance from his materials and the accounts he constructs from them, the communicator generally finds acceptable the interpretations of reality they reflect. He will confess that perhaps his accounts are oversimplified, that considerations of source relationships and editorial policy may colour his selections and interpretations, but he will usually maintain that they remain essentially faithful to reality. Simplification is made necessary by lack of space and considerations of intelligability. Sources deserve the sympathetic treatment they receive. Editorial policies should be respected to some extent. As Richard Hoggart (1973:214) has put it: 'most popular journalists are not, with cynical and detached intent, peddling a certain view of the world; this is their world.' Of course, cynicism and detachment are never totally absent and, at times, when occupational contradictions come to the fore, cynicism and detachment may prove valuable in handling them, providing an emotional and intellectual buffer between the self and the pressure of external constraints.

We cannot hope to understand how 'life-in-the-newspapers' is reproduced until we have explored the relationships within that complex of factors which shape the day-to-day practice of the journalist. Even allowing the overall importance of economic factors we cannot legitimately reduce the explanation of newspaper representations to a single causal factor. This should be clear from the discussion of crime reporting. Police sources exert a more immediate influence on crime reporters' accounts than do newspaper proprietors or even, perhaps, the economic conditions of newspaper production. But while crime reporting is in some ways an unusual specialism it is by no means unique. Tunstall (1971a) has argued that specialists such as crime and football reporters, whose work is most directly related to a goal of attracting audience revenue, tend to be controlled to a considerable extent by news sources. This differentiates them from specialists such as industrial, political, and foreign correspondents whose work is not so directly connected to sales revenue. Any difference that may exist, however, is only one of degree. In all fields of specialist journalism close links are forged between correspondents and powerful sources, whether it be with senior policemen or with members of the CBI, leaders of large unions, ministers, or senior civil servants. The same mechanisms of exchange, dependence, assimilation, and manipulation are to be found even in fields of specialization with 'non-revenue goals'[8]. Crime reporters are atypical in that they are at the mercy of a single institutional source, which means that they are less often able to play one source off against another than many other specialists. Tunstall suggests that crime correspondents are particularly subject to role strain, caught between conflicting expectations of sources and editors. The findings presented in this study, however, indicate that, in practice, this role strain is not as acute as Tunstall's work would lead us to believe. It is generally effectively prevented by the correspondence between newspaper ideology and that promoted by control agencies or it is managed by the mechanism of assimilation.

The choice of crime news, I feel, has been an appropriate one for this analysis both because it is politically significant in itself as a medium through which deviance and opposition within British society is publicly reported and interpreted; and also because it is illustrative of the more general processes by which representations of reality are constructed by the news media. The understanding of the everyday practices and relationships of crime reporters and the pieced-together accounts they, and their fellow journalists, produce is an essential step in grasping how a dominant meaning system is maintained in our society in the face of explicit or implicit challenge. The news media are our central repositories and disseminators of knowledge and, as such, exert a considerable influence over our perceptions of groups and life-styles of which we have little first-hand experience. They have the power to create issues and define the boundaries of debates and, while they may not manipulate our opinions in any direct sense — creating attitudes by changing old ones — they can organize opinion and develop world views by providing structures of understandings into which isolated and unarticulated attitudes and beliefs may be fitted. They provide interpretations, symbols of identification, collective values and myths which are able to transcend the cultural boundaries within a society like Britain. Simultaneously, the news media are able to address factory workers in Wigan and solicitors in Surbiton and can realistically expect to be understood and, in situations which are experienced as unfamiliar and where no contradictory pre-conceptions exist, they can expect to be accepted by both (Halloran 1963, 1970; Hall 1974; Young 1974; Murdock 1973; Muller 1974). This potential power to define reality makes it extremely important that we subject media representations to close, systematic, and critical analysis, and that we understand the interests and considerations which influence their production. This study has been a contribution towards this goal and it is hoped that it may stimulate more researchers to its pursuit.

Chronology of Law-and-Order
News 1945-1975

A Note on the Chronology

Events in the chronology are grouped into five broad and overlapping categories:

Crime: Murders, robberies, arrests, trials etc. without any explicitly political content.

Political deviance: Murders, robberies, bombings, direct action, trials etc. with an explicitly political content; industrial disputes with political overtones.

Youth: Juvenile delinquency and youth cults.

Police: Police activities and organization, especially corruption and changes of policy.

Other events: Chronological landmarks such as General Elections; legislation; events with special relevance to newspapers.

The list of events presented is far from exhaustive and readers are invited to rectify ommissions — the author would be pleased to hear from anyone able to make important additions to the list. It is difficult to locate many of the events referred to here in any of the standard works of reference, and it is hoped that these chronologies will provide a simple and useful source of information by dating incidents, displaying their position in a sequence, and outlining parallel developments in other areas of deviance and control.

Date	Crime	Political deviance
1945	Post-war 'crime wave' of armed robberies, smash and grabs, black market operations, and post office frauds. Murder rate is significantly higher than pre-war years. Elizabeth Jones and Karl Hulton convicted in the 'cleft chin' murder case.	
1946	Neville Heath sex murders. Murder of P.C. Booth	
1947	Recorded indictable crime up 50% on 1939. 'Chalk pit' murder case. Billy Hill establishes a position of supremacy in the London underworld.	
1948	Murder of P.C. Edgar. June Davaney child murder. £338,000 bullion raid at London Airport.	First of what are portrayed as 'politically-motivated' dock strikes in London and Liverpool.
1949	Lynskey Tribunal spotlights white-collar crime and possible political corruption. Haigh (acid bath) murder case. Hume and Setty murder case.	
1950	Messina vice empire exposed by *The People* newspaper. Timothy Evans executed.	Scottish nationalists steal the Stone of Scone from Westminster Abbey. Atom bomb spy, Klaus Fuchs jailed.
1951	4 policemen killed — Sgt. Gibson in May, P.C. Baxter, in June and D.I. Fraser and P.C. Jagger in July. Straffen murders 3 children.	Defection of Burgess and MacLean. 7 dockers charged with inciting strike action contrary to a wartime act.
1952	2 policemen killed — in July Edward Finley (19) kills P.C.	

Youth	*Police*	*Other events*
	Sir Harold Scott succeeds Sir Philip Game as Commissioner of the Metropolitan Police, and institutes a new press relations policy. Fraud Squad created.	Labour General Election victory. Crime Reporters' Association founded.
	Creation of undercover 'Ghost Squad' to infiltrate London's under-world.	
250% more adolescents imprisoned than in 1939. Increasingly violent contact with police.		Royal Commission on the Press appointed.
		Criminal Justice Bill abolishes corporal punishment and opens up debate on hanging.
		Report of Royal Commission on the Press.
		Labour re-elected with reduced majority.
First of a series of moral panics about juvenile delinquency: 'The Cosh Boy menace'.		Conservative General Election victory.
see: Crime		British atom bomb announced.

Date	*Crime*	*Political deviance*
1952 *cont.*	MacLeod in Glasgow, in Nov. Craig and Bentley are involved in the death of P.C. Miles. £ ¼ m post office van raid.	
1953	Christie sex murders case. Crime statistics begin to decrease. 2 mentally-disturbed family murderers, Miles Giffard and Mrs Christophi, executed.	First of a number of raids by IRA on British arms depots.
1954	Chesney double-murder case.	
1955	Wave of 'project crimes' (especially mail van and bullion robberies). Ruth Ellis becomes the last woman to be hanged in Britain. London gangland feud between Jack 'Spot' Comer and Billy Hill.	Docks and rail strikes.
1956	'Scarface' Smithson murdered by gangland racketeers. Crime and violence statistics begin to escalate.	IRA launch border campaign which continues sporadically for 5 years.
1957	'Mad axeman' Mitchell enters the headlines for the first time. Series of spectacular murders including those of Countess Lubienska and Elizabeth Barlow.	
1958	Trial of multiple murderer, Peter Manuel in Glasgow. Insp. O'Donnell killed and another policeman injured by Henry King. P.C. Summers killed during Teddy Boy disturbance.	CND launched. Vast growth in membership over next 3 years. First Aldermaston march.
1959	Guenter Padola kills Sgt. Purdy. His arrest starts a police brutality scandal.	

Youth	*Police*	*Other events*
Murder of youth on Clapham Common is given a new significance by the emergence of 'The Teddy Boy'.	Sir John Nott-Bower is appointed Metropolitan Commissioner.	Coronation of Elizabeth II. Report of Royal Commission on Capital Punishment. Press Council established.
Teddy Boy moral panic and the beginnings of the cult of the rebel.		
	Police corruption becomes a public issue with the trial of Det. Sgt. Robertson.	Conservative General Election victory. Independent Television opens. Fleet St. closures begin with *Sunday Chronicle*.
Rock and roll riots. 'Angry Youth' becomes a focus of media attention.		Suez Crisis. Boom in property and consumer goods. Increase in strikes.
Decline of the Teddy Boy begins as commercial interests promote counter image of the 'Clean-cut Kid'.		*Rent Act* produces increased rents and 'Rachmanism'. Macmillan becomes P.M. End of National Service.
see: Crime.	Brighton bribery scandal.	Notting Hill race riots.
	Royal Commission on the Police announced.	Conservative General Election victory. *Street Offences Act*

Date	*Crime*	*Political deviance*
1959 *cont.*	Patric Byrne YMCA sex murder case.	
1960	P.C. Meehan killed by 'Gipsy' Smith. Manager of the Pen Club in Soho murdered.	Widespread protests against South Africa following the Sharpeville massacre.
1961	John Hall kills 2 policemen before shooting himself. A6 murder case and the arrest of Hanratty. Edwin Simms confesses double murder to *Daily Mirror* crime reporter.	Mass arrests at large CND demo. Portland spy ring is uncovered and Blake, Lonsdale, and the Krogers are arrested.
1962		Vassall security scandal. Fascist demo. in Trafalgar Square.
1963	Great Train Robbery. Rachman housing scandal.	Profumo/Christine Keeler scandal. CND 'Spies for Peace' reveal Regional Seats of Government. Defection of Kim Philby. 2 journalists jailed for refusing to reveal sources concerning Vassall scandal.
1964	First of the London Nudes murders which continue until 1966. *Sunday Mirror* allegations of a relationship between Lord Boothby and Ronnie Kray result in successful libel action and a disruption of police and newspaper investigations into the activities of the Krays.	

Youth	*Police*	*Other events*
		results in increased prosecution of prostitutes.
		4 national newspapers cease publication — *Star*, *Sunday Graphic*, *Empire News*, and *News Chronicle*. *Sunday Telegraph* published.
First crowd invasion of a British soccer pitch marks beginning of soccer hooliganism as a social problem.		*Betting and Gaming Acts* clear path for vast increase in gambling turnover. Second Royal Commission on the Press appointed.
	Royal Commission reports.	Royal Commission reports. *Commonwealth Immigrants Act* heralds influx of Asian immigrants. First edition of 'Z Cars' on BBC TV.
	Sheffield brutality scandal. D.S. Challenor plants half bricks on demonstrators during Greek Royal visit.	Alec Douglas Home becomes P.M. Harold Wilson becomes leader of the Labour Party. *News of the World* pays £23,000 for Christine Keeler confessions.
Mods and Rockers fights at Clacton start fresh moral panic. Vandalism emerges as a social problem. Drugtaking begins to increase.		IPC launches *The Sun* after buying TUC's holding in *Daily Herald*. Labour General Election victory. Drugs (*Prevention of Misuse Bill*) published a few days after Clacton disturbance. *Malicious Damage Act* to help State deal with

Date	Crime	Political deviance
1964 *cont.*		
1965		
Jan	Small-time criminal, Ginger Marks is murdered in Bethnal Green street.	
Feb	P.C. Russell murdered.	
Apr	Kray brothers acquitted on extortion charge.	First protests against Vietnam War at CND demo. in Trafalgar Sq. 2 civil servants, Bossard and Allen are jailed for passing secrets to foreign powers.
July	Train robber, Ronald Biggs, escapes from Wandsworth Prison.	
Aug	D.S. Stanford murdered.	
Oct		
Nov		
Dec	Commital proceedings begin in the Moors Murders case.	
Year		
1966		
Mar	Richardson gang member, George Cornell, killed by Ronnie Kray.	
Apr	Train robber, James White, arrested. Moors Murders trial.	
May		National seamen's strike provokes declaration of state of emergency. 31 arrests at London anti-Vietnam War demo.
Aug	Arrest of the Richardson brothers. 3 policemen murdered at Shepherds Bush.	

Youth	*Police*	*Other events*
		Mods and Rockers. BBC 2 opens.
		Death of Sir Winston Churchill.
		Edward Heath becomes Conservative Party leader.
	Southend Chief Constable charged with fraud.	
		Rhodesian UDI Capital Punishment abolished.
Bank holiday disturbances at seaside resorts deepen public anxiety about Mods and Rockers, vandalism, and drug-taking.	Metro. Police Special Patrol Group established. Regional Crime Squads become fully operational.	First maximum security wings established in selected British prisons.
		Labour increase majority at General Election.
	Leicester Chief Constable Robert Mark, makes early statement of views and policies in TV interview.	England football team wins World Cup.

Date	Crime	Political deviance
Sept	Gateshead police killing. First of a series of confessions to the A6 murder by Peter Alphon.	
Oct		Start of a 30-week lock-out at Barbican building site. George Blake escapes from prison.
Dec	Kray brothers free 'mad axeman' Frank Mitchell from Dartmoor Prison and later murder him.	

Year

1967
Jan	Insp. Bradley killed by Pugh and Woodrow. Murder of fruit machine operator, Angus Sibbet for which Dennis Stafford and Michael Luvaglio were convicted.	'Peace with Rhodesia' rally in Trafalgar Sq. provokes vocal left-wing counter demo.
Mar		Britain's first University occupation at LSE.
May	Murder of racketeer 'Scotch Jack' Buggy in London Club.	
June		
July	Conviction of triple child murderer, David Burgess.	
Sept		
Oct	The Kray twins kill a minor member of their firm, 'Jack the Hat' McVitie.	First Grosvenor Sq. demo. by Vietnam Solidarity Campaign.
Nov	Anthony Cauchi and Tony Galea convicted of conspiracy to cause explosions after the firebombing of Soho strip clubs. Cauchi's	

Youth	*Police*	*Other events*
Europe's first under-ground magazine, *IT*, published. Emergence of 'hippy' counter culture.		Compulsory wage freeze.
		Thompson takes over *The Times*. Mountbatten report on prison security.
Decline of the Mods.		
see: Political Deviance.	Regional Drug Squads formed to combat 'drug problem'. Sir John Waldron succeeds Sir Joseph Simpson as Metro. Commissioner.	
Mick Jagger and Keith Richards of The Rolling Stones convicted of drug offences.		
	Special squad under Supt. Nipper Read begins secret investiga-tion into Krays.	

Date	Crime	Political deviance
Nov cont.	former partner, Frank Mifsud, was convicted in 1976 of suborning witnesses at the trial.	
Year		
1968		
Jan	Train robber, Charles Wilson, escapes from prison.	Spanish Embassy bombed.
Feb		
Mar		Second Grosvenor Sq. demo. by the Vietnam Solidarity Committee. 300 arrests.
Apr		Enoch Powell's 'Rivers of Blood' speech provokes his sacking from the Shadow Cabinet. 1,000 dockers march to Commons in support of Powell.
May	Kray brothers arrested.	Widespread student unrest, especially at Essex University.
June	2 children killed by 11 year old, Mary Bell during the summer.	
July		Legalize Pot rally in Hyde Park.
Oct		Ulster Civil Rights demo. is violently attacked by police. Third and largest anti-Vietnam War demo. in London.
Nov	'Public enemy no. 1', John McVicar, escapes from Durham Prison. Arrests of train robber, Bruce Reynolds and Cannock Chase child murderer, Raymond Morris.	
Dec		London squatters being campaign.
1969		
Jan		Ulster Civil Rights march attacked by Loyalists at Burntollet.

Youth	*Police*	*Other events*
Over 3,000 convictions for drug offences as moral panic is generated.	Introduction of Unit Beat Policing.	
	3 Metro. detectives convicted of corruption.	
		New *Commonwealth Immigrants Bill* introduced.
		Anti-Discrimination Act.
see: Political Deviance.		
First of a series of free pop concerts in Hyde Park. see: Political Deviance.		
	The People accuses members of 2 Regional Crime Squads of arranging for crimes to be committed so that they could arrest those involved.	
		Wooton Report recommending legalization of cannabis is rejected.

Date	*Crime*	*Political deviance*
Feb		Bomb attacks on 2 Spanish banks in Britain.
March	Kray twins receive 30 year prison sentences.	
April		Riots in Derry. Bernadette Devlin elected to Parliament.
May		Widespread strikes against proposed *Industrial Relations Bill*.
June and July		
Aug	P.C. Davies murdered.	Riots in Derry bring Army intervention in Ulster.
Sept	Murder of sub-postmaster during robbery in Luton.	
Nov	2 Glasgow policemen murdered. First of a series of highly-publicized 'hitch-hike' murders: Diana Kemp killed by Ian Troup.	IRA splits into Official and Provisional wings.
Dec		Devlin receives 6 months prison sentence.
Year		

1970		
Jan	Kidnapping of Mrs McKay by Hossein brothers.	
Feb	P.C. Taylor killed by Adamson. £240,000 raid on Barclays Bank in Ilford is one of the biggest in a series of robberies carried out by a group of professional criminals associated with Bruce Brown, Brian Turner, and Bertie Smalls.	Widespread student unrest. Essex University students bomb campus branch of Barclays Bank. Cambridge students attack pro-Greek Junta dinner at Garden House Hotel.
Mar	Gangland killing of Eddie Coleman by Norman Parker.	
Apr		

Youth	*Police*	*Other events*
	Leeds policemen convicted of theft from bodies.	Rupert Murdoch takes over *The News of the World*.
Blind Faith and Rolling Stones concerts in Hyde Park. English Hell's Angels make their first public appearance.		
'Hippy squat' at 144 Piccadilly.		Murdoch takes over *The Sun*. *The Sun* is launched as a tabloid.
	The Times exposes a case of police corruption in London.	
		Capital Punishment abolished in UK.
Emergence of the 'Skinheads'. First newspaper reports of 'Paki-bashing' and 'Queer-bashing'.		
4 skinheads sentenced for the 'queer-bash' killing of Michael de Gruchy.		Attempt to re-introduce Capital Punishment for police murders.
		Misuse of Drugs Bill published.
	4 Bradford policemen convicted of theft.	

Date	*Crime*	*Political deviance*
May		
June		Intensification of sectarian violence in Ulster leads to the imposition of the Falls Rd. curfew.
July		National docks strike. State of Emergency declared.
Aug		Bomb attack on the home of Sir John Waldron (unreported).
Sept	Murder of Nicola Brazier by a hitch-hiker.	Bomb attack on home of Attorney General, Sir Peter Rawlinson (unreported). CS gas canister thrown in Commons.
Oct	Unsolved murder of hitch-hiker, Barbara Mayo.	
Nov	Society hairdresser, Andre Mizelas, murdered in car in Hyde Park. Securicor guard, Raymond Hales, killed in London bank raid. John McVicar recaptured.	Bomb attack on BBC van at Miss World contest.
Dec		Machine-gun attack on Spanish Embassy in London. Bomb attack on Dept. of Productivity in London after large demo. against *Industrial Relations Bill*. Electricity workers work to rule. State of Emergency declared.
Year		
1971		
Jan		Angry Brigade bombs Robert Carr's home after day of protests against *Industrial Relations Bill*. Postal workers strike begins.
Feb		First British soldier killed in Ulster. German student activist, Rudi Deutschke, deported.

Youth	*Police*	*Other events*
	2 Leeds policemen convicted of conspiracy to pervert justice.	After agitation by the 'Stop the Seventy Tour' campaign, the Home Secretary cancels the South African cricket tour. Conservative General Election victory. 4 day strike on Fleet St.
Dylan at Isle of Wight Festival. Hells Angels disturbances.	Police relations with immigrants become a public issue. 3 Leeds policemen convicted of theft.	
Yippies disrupt David Frost television show.	4 Leeds policemen accused of faking evidence. 2 convicted.	
		Daily Mirror Crime Bureau launched.
Skinheads and Hells Angels become premier folk devils of 'The Violent Society'.		
		Publication of *Immigration Bill* placing Commonwealth and alien

Date	*Crime*	*Political deviance*
Feb *cont.*		Jake Prescott charged in connection with Angry Brigade offences.
Mar		Ian Purdie arrested for Angry Brigade offences. Angry Brigade bombs Fords at Ilford. Ulster: 3 off-duty soldiers murdered.
May	Gangland murder of Edward Machin.	Angry Brigade bombs Biba boutique and police computer at Tintagel House.
June	D.C. Coward murdered in Reading by Skingle and Sparrow. Sands drug smuggling trial. Convictions later quashed because of suspect police evidence.	*Little Red Schoolbook* obscenity trial. Angry Brigade bombs home of Ford's managing director, William Batty.
July	Sidney Sporle convicted and T. Dan Smith acquitted, on corruption charges.	Workers take control of Upper Clyde Shipbuilders after closure announced. Angry Brigade bombs home of Minister of Employment, John Davies. Rioting in Derry: Seamus Cusack and Patrick Duffy shot.
Aug	Supt. Richardson murdered in Blackpool by Sewell.	Angry Brigade bombs Army recruiting office in London's Holloway Rd. Stoke Newington 6 arrested. Prescott/Purdie trial opens. Intensified bombing and rioting in Belfast. Tarring and feathering in Ulster.
Sept	Police eavesdrop on radio conversation of gang robbing Lloyds Bank but no arrest.	
Oct	Trial of Skingle and Sparrow. Salah drug smuggling trial: Convictions later quashed because of suspect police evidence.	Angry Brigade bombs home of Birmingham building contractor, Mr Bryant. Bomb attack on Post Office Tower.
Nov	Edward Paisnel sentenced to 30 years for sex crimes in Jersey.	Angry Brigade bombs Royal Tank Regiment's London HQ.

Youth	*Police*	*Other events*
		immigrants under one heading. Brian Faulkner replaces Chichester-Clark as Northern Ireland P.M. *Daily Sketch* stops publication.
	Bomb Squad set up under 'Commander X' (Ernest Bond). 6 Brighton policemen convicted of receiving. First of a number of internal inquiries into the activities of Metro. Drug Squad.	
Oz obscenity trial.	2 senior officers call for tougher approach to violent offenders in an interview in *The Times*. First questions asked in Press about police involvement in porn. trade. Police deviance becomes emergent issue in Press.	Internment introduced in Ulster. *Industrial Relations Act* becomes law.
		Chequers talks on Ireland.
		Immigration Act becomes law.
	2 Leeds policemen convicted of assault on a	*Compton Report* confirms 'ill treatment' of

Date	Crime	Political deviance
Nov *cont.*		
Dec		Prescott sentenced to 15 years for conspiracy. Purdie acquitted.
Year		
1972		
Jan		National miners strike begins. Bloody Sunday: British troops kill 13 men in Derry during a Civil Rights demo.
Feb	3 babies murdered by insane Jordanian doctor, Ahmad Alami. Murder of Margaret Richardson and her son by her brother-in-law.	Official IRA bomb kills 7 at Officers' Mess at Aldershot (Bloody Sunday reprisal).
Mar	Sewell receives 30-year prison sentence.	2 killed and over 100 injured by bomb in Belfast's Abercorn Restaurant. 3-day Provisional ceasefire. 2-day Loyalist strike.
Apr		Rail work-to-rule and overtime ban.
May	£400,000 silver bullion hijack at Mountnessing, Essex.	Stoke Newington 8 trial begins. Official IRA announce ceasefire.
June	Poulson bankruptcy hearings begin.	Belfast: 102nd British soldier to die in Ulster is shot 2 minutes before Provo. IRA truce begins. First Loyalist no-go areas established. see: Police
July	Members of East-End gang led by Philip Jacobs and Dixon brothers receive sentences totalling 61 years. Kristen Bullen babysnatching case.	Bloody Friday: 11 killed by 20 Provo IRA bombs in Belfast. Operation Motorman: Army enters Derry no-go areas. Industrial crisis as 5 dockers are

Youth	*Police*	*Other events*
	Nigerian vagrant, David Oluwale. Inquiry into Leeds police announced.	some detainees in Ulster.
Decline of the Skinheads.		
	Anti-mugging squad established by London Transport Police.	Unemployment in UK reaches one million.
	Sunday People exposes porn. trade and the Cyprus holiday of Commander Drury (Flying Squad) and pornographer James Humphreys.	Government declares State of Emergency in response to miners' strike.
	2 detectives exposed by *The Times* in 1969 are jailed. Drury is suspended. Press identifies crisis of confidence in Police.	Direct rule in Ulster.
	Robert Mark becomes Metro. Commissioner and immediately initiates changes in the detective and uniform branches.	Widgery Report on Bloody Sunday published. Speech by Lord Chancellor Hailsham encouraging a 'tough' attitude to crime.
'Pupil Power' demo. in London by Schools Action Union.	Drury resigns. *Daily Express* poll reveals that public confidence in Police is undamaged.	Death of Duke of Windsor.
	A10 Dept. for investigating serious complaints against the Force is established 'Soir Eire' trial reveals activities of police agent provocateur.	Report of Criminal Law Revision Committee.
	Det. Ch. Supt. Wickstead begins secret investigations into Soho porn. trade.	Home Secretary, Reginald Maudling, resigns over Poulson affair. Replaced by Robert Carr.

Date	Crime	Political deviance
July *cont.*	Manslaughter of Carole Califano by Dr Drinkwater. Murder of Sarah Gibson at Royal Automobile Club by David Frooms. P.C. Guthrie killed in Coventry by Anthony Jeffs.	jailed under the *Industrial Relations Act*. Dock strike begins. Trial of Peter Hail on conspiracy charges, after direct action against South African sporting tours.
Aug	Barclays Bank, Wembley, raided by Brown, Turner etc. Beginning of Mugging moral panic after an old man is murdered at Waterloo Station.	16 prisons involved in inmate demos. Dock strike: 'Battle of Neap House Wharf'.
Sept		
Oct	Leslie Payne (ex-associate of Kray brothers) is jailed for 5 years.	
Nov	Small-time crook, Terence Clark, murdered in Stevenage. Muriel Patience murdered at Barn Restaurant. George Ince charged. David Lee, the murderer of a Northampton nurse, is arrested with the help of The *Sun* newspaper. Anthony Jeffs sentenced to 20 years. Colin Latimer, Ronald Leighton, and Ahmet Salih wrongly convicted of the murder of homosexual prostitute, Maxwell Confait 3 years before, have sentences quashed.	Provo. IRA Chief of Staff, Sean MacStiofain arrested.
Dec	Kensington bank robber killed by armed policeman.	2 killed, 140 injured in 2 explosions in Dublin as the *Offences Against the State (Amendment) Act* is being passed. It is unclear who is responsible, but British Intelligence are blamed by IRA. 4 of the Stoke Newington 8 are convicted of conspiracy to cause explosions.

Youth	*Police*	*Other events*
see: Crime.		Ugandan Asians expelled. State of Emergency. Government offers £50,000 reward for information on 60 'motiveless' murders in Ulster.
	Special squads set up in mugging blackspots. Home Secretary writes to police chiefs for information on mugging and also promises anti-picket flying squads. Robbery Squad set up.	Darlington conference on future of Ulster. *Criminal Justice Act.*
3 Hells Angels jailed for raping a 14 year-old girl guide.	*Sunday Times* article on Sands case and Metro. Drug Squad. 5 members of squad charged with conspiracy to pervert the course of justice. Mark unveils new press relations policy. New Obscene Publications Unit of the uniform branch announced. Discontent at high level among CID.	*News of the World* exposes 'the Strifemakers in British Industry'.

Date	Crime	Political deviance
Dec *cont.*		Ulster: 2 workmen killed by soldier who mistook them for snipers.
1973 Jan	Tibbs gang sentenced to a total of 58 years imprisonment.	Michelle O'Callaghan sentenced to 18 months for possession of explosives. Clay Cross councillors refuse to implement *Fair Rents Act*.
Feb	Killing of milkman, Frank Kidwell, during raid on Ewell dairy.	Industrial action by gas workers.
Mar	16 year-old, Paul Story, sentenced to 20 years detention in Handsworth mugging case.	Provo. IRA car bombs in London kill one and injure 700. Price sisters and 8 co-conspirators are arrested at London Airport (Belfast 10). Strike of hospital ancilliary workers. Ulster: 3 British soldiers are 'lured' to a party by 2 girls and are murdered.
Apr	Arrest of group responsible for series of bank raids between 1969 and 1972. 3 children murdered by David McGreavy in Worcester.	
May	Handcuffed body of 'small-time crook', Michael St John, washed up at Rotherhithe. George Ince stands trial twice for Barn Restaurant murder and is acquitted.	Lord Lambton and Lord Jellico resign over Norma Levy scandal.
June	James Humphreys arrested in Holland.	Rose Dugdale and Wally Heaton arrested for the theft of £80,000 worth of antiques from Dugdale's father. Convicted in Oct.
July	Humphreys' wife, Rusty, acquitted of charges arising from an attack on her lover, Peter Garfarth; but is later convicted of keeping a	Littlejohn brothers convicted of armed robberies in Eire claim they are British agents.

Youth	*Police*	*Other events*
	Officer in charge of 'Buggy' file convicted of corruption. £500,000 worth of porn. seized in 50 raids. Discovery of 'top people's' vice ring (Lambton scandal). 2 members of Metro. Special Patrol Group kill 2 Pakistani boys armed with toy guns who are holding hostages at Indian High Commission.	
'Gang bang' case: 6 Hells Angels acquitted of raping a 17 year-old WRAC. see: Crime.	National Drugs and Immigration Intelligence Units created.	
Hells Angels murder of Clive Olive discovered.	Wickstead congratulates *News of the World* on its investigations into West End porn. and vice.

Home Secretary tells police to 'hot up' war against muggers. Fresh investigation into corruption launched. | Bill to restore hanging rejected. |
| | | Northern Ireland Assembly elected. |
| 16 year-old convicted of 'clockwork orange' killing of an old tramp in Bletchely. | | |

Date	Crime	Political deviance
July *cont.*	brothel and possessing a firearm. Poulson scandal: Andrew Cunningham arrested. Brook and Johnson charged with Barn Restaurant murder. German student, Heidi Mnilk, murdered on London train.	
Aug		'Freedom Fighters For All' bombings. Provo. IRA autumn bombing campaign begins: 14 incendiaries in West End stores, 3 other London bombs.
Sept	Committal hearings in bank robberies case: Bertie Smalls, 'the squealer', becomes focus of media attention. George Ince and 3 others convicted of Mountnessing bullion robbery. Mrs Iris Thompson dies in the first of a series of 5 fatal stabbings over the next 6 months in Essex/Herts area.	25 IRA bombings in Britain, including 3 London rail stations. Trial of Belfast 10 begins at Winchester.
Oct		End of IRA autumn campaign: 8 bombs in Britain.
Nov		Industrial action by miners and electrical power engineers. Belfast 10 convicted. 200th British soldier killed in Ulster.
Dec	4 people, including P.C. Smith killed in Torquay by Martin Fenton.	ASLEF overtime ban. Provo. IRA winter bombing campaign begins: 19 bombings in 9 days around Christmas. Arab gunman injures Marks & Spencer president, Joseph Sieff.

Youth	*Police*	*Other events*
	Robbery Squad make 100th arrest.	
	Size of Bomb Squad trebled to 120.	
	Police name McMorrow and Coyle as bombers.	Conservative Party Conference votes to restore death penalty.
	3 Metro. Drug Squad officers convicted of perjury. 3 others, including Ch. Insp. Kellaher, acquitted. Ch. Insp. Hales receives first of two 5 year sentences on conspiracy charges. Robert Mark gives Dimbleby Lecture on BBC TV.	State of Emergency declared. Wedding of Princess Anne and Capt. Mark Phillips.
	Series of anti-porn. and vice raids: Numerous arrests including Silver and Miscallef.	3 day week and other crisis measures. Sunningdale agreement on Northern Ireland.

Date 1974	Crime	Political deviance
Jan	Humphreys extradited and 8 of his associates jailed. Silver and Mangion charged with Smithson murder. Philip Morris jailed for 17 years for the manslaughter of Frank Kidwell.	Ulster: Disappearance of West German Consul, Thomas Niedermayer. Rose Dugdale and IRA unit drop milk churn bombs from helicopter on police station. 16 bomb attacks in England, including Boat Show.
Feb	Bank robberies trial opens. Poulson and Pottinger jailed for corruption. 'The Black Panther' kills sub-postmaster, Donald Skepper in Harrogate.	Miners vote for strike action. Vermeer painting stolen. Reginald Maudling receives letter bomb. 12 die in M62 coach bombing.
Mar	Ian Ball attempts to kidnap Princess Anne as she is driven down the Mall. Ex-bookmaker, Francis Daniels charged with Buggy murder.	Police enter Essex University campus to break student picket: 105 arrests. Dublin: Littlejohn brothers escape from Mountjoy Prison.
Apr	Humphreys jailed for 8 years for attack on Garfath. T. Dan Smith and Andrew Cunningham jailed for corruption.	Murder of Special Branch informer Kenneth Lennon. Murder of Colonel Stevenson at Otterburn camp. Rose Dugdale and IRA unit steal paintings from the home of Sir Alfred Beit.
May	Gerald Citron fined £50,000 on porn. charges. Brown, Turner, and 5 others sentenced to a total of 113 years for bank robberies.	Loyalist strike brings collapse of Ulster executive. Provo. IRA command structure damaged after house raid in fashionable area of Belfast. 26 killed by car bombs in Dublin. 3 hurt in blast at Heathrow.
June	Fenton jailed for life.	Price sisters' hunger strike. Student, Kevin Gately, killed during a protest against the National Front in London's Red Lion Square. Bomb at Westminster Hall.
July	P.C. Schofield killed by Egon Von Bulow.	Bomb at Tower of London is most serious of 30 attacks.

Youth	*Police*	*Other events*
	Vice and porn. raids continue: half of the strip clubs in Soho are closed. First of the joint Army/ Police exercises at Heathrow.	Price of Persian oil doubles.
		Conservatives defeated in General Election. Labour minority Government. *Daily Express* finds Ronald Biggs in Rio.
	Press reports that 25 officers may be suspended after allegations by Humphreys and Citron.	
	Ex-head of Obscene Publications Squad, Ch. Supt. Moody, suspended. Yard issues statement that rumours of large-scale suspensions are 'fictional nonsense'. Policeman jailed for 7 years for rape (case of the 'Copper and the Topper').	

Date	*Crime*	*Political deviance*
July *cont.*	Frank Mifsud arrested in Switzerland: later acquitted of murder but convicted of suborning a witness.	
Aug	Over 90 held after Yard raids directed at smashing large car-stealing syndicate. Ex-Broadmoor patient, Barry Robinson, hijacks police panda car.	Eire: 19 IRA men escape from Portlaoise Prison.
Sept	Maurice O'Mahony jailed for 5 years for robbery. It is revealed that he is to give evidence in up to 30 forthcoming major ciminal trials.	Private armies formed to combat 'Civil Emergencies' become focus of media attention.
Oct	Cambridge Rapist makes his first attack.	3 exclusive London clubs bombed.
Nov	Lord Lucan disappears after the murder of Sandra Rivett. Ronald Milhench jailed for forging Harold Wilson's signature. The Black Panther kills third sub-postmaster, Sidney Grayland.	Judith Ward sentenced to 30 years for M62 coach bombing. Rose Dugdale jailed for 9 years. Death of IRA man, Frank Stagg, after hunger strike. Woolwich pub bomb. 20 killed by Birmingham pub bombs. London pillar box bombs.
Dec	Gangland killing of William Moseley. Bernie Silver jailed for 6 years. 6 other members of his syndicate are also convicted.	Provo. IRA ceasefire declared after attacks on 2 London clubs, 3 post offices, Harrods, Selfridges, and the home of Edward Heath.
1975 Jan	Kidnap and murder of Lesley Whittle by 'The Black Panther'. George Brett and his son disappear: Brett is the brother of one of those convicted of the Mountnessing bullion robbery. Jeremiah Callaghan, Alfred Geard, and Ronald Everett charged with Ginger Marks murder.	6 bombs in London.

Youth   *Police*   *Other events*

250 arrests as 600 police
break up Windsor pop
festival.

Labour increases majority
at General Election.
Paul Foot of *Socialist
Worker* fined for
publishing article in
contempt of court.
Trevor Aspinall of
Sunday People acquitted
of incitement.
Starritt Report on Lennon
case clears police of
misconduct.
*Prevention of Terrorism
(Temporary Provisions)
Act.*
Attempts to restore
Death Penalty defeated.

2 Metro. detectives jailed
after *Guardian*
corruption exposé.

Date	*Crime*	*Political deviance*
Feb		P.C. Tibble killed by IRA gunman: Bomb factory discovered in Kensington. Provo. IRA ceasefire begins.
Mar	Bunny Girl, Eve Stratford, murdered. Body of Lesley Whittle found. Von Bulow sentenced to life imprisonment.	
Apr	£1m Mayfair bank raid. Information from underworld informant leads to immediate arrests.	
May	Maurice O'Mahoney begins to give evidence in a series of old Bailey trials.	7 convicted in 'Tartan Army' trial.
June	Cambridge Rapist arrested.	
July	P.C. Green killed in Birmingham by young West Indian. Bernie Silver receives life sentence for Smithson murder.	Insp. Watkins shot by IRA men in Manchester. Sgt. Davies shot in police raid on Liverpool bomb factory. Police search for 'The Jackal', Carlos Martinez, after arms cache is discovered in London flat.
Aug	£1m Hatton Gardens gems raid.	Supporters of the 'Free George Davis' campaign dig up test pitch at Headingly. Birmingham pub bombers jailed for life. Bombings at Oxford St. and Caterham pub.
Sept	Sgt. Dawson, an ambulance man, and a woman killed after domestic disturbance in Leicester. Gangland killing of Michael Cornwall.	Bombs at London's Hilton and Portman Hotels.
Oct	Cambridge Rapist, Peter Cook, jailed for life.	Knightsbridge Spaghetti House siege ends after 5 days. 3 Irishmen and an English girl convicted of Guildford pub bombings.

Youth

Police

Ex-Commander Drury is
the subject of more alle-
gations of misconduct at
the appeal of those con-
victed of the Luton post
office raid and murder.
News of the World
reveals that 22 detectives
alleged to have been on
Humphrey's pay roll
have resigned or retired.
3 Appeal Court judges
criticize police deals with
underworld 'squealers'.

Home Office meetings to
consider the possibility of
a national CID.

Police appeal for inform-
ation on Margaret
McKearney.

Other events

Scarman Report on Red
Lion Sq. disturbances
clears police of using
excessive force and
blames IMG for much of
the violence.

Freelance crime reporter
Thomas Bryant cleared of
47 charges of dishonestly
handling police docu-
ments.

David May of *Time Out*
acquitted of dishonest
handling charge.

Date	*Crime*	*Political deviance*
Oct *cont.* Nov		Series of bomb attacks against prominent people begins. Eire: Kidnappers of Dr Herrema, Eddie Gallacher, and Marion Coyle, surrender after 18 day siege at Monasterevin. Assassination of Ross McWhirter. Bomb attacks on expensive London restaurants. Bomb cache found in Southampton.
Dec	Black Panther, Donald Neilson arrested.	4 IRA men surrender after 6 day siege at Balcomb St., London. 2 bomb factories discovered in London. 14 pacifists acquitted of conspiracy to incite disaffection.

Youth   *Police*   *Other events*

Police win co-operation
of news media in news
blackout on the kidnap-
ping of Alio Kaloghirou.

Ulster: Internment ends.
Attempt to re-introduce
Capital punishment
defeated in Commons.

References

Adamson, I. (1966) *The Great Detective*. London: Muller.

Alberoni, F. (1972) The Powerless 'Elite': Theory and Sociological Research on the Phenomenon of the Stars. In D. McQuail (ed.), *Sociology of Mass Communications*. Harmondsworth: Penguin.

Althusser, L. (1969) *For Marx*. London: Allen Lane.

———(1971) Ideology in the State. In *Lenin and Philosophy*, and other Essays. London: New Left Books.

Barnett, A. (1973 Class struggle and the Heath Government. *New Left Review* 77.

Barthes, R. (1972) *Mythologies*. London: Cape.

Bass, Z. (1969) Refining the Gatekeeper Concept. *Journalism Quarterly* 46(1): 69-72.

Becker, H. (1967) Whose Side Are We On?. *Social Problems* 14: 239-47.

Bensman, J. and Lilienfield, R. (1973) *Craft and Consciousness*. New York: Wiley.

Berger, P. and Luckmann, T. (1967) *The Social Construction of Reality*. London: Allen Lane.

Birnbaum, N. (1955) Monarchs and Sociologists: A Reply to Professor Shils and Mr Young. *Sociological Review* 3(1): 5-23.

Blom-Cooper, L. (1963) *The A6 Murder*. Harmondsworth: Penguin.

Booker, C. (1970) *The Neophiliacs*. London: Fontana Books.

Boorstin, D. (1963) *The Image*. Harmondsworth: Penguin.

Borrell, C. and Cashinella B. (1975) *Crime in Britain Today*. London: Routledge & Kegan Paul.

Box, S. (1971) *Deviance, Reality and Society*, London: Holt, Rinehart and Winston.

Breed, W. (1955) Newspaper Opinion Leaders and Processes of Standardization. *Journalism Quarterly* 32: 277-84.

Bunyan, T. (1976) *The Political Police in Britain*. London: Julian Friedmann.

Burgelin, O. (1971) Structural Analysis of Mass Communication. In D. McQuail (ed.), *Sociology of Mass Communications*. Harmondsworth: Penguin.

Butler, D. and King A. (1966) *The British General Election of 1966*. London: Macmillan.

Cain, M. (1971) On the Beat. In S. Cohen (ed.), *Images of Deviance*. Harmondsworth: Penguin.

———(1972), *Society and the Policeman's Role*. London: Routledge & Kegan Paul.

Carey, J. (1969) The Communications Revolution and The Professional Communicator. *Sociological Review Monograph* 13.

Carr, G. (1975) *The Angry Brigade*. London: Gollancz.

Chibnall, S. (1975a) The Crime Reporter: A Study in the Production of Commercial Knowledge. *Sociology* 9(1): 49-66.

_____(1975b) The Police and the Press. In J. Brown and G. Howes (eds.) *The Police and the Community*. Farnborough: Saxon House.

Cobb, B. (1961) *Murdered on Duty*. London: W.H. Allen.

Cockburn, A. and Blackburn, R. (1969) *Student Power*. Harmondsworth: Penguin.

Cockerell, M. (1975) How Good is Scotland Yard Now?. *The Listener* 6.2.75.

Cohen, B. (1963) *The Press and Foreign Policy*. Princeton: Princeton University Press.

Cohen, P. (1972) Subcultural Conflict and Working Class Community. *Working Papers in Cultural Studies 2*. University of Birmingham.

Cohen S. (1972) *Folk Devils and Moral Panics*. London: MacGibbon & Kee.

Cohen, S. and Rock P. (1970) The Teddy Boy. In V. Bogdanor and R. Skidelsky, *The Age of Affluence 1951-1964*. London: Macmillan.

Cudlipp, H. (1962) *At Your Peril*. London: Weidenfeld & Nicolson.

Daniels, S. (1974) The Weathermen. *Government and Opposition* 9: 430-59.

Deeley, P. and Walker, C. (1971) *Murder in the Fourth Estate: An Investigation into the roles of Press and Police in The McKay Case*. London: Gollancz.

Driver, C. (1964) *The Disarmers*. London: Hodder & Stoughton.

Enzenberger, H.M. (1970) Constituents of a Theory of the Media. *New Left Review* 64: 13-36. November-December.

Erikson, K. (1964) Notes on the Sociology of Deviance. In H. Becker (ed.), *The Other Side: Perspectives on Deviance*. New York: Free Press.

Evans, P. (1974) *The Police Revolution*, London: Allen & Unwin.

Farren, M. (1972) *Watch Out Kids*. London: Open Gate Books.

Ferris, P. (1973) Why Mark Laid Down The Law. The *Observer* 11.11.73.

Firmin, S. (1948) *Scotland Yard: The Inside Story*. London: Hutchinson.

Foot, P. (1971) *Who Killed Hanratty*. London: Cape.

Forbes, I. (1973) *Squad Man*. London: W.H. Allen.

Fordham, P. (1965) *The Robbers' Tale*. London: Hodder & Stoughton.

_____(1972) *Inside The Underworld*. London: Allen & Unwin.

Fox, J. (1974) Top Of The Cops. The *Sunday Times Magazine* 3.11.74.

Galtung, J. and Ruge M. (1965) The Structure of Foreign News. *Journal of International Peace Research* 1 (1): 64-90.

Gieber, W. (1956) Across the Desk: A Study of 16 Telegraph Editors. *Journalism Quarterly* 33: 425-32.

_____(1960) Two Communicators of the News: A study of the Roles of Sources and Reporters. *Social Forces* 39 (1): 76-83.

Gieber, W. and Johnson, W. (1961) The City Hall Beat: A study of Reporters and Source Roles. *Journalism Quarterly* 38: 289-97.

Glucksmann, M. (1974) The Structuralism of Levi-Strauss and Althusser. In J. Rex (ed.), *Approaches to Sociology*. London: Routledge & Kegan Paul.

Golding, P. (1975) *The Mass Media*. London: Longman.

Grigg, M. (1965) *The Challenor Case*. Harmondsworth: Penguin.

Hall, S. (1972) External Influences on Broadcasting. Stencilled *Occasional Paper No. 4*. Centre for Contemporary Cultural Studies, University of Birmingham.

_____(1973) The Structured Communication of Events. Stencilled *Occasional*

Paper No. 5. Centre for Contemporary Cultural Studies, University of Birmingham.

———(1974) Deviance, Politics and the Media. In P. Rock and M. McIntosh (eds.), *Deviance and Social Control*. London: Tavistock.

———(1975) Mugging: A Case Study in the Media. *The Listener* 1.5.75.

Halloran, J. (1963) *Control or Consent*. London: Sheed and Ward.

———(1965) (ed.), *The Effects of Television*. London: Panther Books.

Halloran J, Elliot, P., and Murdock, G. (1970) *Demonstrations and Communication: A Case Study*. Harmondsworth: Penguin.

Harrison, S. (1974) *Poor Men's Guardians*. London: Lawrence & Wishart.

Hartmann, P. and Husband, C. (1974) *Racism and the Mass Media*. London: Davis-Poynter.

Hebdige, D. (1974) The Kray Twins: Study of a System of Closure. Stencilled *Occasional Paper No. 21*. Centre for Contemporary Cultural Studies, University of Birmingham.

HM Govt. (1962) *Report of the Royal Commission on the Police*. Cmnd. 1728. London: IIMSO.

Hill, B. (1955) *Boss of Britain's Underworld*. London Naldrett Press.

Hindess, B. (1974) *The Use of Official Statistics in Sociology*. London: Macmillan.

Hirsch, P. and Gordon, D. (1975) *Newspaper Money*. London: Hutchinson.

Hirst, P. (1973) Some Problems of Explaining Student Militancy. In R. Brown (ed.), *Knowledge, Education, and Cultural Change*. London: Tavistock.

Hoch, P. (1974) *The Newspaper Game*. London: Calder and Boyars.

Hoggart, R. (1973) *Speaking to Each Other*. Volume 1. Harmondsworth: Penguin.

Hoggart, S. (1973) The Army PR Men of Northern Ireland. *New Society* 11.10.73: 79-80.

Horowitz, I. and Liebowitz, M. (1968) Social Deviance and Political Marginality: Towards a Redefinition of the Relation between Sociology and Politics. *Social Problems* 15: 280-96.

Howe, Q. and Nowell-Smith, G. (eds.) (1971) *Antonio Gramsci: Selections from Prison Notebooks*. London: Lawrence & Wishart.

Hughes, D. (1963) The Spivs. In M. Sissions and P. French (eds.), *Age of Austerity 1945-1951*. London: Hodder and Stoughton.

Jackson, Sir R. (1967) *Occupied with Crime*. London: Harrap.

Jacobs, H. (ed.) (1970) *Weathermen*. Berkeley: Ramparts Press.

Jefferson, T. (1973) The Teds: A Political Resurrection. Stencilled *Occasional Paper No. 22*. Centre for Contemporary Cultural Studies, University of Birmingham.

Jefferson, T. and Clark, J. (1973) 'Down These Mean Streets' — The Meaning of Mugging. Stencilled *Occasional Paper No. 17*. Centre for Contemporary Cultural Studies, University of Birmingham.

Jefferson, T., Critcher, C., Hall, S., Roberts, B., and Clark, J. (1975) Mugging and Law 'n' Order. Stencilled *Occasional Paper No. 35*. Centre for Contemporary Cultural Studies, University of Birmingham.

Judd, R. (1961) The Newspaper Reporter in a Suburban City. *Journalism Quarterly* 38 (1): 35-42.

Justice, J. (1964) *Murder versus Murder*. Paris: Olympia Press.

Klapper, J. (1960) *The Effects of Mass Communication*. New York: Free Press.

La Bern, A. (1974) *Haigh: The Mind of a Murderer*. London: W.H. Allen.

Lang, K. and Lang, L. (1965) The Inferential Structure of Political Communications. *Public Opinion Quarterly* 19.

Laurie, P. (1965) *The Teenage Revolution*. London: Anthony Blond.

———(1972) *Scotland Yard*. Harmondsworth: Penguin.

———(1973) The Man Who Purged Scotland Yard. *Inside London* No. 1. 11.10.73.

Lefeburg, M. (1958) *Murder With A Difference*. London: Heinemann.

Lenin, V.I. (1970) *Selected Works, Volume I*. Moscow: Progress Publishers.

Lewin, K. (1943) Forces Behind Food Habits. *Bulletin of the National Research Council*.

Longford, The Earl of (1972) *Pornography: The Longford Report*. London: Coronet Books.

Lucas, N. (1969) *Britain's Gangland*. London: W.H. Allen.

———(1970) *The Child Killers*. London: Barker.

———(1973) *Spycatcher*. London: W.H. Allen.

———(1974) *The Sex Killers*. London: W H Allen.

Lukacs, G. (1971) *History and Class Consciousness*. London: Merlin Press.

MacDougall, C. (1968) *Interpretative Reporting*. New York: Macmillan.

MacInnes, C. (1960) *Mr Love and Justice*. London: MacGibbon & Kee.

Mack, J. (1975) *The Crime Industry*. Farnborough: Saxon House.

Marchbanks, D. (1966) *The Moors Murders*. London: Frewin.

Marcuse, H. (1964) *One Dimensional Man*. London: Routledge & Kegan Paul.

Marcuse, H., Wolfe, R., and Moore B. (1965) *Critique of Pure Tolerance*. Boston: Beacon.

Mark, Sir R. (1973) Minority Verdict. The Dimbleby Lecture, BBC 1, 6.11.73; printed in *The Listener* 8.11.73.

———(1975) Why Help the Police ... When there's a gun to the head of your readers. *U.K. Press Gazette*. 21.12.75.

Marx, K. and Engels, F. (1846) *The German Ideology*. London: Lawrence & Wishart 1965.

McCann, E. (1971) *The British Press and Northern Ireland*. Northern Ireland Socialist Research Centre. London: Pluto Press.

McConnell, B. (1970) *The Evil Firm: The Rise and Fall of the Brothers Kray*. London: Mayflower Books.

———(1974) *Found Naked and Dead*. London: New English Library.

McIntosh, M. (1971) Changes in the Organsation of Thieving. In S. Cohen (ed.), *Images of Deviance*. Harmondsworth: Penguin.

———(1976)*The Organisation of Crime*. London: Macmillan.

McLellan, D. (1973) *Karl Marx*. London: Macmillan.

McQuail, D. (1969) *Towards a Sociology of Mass Communications*. London: Collier-Macmillan.

Mepham, J. (1973) The Theory of Ideology in Capital. *Radical Philosophy* 6.

Miliband, R. (1973) *The State in Capitalist Society*. London: Quartet Books.

Millen, E. (1972) *Specialist in Crime*. London: Harrap.

Molotch, H. and Lester, M. (1974) News as Purposive Behaviour: On the Strategic

Use of Routine Events, Accidents and Scandals. *American Sociological Review* 39: 101-12.

Morley, D. (1974) Industrial Conflict and the Mass Media. Stencilled *Occasional Paper No. 8*. Centre for Contemporary Cultural Studies, University of Birmingham.

Mueller, C. (1974) *The Politics of Communication*. New York: Oxford University Press.

Murdock, G. (1973) Political Deviance: the press presentation of a militant mass demonstration. In S. Cohen and J. Young (eds.), *The Manufacture of News: Deviance, Social Problems and the Mass Media*. London: Constable.

Murdock, G. and Golding, P. (1974a) For a Political Economy of Mass Communications. In R. Miliband and J. Saville (eds.), *Socialist Register 1973*. London: Merlin Press.

———(1974b) Communications: The Continuing Crisis. *New Society* 25.4.74: 179-81.

Newman, G. (1970) *Sir, You Bastard*. London: W.H. Allen.

———(1972) *You Nice Bastard*. London: New English Library.

———(1974) *The Price*. London: New English Library.

O'Higgins, P. (1972) *Censorship in Britain*. London: Nelson.

Orwell, G. (1946) Decline of the English Murder. In S. Orwell and I. Angus (eds.), *The Collected Essays, Journalism and Letters of George Orwell: Volume 4*. London: Secker & Warburg 1968.

Packer, H. (1964) Two Models of the Criminal Process. *University of Pennsylvania Law Review*. 113: 1-68.

Parker, T. (1965) *The Plough Boy*. London: Hutchinson.

Parkin, F. (1968) *Middle Class Radicalism*. Manchester: Manchester University Press.

Payne, L. (1973) *The Brotherhood*. London: Michael Joseph.

Pearson, J. (1972) *The Profession of Violence*. London: Weidenfeld and Nicolson.

Phelan, J. (1953) *The Underworld*. London: Harrap.

Procter, H. (1958) *The Street of Disillusion*. London: Wingate.

Rees-Davies, W. (1970) *The Conquest of Crime: a proposed programme for the 70s*. London: Conservative Political Centre.

Robertson, G. (1976) *Reluctant Judas*. London: Temple Smith.

Rock, P. (1973) News as Eternal Recurrence. In S. Cohen, and J. Young (eds.), *The Manufacture of News: Deviance, Social Problems and the Mass Media*. London: Constable.

Rose, J. du (1973) *Murder Was My Business*. St. Albans: Mayflower Books.

Roshier, R. (1971a) *Crime and the Press: A Study of the Reporting of Crime in the English National Daily Press*. Ph.D. Thesis, University of London.

———(1971b) Crime and the Press. *New Society* 16.9.71: 502-6.

Russell, Lord (1965) *Deadman's Hill: Was Hanratty Guilty*. London: Secker & Warburg.

Rutherford, W. (1973) *The Untimely Silence*. London: Hamilton.

Schutz, A. and Luckmann, T. (1974) *The Structures of the Life World*. London: Heinemann.

Scott, Sir H. (1954) *Scotland Yard*. London: André Deutsch.

Shils, E. and Young M. (1953) The Meaning of the Coronation. *Sociological Review* 1(1): 63-81.

Sigal, L. (1973) *Reporters and Officials*. Lexington: D.C. Heath.

Sigalman, L. (1973) Reporting the News: An Organizational Analysis. *American Journal of Sociology* 79: 132-51.

Skolnick, J. (1966) *Justice Without Trial*. New York: Wiley.

Slater, M. (1971) *Levi-Strauss in Fleet Street*. M.A. Thesis, University of Essex.

Smith, A. (1975) *Paper Voices: The Popular Press and Social Change 1935-1965*. London: Chatto & Windus.

Sparrow, Judge G. (1969) *Gang-Warfare*. London: Feature Books.

Steck, H. (1965) The Re-Emergence of Ideological Politics in Great Britain: The Campaign for Nuclear Disarmament. *Western Political Quarterly* 18(1): 87-103.

Stephen, A. (1976) A Reporter's Life in Ulster. *Observer* 29.2.76.

Taylor, I., Walton, P., and Young, J. (1973) *The New Criminology: For a Social Theory of Deviance*. London: Routledge and Kegan Paul.

_____(eds.), (1975) *Critical Criminology*. London: Routledge and Kegan Paul.

Taylor, L. (1975) A Cure for Fame. *New Society* 1.5.75: 279-81.

Taylor, R. (1970) The Campaign for Nuclear Disarmament. In V. Bogdanor and R. Skidelsky (eds.), *The Age of Affluence 1951-1964*. London: Macmillan.

Thompson, E. (1970) Sir, Writing By Candlelight. *New Society* 24.12.70:1135-6.

Traini, R. (1971) *The Work of the Crime Reporters Association*. Paper to 8th National Deviancy Symposium. University of York.

Tuchman, G. (1972) Objectivity as Strategic Ritual: An Examination of Newsmen's Notions of Objectivity. *American Journal of Sociology* 77: 660-79.

_____(1973) Making News by Doing Work: Routinizing the Unexpected. *American Journal of Sociology* 79: 110-31.

Tullett, T. (1967) *No Answer from Foxtrot 11*. London: Michael Joseph.

Tunstall J. (1971a) *Journalists at Work*. London: Constable.

_____(1971b) *The Westminster Lobby Correspondents*. London: Routledge & Kegan Paul.

Walton, P. (1973) The Case of the Weathermen: Social Reaction and Radical Commitment. In I. Taylor and L. Taylor (eds.), *Politics and Deviance*. Harmondsworth: Penguin.

Whale, J. (1971) *Journalism and Government*. London: Macmillan.

Whitaker, B. (1964) *The Police*. Harmondsworth: Penguin.

White, D. (1950) The Gatekeeper: A Case Study in the Selection of News. *Journalism Quarterly* 27: 383-90.

Wilkinson, L. (1957) *Behind the Face of Crime*. London: Muller.

Williams, F. (1973) *No Fixed Address: The Great Train Robbers on the Run*. London: W.H. Allen.

Willis, P. (1971) What is News. *Working Papers in Cultural Studies 1*. University of Birmingham.

Wilson, C. (1969) *A Casebook of Murder*. London: Frewin.

_____(1972) *Order of Assassins*. London: Hart-Davis.

Wilson, C. and Pitman, P. (1964) *Encyclopaedia of Murder*. London: Pan.

Winchester, S. (1975) *In Holy Terror*. London: Faber.

Yallop, D. (1971) *To Encourage the Others*. London: W.H. Allen.

Young, J. (1971) *The Drugtakers*. London : Paladin.

_____(1974) Mass Media, Drugs, and Deviance. In P. Rock and M. McIntosh (eds.), *Deviance and Social Control*. London: Tavistock.

Notes

Notes to Introduction

1. Crime is one of those 'meaningless realities which, according to Berger and Luckmann, continually threaten the legitimation of the established order:

'The institutional order ... is continually threatened by the presence of realities which are meaningless in *its* terms. The legitimation of the institutional order is also faced with the ongoing necessity of keeping chaos at bay. *All* social reality is precarious. All societies are constructed in the face of chaos. The constant possibility of anomic terror is actualized whenever the legitimations that obscure the precariousness are threatened or collapse.' (Berger and Luckmann 1967: 121)

2. The means by which these aims are accomplished by two popular newspapers (the *Daily Mirror* and the *Daily Express*) have been elegantly explicated by the recent Rowntree study of the popular press and social change (Smith 1975). It takes, for instance, the *Mirror*'s Old Codgers' column as

epitomizing the paper's tone and linguistic style. The column is:

'... much more than a way of publishing readers' letters. It is a daily rehearsal of a particular humour, the humour of everyday life, of Us, neighbours, always ready with a cup of tea and a laugh when things aren't going too well, the laugh that compensates for the impossibility of actually changing the real situation, out there ... A way of talking that grew up in the working-class, and was a cultural defence against articulacy of the dominant class, is being imitated now in a newspaper which elsewhere is closely related to that dominant culture.' (Smith 1975: 234)

This expropriation of working class speech forms allows the *Mirror* to sustain its 'facade of radicalism' by which the rich and powerful are the subject of 'plain speaking' and 'commonsense' critiques, but the structure of power and privilege remains unchallenged.

Notes to Chapter 1

1. For a summary of the findings of this research see either Klapper

1960 or Halloran 1965.

2. For a convincing critique of con-

ventional social science approaches to content analysis see Burgelin 1972.

3. Jeremy Tunstall's work on journalists is a notable exception (Tunstall 1971a and b).

4. The Origin of the concept lies in Kurt Lewin's (1943) studies of food marketing, but it was first introduced into media sociology by D.M. White (1950). It has since undergone numerous refinements (see Gieber 1956: Bass 1969).

5. Again, there are exceptions. See Gieber 1960; Gieber and Johnson 1961; Judd 1961; Cohen 1963; Tunstall 1971b; Sigal 1973.

6. Work of this kind has already been started in the USA, notably by the Californian school of phenomenologists: see Tuchman 1972, 1973; Molotch and Lester 1974.

7. In Jeremy Tunstall's study (1971a: 130) 71% of the specialist correspondents surveyed claimed that over 80% of their copy appeared in the paper. This included 13 of the 14 crime reporters consulted. Non-specialists and inexperienced reporters are perhaps less likely to get their copy past the sub-editors unchanged, especially on mass-circulation papers.

Notes to Chapter 2

1. Althusser is apparently operating with a similar conception of ideology when he writes:

   'Ideology is indeed a system of representations, but in the majority of cases, these representations have nothing to do with "consciousness": they are usually images and occasionally concepts, but it is above all as *structures* that they impose on the vast majority of men, not via their "consciousness".' (1969: 233)

2. Clearly, any elucidation of 'the ideology of the press' must be a candidate for charges of overgeneralization. I agree that the press is far from being a homogeneous collection of papers and I have no desire to portray it as an ideological monolith, but there are sufficient similarities among the various newspapers to justify discussion of core elements of a general world view (even though

the ideology of a particular newspaper may not possess all those elements in the same combination). The popular press probably conforms more closely to the ideal type outlined here than do the 'heavies' which tend to surround their ideological themes with a more complex network of qualifications. The small-circulation, communist *Morning Star* is excluded from present consideration.

3. This should not be considered an exhaustive list.

4. These concrete evaluations will be further analyzed in due course.

5. As Galtung and Ruge (1965) point out, this approach fits very well with modern techniques of newsgathering and presentation: 'It is easier to take a photo of a person than of a structure ... and, whereas one interview yields a necessary and sufficient basis for a one person-centred news story, a

structure-centred news story will require many interviews, observation techniques, data gathering etc.'

6. However, the 'quality' press should not be thought immune from the temptation to titillate. The reader is invited to examine, for example, the *Daily Telegraph's* 'full and frank' coverage of the case of 'the topper and the copper' in 1974 (the rape of a show girl by a policeman).

7. I am indebted to James Curran of Central London Polytechnic for pointing this out.

8. Specialist correspondents usually employ conventionalized interpretations in their private as well as their public constructions of reality. The discontinuity between private thoughts and public words is characteristic of the generalist rather than the specialist — the strong element of natural selection in specialist recruitment sees to this (Sigalman 1973).

9. Roshier's study (1971) of crime news is notably sceptical about the effects of media representations on public perceptions of, and opinions about, crime. He stresses the ability of readers to differentiate and interpret the information they receive. The evidence he presents, however, is far from conclusive and his methodology leaves much to be desired.

Notes to Chapter 3

1. For instance, it was 1950 before the first major newspaper exposé of the Messina vice empire was undertaken (by *The People*).

2. Heath was convicted of the sadistic killing of two young women. Haigh, 'the acid-bath killer', was responsible for the murder of at least six people during the 1940s. The *News of the World* paid for his defence. For further discussions of these cases see Wilson and Pitman, 1964; Scott 1954; Procter 1958; Lucas 1974. For the Haigh case see Lefebury 1958; La Bern 1974.

3. The Metropolitan Police Commissioner, Sir Harold Scott, clearly felt that it was desirable to counteract the corrupting effect of a film like 'Miss Blandish'. In his account of his new public relations policy he tells us that he co-operated with Ealing Studios in making 'The Blue Lamp', the rather sentimental precursor of 'Dixon of Dock Green' which he claims gave 'a faithful picture of the policeman's life and work in the form of an exciting crime story' and constituted 'a valuable means of spreading a knowledge of the efficiency and high traditions of the Metropolitan Police' (Scott 1954: 91).

4. 'Redevelopment meant the destruction of the neighbourhood, the breakdown of the extended kinship network, which ... combined to exert a powerful force for social cohesion in the community — The first effect of the high density, high rise schemes, was to destroy the function of the street, the local pub, the corner shop, as articulations of communal space. Instead there was only the privatised space of the family unit, stacked one on top of each other, in total isolation, juxtaposed with the totally public space which surrounded it and which lacked

any of the informal social controls generated by the neighbourhood (Cohen 1972:16).

5. Accounts of these and other murders of policemen can be found in Cobb 1961.

6. The Craig/Bentley case is the subject of a comprehensive and perceptive study by David Yallop (1971) entitled *To Encourage The Others*.

7. Competition was intensified in the 1950s by the relaxation of newsprint restrictions and the introduction of commercial television.

8. This analysis of social order and change in British society was, of course, not shared by all our sociologists, see Birnbaum 1955.

9. Cohen and Rock's analysis concentrates upon the social reaction to the Teddy Boy, rather than his motivations and social origins. Their study is complemented by that of Tony Jefferson (1973) which re-emphasizes the need to see the activities of the Teds as authentic responses to objective social conditions. Briefly, Jefferson relates the emergence of the Teds to 'the worsening position of lumpen proletariat youth' in the early fifties. As evidence of the decline of lumpen youth relative to more respectable sections of the working class he cites the break-up of traditional working-class communities the influx of immigrants which accompanied it, the debilitating effects of the meritocratic myth carried in the 1944 *Education Act*, and the increasing isolation of unemployed youth at a time of 'full employment'. These developments engendered grievances which were 'worked

out' in the impoverished sphere of leisure.

10. It is interesting to note how closely these remarks echo Orwell's on the classic English murderer (Orwell 1946).

11. During a murder inquiry at Bury St. Edmunds in 1938, the Scotland Yard detective investigating the case wrote to his wife: 'The press are here in large numbers, very inquisitive and following us about if they can' (Adamson, 1966: 81).

12. The heavy sentences meted out to the robbers can be seen as an expression of opposition on behalf of the established order to the emergent theme of vitality and change. As Mr Justice Edmund Davis put it during his sentencing: 'Let us clear out of the way any romantic notions of dare-devilry. This is nothing less than a sordid crime of violence inspired by vast greed' (Fordham 1965: 128).

13. The debate crystallized to some extent around the form of the BBC's new 'realistic' drama series, 'Z Cars' which defenders of the established order found dangerously irreverent and amoral. Donald Soper wrote of the series in the *Tribune*, 'Z Cars destroys genuine respect for the law by blurring the real divisions between right and wrong. Both sides of the law are smeared with self-indulgence and moral indifference ...'

14. Significantly, 'Squad Man' was the title of a recent autobiography by a retired Metropolitan CID officer (Ex-Deputy Assistant Commissioner, Ian Forbes).

15. In quoting these statistics I am not ignoring justified sociological

scepticism about the correspondence between official statistics and reality (Hindness 1974). They are supplied as 'evidence' upon which newspapers might have drawn in persuading their readers that the new police image was plausible. Other grounds for acceptance were, of course, provided by real changes in the organization of police work e.g, the change from beat policing to the use of crime cars, the development of regional crime squads, etc.

16. It should be stressed that this is only a decline and not an eradication. Newspaper coverage of cases such as those of the Black Panther and the Cambridge Rapist, and the lively competition for the memoirs of the Great Train Robbers, testify that cheque-book journalism still survives in the 1970s.

17. Murder remained a focal concern of crime reporting, and the sixties saw the continued development of Wilson's new pattern of murder; but only the most extraordinary cases surfaced on the front pages after about 1961 and the A6 killing (Blom-Cooper 1963; Justice 1964; Russell 1965; Foot 1971). The watershed came in the years 1965-6 with the unsolved 'London Nude Murders' (du Rose 1973; Wilson 1972; McConnell 1974), the suspension of the Death Penalty, and, finally, the Moors Murders (Lucas 1970; Marchbanks 1966; Wilson 1972). If the Great Train Robbery had 'put robberies in perspective' as one crime reporter suggested to me, Brady and Hindley did much the same for murder.

18. The declared aim of the Crime Bureau was to help the police track down criminals by presenting dossiers on recent offences.

Notes to Chapter 4

1. There are exceptions to this generalization notably the *Sunday Times* 'Thalidomide' campaign.

2. For an account of the killings and the hunt which followed them see Tullett 1967.

3. Some newspapers, of course, — like the *Guardian*, the *Observer* and the *Sunday Times* — rallied less enthusiastically than others.

4. This response of course mainly took the form of news reports and editorials, but it was also widely believed at the time that a mass circulation Sunday Newspaper had been directly instrumental in the arrest on drug charges of Mick Jagger and Keith Richards of the Rolling Stones in the most celebrated case of the period.

5. A useful, if rather academic, exposition of the New Left critique of modern capitalist society is provided by the contributors to Cockburn and Blackburn 1969.

6. One of its more recent applications was in the coverage of militant protest by English schoolchildren which culminated in the London 'pupil power' demonstration of May 1972. The organizers of the demonstration, the executives of the Schools Action Union, were portrayed as a mere link in a chain of corruption which could be traced back through left-wing teachers and extremist political groups to the machinations of mysterious foreign powers. All were apparently conspiring to

overcome the inherent goodness of weak-willed schoolchildren.

7. Clearly, this is an oversimplification of the Tory election victory, but that result was symbolic of the reassertion of right-wing sentiment evident in the late sixties.

8. Statistically, the largest increase in crime took place in the fifties.

9. Shortly after the attack on his home, The Attorney General also took up the Law and order theme:

'No free society can tolerate a minority, often a minute minority, unable to persuade and convince by argument, who bludgeon or terrorise the majority into acceptance of social and political demands The assassins, the kidnappers, the terrorists, the rioters all in different degrees are seeking to impose by force their will upon the majority ...' (*The Times* 28.1.71)

10. Increasing use has been made of confidential memoranda since the war. For an account of their use in one particularly delicate case (the kidnapping of Mrs Muriel McKay in 1970) see Deeley and Walker 1971.

11. These figures are taken from 'Guerilla War in The U.S.A.', *IT* (109) 29.7.71. For other accounts and explanations of Weathermen activities see Jacobs 1970; Walton 1973; Daniels 1974.

12. The *Industrial Relations Bill* was designed to bring the domain of strike action more closely within the Rule of Law by institutionalizing an enforced 'cooling off' period between a dispute and industrial action, and instituting a new court to regulate industrial relations.

13. This was the phrase used by Mr Justice Melford Stevenson in sentencing Jake Prescott for addressing the Angry Brigade communiqué's after the attack.

14. 300 must have represented almost the entire establishment of Special Branch in 1971.

15. For an account of police activity during late January and early February 1971 see Carr 1975, chap. 5. The essential point is that the involvement of Jake Prescott in the 'conspiracy' was discovered while he was on remand in Brixton Prison on a fraud charge. On February 3rd he was released on bail and kept under close surveillance so that he could lead police to other conspirators.

16. There are several reasons for this; one is increasing financial instability which will not allow editors the luxury of a specialist for every story; another is the influx of radical journalists who wish to retain broad and flexible frames of reference.

17. Part of the Association's letter of protest to the *Evening Standard's* Editor reads:

'Our members are reporters of long experience in Fleet Street and elsewhere, who are justly proud of their reputation of providing responsible day-to-day coverage of trials at a place that the Lord Chancellor described last month as ''... par excellence, the premier criminal court in the Commonwealth, and perhaps the world''. We object, therefore, to being identified ... with a person who has a conviction for sending an obscene article, viz. Oz No 28, Schoolkids issue, through the post

... Our members feel that, in these days of declining standards, our voice must be raised in the hope that eventually, with others, it will be heard.'

18. With language like this it is perhaps not surprising that Stuart Christie compared the *News of the World's* coverage to *Die Stürmer*, the Nazi's vehicle for anti-Jewish propaganda.

19. This is the process Berger and Luckmann (1971: 132-33) term 'nihilation'.

20. In attacking 'the pub' the IRA were extracting the last drop of paranoia from the fear of the bombing conspiracy because they were attacking a powerful cultural symbol of the ordinary man's leisure hours.

21. *20 Years* pamphlet produced by the Paul, Jimmy, and Mustafa Support Committee p.31. See also Jefferson 1975.

22. British journalists are, by and large, acutely aware that any story with a racial content requires sensitive handling in order to avoid allegations of prejudice (Hartmann and Husband 1973: 163-65).

23. It is interesting to note that an opinion poll carried out four years later by Marplan arrived at very similar findings. The problem of 'violence and vandalism' (along with that of unemployment) was rated by respondents as 'the most important facing Britain today' in 37% of cases, more often than any other 'problem' including inflation, the value of the pound, race and immigration, housing, tax and pension levels, strikes, and trade unions and nationalization. Mugging was ranked second only to bombing in seriousness, 81% of respondents calling for very much more severe sentences. (Source: *Sun* 22.6.76)

24. The pamphlet *20 Years* described the Handsworth case and the media reaction to it in detail. The case constitutes remarkable evidence of the depth of feeling aroused by mugging in certain sections of both the press and the judiciary, and provided a focus of the debate surrounding the issue. It captured the headlines when sixteen year-old Paul Storey and two friends were given detention orders of 20 years and 10 years respectively after assaulting and robbing an Irish building worker, Robert Keenan.

Notes to Chapter 5

1. For a further discussion of the presentation of the police in the press see Chibnall 1975b.

2. As one senior crime reporter on a popular daily expressed it:

'Lots and lots of criminals have gone the way they've gone because of environment — it doesn't necessarily have to be last-ing but I think it kicks people off in a certain way, which could happen to anyone, it's just a trick of birth or where you live. I think you've got to be lucky to be born in the East End and not get involved with criminal people, or any area which has a large percentage of criminals. Young children of criminal families tend to follow their elders and you've got to be very lucky to survive that situation and not get pinched for something or other.'

3. This section draws extensively on Chibnall 1975a.

4. The idea that reporters thrive on 'scoops' is a truism. Exclusive material creates problems of validation and involves the journalist in risk taking. A major channel for testing both the veracity and newsworthiness of information — the opinions of other journalists — is effectively closed. See Breed 1955; Cohen 1963: 81-2; Sigal 1973: 71-2.

5. The existence of these unofficial relationships often proves embarrassing to the Press Bureau where the situation of denying what some journalists already know is a familiar one to the press officer: 'We are often undercut by police officers who are saying one thing while we say another.' For a specific example of Press Bureau embarrassment see Deeley and Walker 1971 especially p. 114.

6. In his autobiography, ex-Assistant Commissioner, Sir Richard Jackson, recalls going to a football match while in Madrid for an Interpol conference: 'With me were my wife, my daughter, Virginia, and the crime reporters of the *Daily Express* and the *Daily Mirror*, Percy Hoskins and Tom Tullett, both old friends of mine' (Jackson 1967: 283).

7. A graphic example of the way in which a crime reporter can participate in a police investigation can be found in Norman Lucas's book *The Child Killers*. Lucas, one of the most prolific of crime correspondents, records how he was

granted permission to question the mother of a murdered Eastbourne baby and how he was able to elicit her confession to the crime (Lucas 1970: chap. 6).

8. It is, of course, possible for the crime reporter to promote the interests of individual policemen as well as those of the Force. My informants were generally uncertain of the influence of their reports on the career prospects of policemen. Most felt that senior officers at the Yard are suspicious of publicity-seekers, but some were prepared to entertain the possibility that press reports might influence the decision to promote an officer:

'Normally, if they're efficient and don't blot their copy book, promotion comes to some extent in time, up to certain ranks ... It is possible, of course, that the attention of very senior officers inside the Metropolitan Police to a particular middle-ranking officer is drawn rather more often by the fact that he's hit the headlines on certain cases. It may be that they become more familiar with his name and may give him some sort of preferential treatment when they come to consider his promotion. It's possible, but certainly I've no evidence of it at all.'

(Crime Correspondent)

For a fictional account of the role of the press in police promotion see Newman 1970: 8-9.

9. For other discussions of assimilation in this context see Gieber and Johnson 1961; Judd 1961; Cohen 1963: 144-53; Tunstall 1971a: 173-201; Sigal 1973; chap. 3.

10. A journalist on the *Sunday Times*

told me that his paper has requests from about six young Fleet Street journalists per year to investigate cases of police deviance which they are convinced their own papers would not handle.

11. Few of Sir Robert Mark's policy moves and initiatives can be adequately understood in isolation. His policies towards the news media, police reorganization and methods of investigation, Judges Rules and the jury system form a complexly-integrated whole, displaying considerable organizational vision, and political sophistication. There is no space here to unpack Sir Robert's policy programme, but readers interested in this task are referred to Laurie 1973; Fox 1974; Evans 1974: chap. 6; Cockerell 1975.

12. In a later editorial (27.6.73) the *Sun* praised the two journalists directly responsible for the exposé 'who saw their duty and did it'.

13. There can be little doubt about Mark's sincerity. In his first four years as Commissioner almost 100 officers per year were dismissed from the Metropolitan Force or left voluntarily during Criminal or disciplinary inquiries. In the decade before Mark's appointment the average was only sixteen per year.

Notes to Chapter 6

1. The army is included in the analysis for a number of reasons, primarily because its immediate aims and long-term goals in Ulster are very similar to those of the police: i.e. 'peace-keeping', the detection and surveillance of offenders, the establishment and maintenance of a favourable public image, etc. Moreover, the way in which the army handles reporters in Northern Ireland provides an interesting comparison with the relations between the police and Fleet Street journalists.

2. The crime correspondent of one of Fleet Street's quality dailies told me that, while waiting for the verdicts in the Winchester Bomb Trial in 1973 he had taken the two senior officers involved in the case to dinner. Over the meal they discussed the background to the case and the story the reporter was going to write. He told them that he planned to refer to one of them as 'Uncle George' but that he had no nickname for the other officer. The final report, however, was enriched by the officer's own suggestion: 'The Evil Genius'.

3. This is not to deny that journalists do have regular contacts representing the protestant and catholic para-militaries who they frequently quote.

4. For example:

'... suppression goes against the grain for newspapers ... If and when another victim is kidnapped and if the police again ask for secrecy; newspapers will have to make another difficult decision. It must be made at the time on the merits of the particular case.' (*Daily Mirror* 17.11.75)

'... In any democratic country, the police, like all other powerful institutions, must expect to be scrutinised and reported upon continuously. That is the rule.

The nine-day suspension of news coverage in the Kaloghirou kidnap was the exception.' (*Daily Mail* 17.11.75)

'Pacts of silence of this kind are proper so long as it remains a matter of unfettered discretion for the media concerned whether to co-operate and for how long. There should be no question of pressure from the police in the form of threats to deny information in future cases, let alone any legal prohibitions.' (*The Times* 17.11.75)

5. Source: *Times* Correspondent, Robert Fisk, interviewed on BBC TV's 'Inside the Press' 26.1.75

6. Similar tactics had been employed

by press officers of the Ministry of Defence just before the publication of the Widgery report on 'Bloody Sunday' in April 1972. They had telephoned Fleet Street defence correspondents and leaked those comments in the report most favourable to the army. Simon Winchester who was prevented from attending the press conference on the report because he was not an 'accredited defence correspondent' has commented that, as a result of this particular piece of news management, Blood Sunday became 'a closed book with the Irish fully to blame'.

7 Quoted in the *Daily Telegraph* and the *Guardian* 20.5.76.

Notes to Chapter 7

1. Lukacs (1971) agrees that the bourgeoisie are condemned to false consciousness by their material interests, that they are largely unaware of the 'true' nature of their social and historical position. However, their experience of defending their class position against the rising tide of proletarian consciousness may bring them an increasing awareness of the reality and meaning of the class struggle, which may, in turn, lead to an increasingly conscious and cynical manipulation of the existing dominant ideology for directly repressive purposes. (I take this to be the gist of his argument in *History and Class Consciousness*.)

2. Marx identified many of the components of the dominant ideology in capitalist society — the idea of the state as a disinterested third

party in the interaction between labour and capital, of the wage contract as an equal exchange, of poverty and deviance as the consequence of individual failure or wickedness etc. This dominant ideology constitutes the basis of the newspaper ideology discussed in chapter 2.

3. The relevant writings of Frankfurt School theorists such as Adorno, Horkheimer, and Habermas cannot justifiably be said to constitute a theory of mass communication. They are predominantly aesthetic critiques of a mass culture which reduces art to the level of a commodity. They pay scant attention to the process of news production and reception.

4. The others being: The Religious ISA, The Educational ISA, The Family ISA, The Legal ISA, The Political ISA, The Trades Union

ISA, and The Cultural ISA.

5. Questions of this type are not central to Althusser's structuralism which seeks explanations of social formations in the combined actions of impersonal elements of those formations. In one attempt to explicate Althusser's conception of causality, Miriam Glucksmann notes that it is very different from traditional concepts of cause:

'Causation is to be sought within the process and consists in showing how the social formation works and hangs together, and what its strong and weak links are. Althusser describes this type of cause operating in the combination as an "immense machine", or "play without an author" or "the presence of an absence", since the internal articulation of the social formation does not rest on the activity of men as individuals or groups. Relations of production constitute the unit of analysis, not men, and rather than looking for external causes of structures, it is more pertinent to think in terms of an absent cause or the existence of a structure through its effects.' (Glucksmann 1974: 230-45)

6. This last sentence, of course, recalls Marcuse's (1965) concept of 'repressive toleration'.

7. Stanley Harrison's (1974) study of the radical press and its changing social context is a notable exception.

8. See, for instance, Jeremy Tunstall's (1971b) study of Lobby correspondents and Bernard Cohen's (1963) and Leon Sigal's (1973) studies of the Washington press corps.

Index

newspapers
  competition with television, 73-4
  economic crisis of, 73
  ideology of, 33-6; role of police in,
    142-46;
  and violence, 79, 83-4, 88
  ownership of, 5-6
  partiality of, 3-4
  values of, ix
  see also names of newspapers
Niedermayer, Thomas, kidnapped
    West German consul, 190, 254
'No Orchids for Miss Blandish'
    gangster film, 55
Northern Ireland, see Ireland,
    Northern
Nott-Bower, Sir John, Metropolitan
    Commissioner, 162, 231

objectivity in reporting, 33-4
Observer, 87, 107, 161
'olds', news set in existing framework,
    35

Paisnel, Edward, Jersey sex criminal,
    66, 244
Paki-bashing, 126, 241
Pall Mall Gazette, 49
parental control, lack of and crime, 81
'Pentonville five', jailed dockers, 127,
    246, 248
People, 96, 228, 239
personalization, 26-9, 68
picketing, violent, 127
  as intimidation, 130, 132
  as threat to order, 76
police
  arming of, 87
  attitude to political deviants of, 96,
    106-107
  complaints against, 70
  deviance in, 65, 69, 142-71, 233
  image of, 68-72
  killing of, 54, 86, 88, 116-20
  and mugging, 122
  role of, 81; as 'thief-taker', 106
  Royal Commission on, 69, 70, 231,
    233

police, *cont.*,
  as source of crime news, 49, 146-54,
    172-205
  technology and, 71
  and 'The Violent Society', 118
Police Chronicle, The, 55
Police Federation, 85
Police Gazette, 49, 183
politics, 27
  deviant, 62-3, 89-94; police lack of
    understanding of, 108; police
    view of, 106-107
  diversion from, 33
  in newspaper ideology, 22, 105
pollution, environmental, as violence,
    78
Ponder, John, *Evening Standard* crime
    reporter, 203-204
Poole, Derek, murderer of policeman,
    56
popularism, ideology of, 58
Portland spy ring, 63, 232
Powell, Enoch, 94, 238
Prescott, Jake, Angry Brigade member,
    109, 112, 244, 246
press
  access to, 37-9
  as defender of dominant ideology,
    115
  ideology of, 11-45
  police and, 70, 72; deviancy of,
    142-71
  role in fight against deviancy and
    crime, 173
  Royal Commission on, 229; second,
    233
  see also newspapers
Press Association, 95, 186, 188
press cards, in news management, 178
pressurization, in news management,
    194-96
Price sisters, IRA bombers, 78, 107,
    250, 254
prisons, in newspaper ideology, 20
Private Eye, 102, 189
Procter, Harry, journalist, 57-9, 65
propaganda
  by control agencies, 201-205